# BRIGHT MORNING STAR

Ginny Nieukirk van der Steur

**Companion Press**
**P.O. Box 310**
**Shippensburg, PA 17257-0310**
**Internet: http://www.reapernet.com**

"Good Stewards of the
Manifold Grace of God"

ISBN 1-56043-216-0

For Worldwide Distribution
Printed in the U.S.A.

Author photograph by Robert Roos van Raadshooven.

# DEDICATION

With all my heart I dedicate this book to JESUS, the Messiah,
who is the BRIGHT MORNING STAR!
Thank You, Lord,
for Your light and love every new morning!

To my precious husband, Peter: You are God's gift to me and
I'm so thankful to love and serve our Lord together!
I love you so much!

To our little son, Joshua: You are our joy and delight!
God is with you!

To my father, Jim Nieukirk: Thank you for all the years of
your constant love and kindness to me!
You're the best!

In loving memory of my mother, Martha Nieukirk:
Thank you for your sweetness and
the way you raised me!

# ACKNOWLEDGMENTS

I am thankful forever for the very loving family that the Lord has given me, and I carry each one in my heart! He has also given me a few lifetime friends, who are a continual blessing to me!

I want to thank Alice Alexander for leading me to Yeshua (Jesus) who changed my life so gloriously!

In writing BRIGHT MORNING STAR I want to say: Thank you, Anne and Jordana Jiles, for your long hours in getting it ready. Thank you, Carol Huffman, for your help in getting started. Thank you, Richard and Vicki Shirley, for your encouragement and on-going help. Thank you, Suzy Stuart, for your love and help at the end. Thank you, Gail Watson, for your constant help and diligence in the finishing! May the Lord Himself reward you in His own way!

# INTRODUCTION

There is something sacred about the morning hours before the sun rises and there is just one star left in the sky. It is the BRIGHT MORNING STAR! Jesus calls Himself the Bright Morning Star in Revelation 22 and He promises to give the Morning Star to those who overcome in their faith and love for Him. He gives Himself to us! His eternal light and love shine in us brighter and brighter until the full day when He will return!

If you find yourself LONGING TO KNOW JESUS MORE DEEPLY, OR EVEN WANTING THIS DESIRE, then this devotional is for you. I wrote it with this in my heart. As a matter of fact, it IS my heart poured out. May the beauty of the Lord's presence be yours as you read it each day! Read it carefully and slowly, searching for the treasure of His love daily. He loves you and knows the deepest place of your heart. He will come to you. Be devoted to Him and He will reveal Himself and His will for you.

Sometimes unanswered prayer seems difficult or a circumstance holds you back, or walking in holiness seems so impossible. You may not feel you can be devoted to the Lord. If you will take the first step, He will come and lead you with His patient love. He will give you His own love and peace and joy in life! You must be willing to forsake your sins and follow Jesus with all your heart. Jesus was actually God Himself in a human body. He came for one purpose—to give His life, even His holy blood for you. He took your sins (and mine) upon Himself and suffered untold agony for you. Then He rose up from the dead and is alive forever! He is full of grace and glory! He gives you His holiness in exchange for your sins. By the cross He gives you eternal life and a personal relationship now with Himself. It is for this relationship that He gave His life. It cost Him everything. Will you give yourself to Him? If you can say "Yes!" from your heart, then stop reading now and take a few minutes to pray:

> *Dear Loving Father, God of Abraham, Isaac & Jacob, I come to You and thank You for Your love for me that is greater than I can understand. Thank You for sending Your Son Jesus to give His life for me. Thank You, dear Jesus, Yeshua, for suffering for my sins. Please forgive me for all of them and make me the way You want me to be. Come into my heart. I give You my life. I will love You and follow You. Fill me with Your Holy Spirit and make me Yours. Give me understanding of Your Word, the Holy Scriptures, day by day. Amen.*

If you have prayed this in these last moments for the first time, then be joyful! All of heaven rejoices over you right now! God will be with you with His precious love every moment (whether you feel it or not). You are His child and He will never leave you. He loves you with an ETERNAL LOVE that is different than human love. PLEASE WRITE ME A LETTER at the address on the Order Form in the back of this book. I am interested in your life and walk with the Lord!

IF YOU HAVE WALKED WITH THE LORD FOR SEVERAL YEARS, REJOICE ALSO BECAUSE HE WILL GIVE YOU MORE than what you have asked Him for! His ultimate desire is increasing intimacy with you, moment by moment. YOU CAN BE AS CLOSE TO THE LORD AS YOU WANT if you will moment by moment seek Him, enjoy Him, and surrender to Him. He delights in you and rejoices over you! Above all, keep your eyes on Jesus! By faith look into His eyes and see His tender kindness and love for you! Keep looking for He never takes His eyes off of you! His eyes are as a holy and glorious light causing you to become pure and to be able to see Him as He really is. You will reflect Him! You are the very jewel of His heart!

You were created to know Him and love Him and shine as a BRIGHT MORNING STAR with His glory, bearing His eternal light to the world around you! It is in these moments, the moments of the MORNING STAR that you will reflect His love!

*"ARISE, SHINE, FOR YOUR LIGHT HAS COME*
*AND THE GLORY OF THE LORD*
*HAS RISEN UPON YOU!"*
*Isaiah 60:1*

# JANUARY 1

*"The Lord your God is in your midst, A victorious warrior. He will exult over you with joy! He will be quiet in His love. He will rejoice over you with shouts of joy."*
*Zephaniah 3:17*

He is in your midst, in the very deepest part of your being! He fights for you. He is for you and not against you. He will surely renew your love. His presence will come to you quietly. In the silence you will feel the strength of His presence and love for you.

Be filled this day! Let Him dwell in the depths of stillness in you. Let His sweet peace well up inside of you. Let His pure love saturate your heart.

Embrace your God! He longs for you! He is pleased with you, devoted to you! He even rejoices over you—not quietly but with heartfelt shouts of joy! Your God quietly fills you with His sweet love and then He shouts for joy over you! He shouts!

———————————◇———————————

Get alone with the Lord this New Year's Day and shout for joy over His great love for you!

# JANUARY 2

*"Do not call to mind the former things or ponder things of the past. Behold, I will do something new. Now it will come forth. Will you not be aware of it? I will even make a roadway in the wilderness, rivers in the desert." Isaiah 43:18-19*

Do not live on the past or for the future. Resist the temptation to dwell on the good or bad that has happened. Let the anointing to forgive and forget fill  your heart. Press on to the will of God.

BEHOLD! He will do a new thing. It *will* come about. Do not miss it. Behold your God! Keep your eyes on Him and you will see it come to you. Sing a *new* song. Break routines and be free to love the Lord in fullness!

Are you in the wilderness? Do you long for more of Him? Drink in the living waters of His sweet love. He makes a way for you, a highway of holiness. Come to Me and let Me fill you with new wine. My lovingkindness is better than life. Dwell in Me, for I love you with an everlasting love.

———————————◇———————————

Today, express your love for the Lord in a new way — a song, a letter, a poem. Be blessed. His love is fresh and new for you today.

# JANUARY 3

*"Thou wilt make known to me the path of life;*
*in Thy presence is fullness of joy; in*
*Thy right hand there are pleasures forever."*
*Psalm 16:11*

Your God will come to you and make known the way you should go. He is faithful and committed to you. He delights in giving you light and life. He delights in giving you His treasures, even Himself. **HE** alone is your life, your treasure. He is your breath and peace forever. He is your great reward. In His presence is ***fullness of joy!*** Not earthly joy but heavenly raptures! You are the love of His heart!

Think not on things of the earth. Rise above them and dwell in His presence. He has called you with an everlasting love to enjoy His communion with you. He wants to ***be*** with you!

Tell Him you love Him throughout the day and let His presence be your supreme joy!

---◇---

Put love notes to Jesus in every room at home, at work and in your car (or pocket if you take a bus). Say, "I love you, Jesus" throughout the day!

# JANUARY 4

*"He is a rewarder of those who diligently seek Him." Hebrews 11:6*

Oh, how He loves to reward you. His reward is everlasting. His reward is excellent and high and lofty, above all that you know to ask for. He looks, He waits, He longs to lavish His reward upon you!

Are you a diligent seeker? Does your heart search for Him daily? Do you pursue the Lord of your life and desire more and more of Him? Do you seek His revelation to you? He sees your smallest attempt to seek Him and He will reward you in ways you do not know—beyond your comprehension!

Seek your Lord today in newness and let Him pour His great reward upon you! **HE** is your all consuming reward! He gives you Himself!

———————————◇———————————

Set aside this week to **diligently** seek the Lord in new ways. Receive His sweet reward!

# JANUARY 5

*"Mary therefore took a pound of very costly ointment, and anointed the feet of Jesus, and wiped His feet with her hair; and the house was filled with the fragrance of the ointment." John 12:3*

Oh, the SWEETNESS of His presence! Mary lavished the costly ointment on Him. She gave Him the best! She abandoned herself to Jesus in sweet surrender. She wiped His feet with her hair. As she did, the anointing came back on her and filled the house with His fragrance. She gave and He filled the room.

Will you give your best to Jesus today? Your most costly? Will you give it to Him in abundance and cast yourself before Him? Become *His*—all that you are, and all that you are not yet. Give Him *all* of yourself so that He might fill you with sweet fragrance and anointing, that you might overflow to all who meet you today! The sweet fragrance of His presence is in you! It will fill the house!

———————————◇———————————

In your mind anoint the feet of Jesus and in your heart give Him all today. Pour yourself upon Him and let Him fill you and anoint you with fresh wine!

# JANUARY 6

*"Keep me as the apple of the eye; Hide me in the shadow of Thy wings." Psalm 17:8*

You are the very apple of His eye, His choice, the love of His life. What is the "apple" of His eye? It is translated "pupil." And what is the "pupil" of the eye? It is the most sensitive part of the body. You have the most sensitive part of Him! He loves you with an everlasting love.

And He will hide you in the shadow of His wings. He will keep you in the hidden place with Himself and carry you away from evil. Abide in Him today in that secret place, for He is the very apple of your eye too! Give Him the most tender, the very deepest part of you. Give Him all. He is the apple of your eye!

---◇---

Draw an apple and write this verse on it and put it up somewhere to remind you of the sensitive place you have with the Lord.

# JANUARY 7

*"Though He slay me, I will hope in Him."*
*Job 13:15*

When the dark night comes and you can't see where the Lord is—when you don't feel His presence or hear Him as clearly—when you suffer great loss or pain—what then will you do?

This is where our faith is tested. This is where our faithfulness is seen. In the darkness.

Deep in the human heart is buried a reaction of blaming God when tragedy or calamity hits. But deeper in the human heart, for those who are His, is the grace of God to trust Him no matter what. To keep your hope in Him. To be faithful to Him forever.

Job had lost wealth, family and health. Even his wife had turned against him. Yet he trusted the Lord *no matter what*. He clung to the Lord.

Are you determined to trust God in that way—when all is lost? It's a type of crucifixion, but afterwards comes the resurrection! You will rise up afterwards reflecting Jesus!

---◆---

Write Job 13:15 on a piece of paper and keep it for when things get rough. God is trustworthy above all!

# JANUARY 8

*"But from there you will seek the Lord your God, and you will find Him if you search for Him with all your heart and all your soul."*
*Deuteronomy. 4:29*

This promise is all through the Scriptures. You will find Him when you **seek Him** with all your heart. Seek the Lord while He may be found. How gracious the Lord is. How He longs to be found by you. He makes Himself constantly available to you.

A worshipper in the cult of Hari Krishna stood at that false altar and called out, "Lord God I want to know You!" Instantly he saw a vision which flashed before his eyes—of Jesus on the cross! He ran out and repented and gave his heart to Jesus. His life was radically changed. He was searching.

The Lord is as near as your breath. He wants the most intimate relationship with you. It can be as deep with Him as you want—if you will seek Him with all your heart. Is He your life, your very love? Are you a diligent seeker of the Lord? Run to Him! He is there for you in great depth!

---◇---

Set your mind to seek the Lord early each day this week. Study His word. Throw yourself into prayer. Lean on Him.

# JANUARY 9

*"Blessed be the God and Father of our Lord the Messiah who has blessed us with every spiritual blessing in heavenly places in the Messiah."*
*Ephesians 1:3*

Do you know that you are a blessed person? That you walk with the blessings of God upon your head?

Because Jesus has made a covenant with you with His own holy blood, all that He has now belongs to you. *All* that He has. You have every spiritual blessing in heaven because of Jesus.

You have His name in which to pray and receive. You have His Holy Spirit in which to live on earth and in heaven. He even promises to change you into His own image if you are willing. No good thing will He withhold from you if you walk uprightly with Him. You have His word in which to dwell and to keep evil away. You have His promise that nothing is impossible with Him and that He will be with you until the end of time. His goodness and mercy will follow you all of your days. You have JESUS! You are rich!

---

Make a list of all the spiritual blessings the Lord had given you. Thank Him all day long. Share it with someone you love.

# JANUARY 10

*"The Lord gave and the Lord has taken away. Blessed be the name of the Lord." Job 1:21*

Who is the Lord, but the giver of life. The giver of every breath. The giver of every heartbeat. Yes, He is the giver of every good blessing under heaven.

If He is really the Lord of your life, then you have found Him to be trustworthy. He is not like people, sometimes faithful and true, sometimes not. He is God: wholly faithful and true for all eternity. As Lord He has taken the sovereign right to take from our lives any time He wants to.

Job had lost all—family, wealth, his wife's support and eventually his health. But he did not sin against the Lord with his lips. Instead he **worshipped** the Lord. "Blessed be the name of the Lord!" His trust in God stood mightily in the midst of ruins. How pleased the Lord must have been to receive Job's true love from his heart Job had lost all—family, wealth, his wife's support and eventually his health. But he did not sin against the Lord with his lips. Instead he **worshipped** the Lord. "Blessed be the name of the Lord!" His trust in God stood mightily in the midst of ruins. How pleased the Lord must have been to receive Job's true love from his heart and the Lord restored him doubly in the end.

Bless the Lord in the midst of your heartaches and losses. Bless His name.

---◇---

In your heart give all you are and all you have to the Lord in a fresh, new way. Proclaim Him as **Lord of all**!

# JANUARY 11

*"Delight yourself in the Lord and He will give you the desires of your heart." Psalm 37:4*

As you delight in Him, rejoice that He's yours, and minister to Him—He will be so very faithful to give you the desires of your heart.

But have you given Him your desires? Not just praying about them, but giving them completely to Him? This is what you must do, for every good gift (and desire) comes from the Father of lights. Have you laid each one before Him and said, "Not my will but *Thy* will be done"?

The Lord will not only give you the desires of your heart in His good timing, but He will place in your heart *His very own* desires. You will be one with Jesus as He gives you His desires. Delight, yes, delight in the Lord today! He will truly give you the deepest desires of your heart according to His perfect and loving will for you!

---

Write your most precious desires on a little piece of paper. Put them in a tiny box or container with a lid. Hand them to the Lord and delight in Him!

# JANUARY 12

*"All the paths of the Lord are lovingkindness and truth to those who keep His covenant and His testimonies." Psalm 25:10*

Which paths? ***All*** the paths of the Lord are lovingkindness and truth. Even this dark and lonely path? Even this heavy trial? Even this injustice? This pain? This heartbreak?

What path did Jesus take? He took the way of the crucifixion. The "Via Dolorosa" (way of pain). He was despised and rejected. He was marred beyond recognition. He even sweat great drops of blood in the Garden over our sins.

You have not resisted sin to the point of bloodshed as He did.

Yes, all the paths of the Lord are lovingkindness. Even His judgment is merciful. He is not willing for any to perish. You shall come forth as gold! Yes, His path leads to purity and you will shine with His reflection if you go His way—the way of crucifixion.

---

◇

Take a few minutes to thank the Lord that through your trials, on the other side—you will come forth as gold and be more like Jesus! His path is kind.

# JANUARY 13

*"The lovingkindness of God endures all day long." Psalm 52:1*

Oh, yes it does! His lovingkindness endures all day long for you. Does it endure when I fail? Yes, it does. Does it endure when my priorities have gotten off course? Yes, it does. Does God's lovingkindness endure even when I can't feel His presence? When He seems far away? Yes, indeed, it does. It endures all day long—for you. Does it even endure when I have been treated unfairly, or when I have neglected Him? His lovingkindness endures for you.

Dear lover of God, take hold of His lovingkindness for you today. His mercy is everlasting and His lovingkindness ***endures*** with you all day long. It endures your ups and downs. It endures your circumstances. It endures all for you. Rest in His everlasting arms as His love endures with you all day long. It is there for you all day long. His sweet lovingkindness is never missing. It's there. Drink it in. Let it fill your heart over and over again.

Oh taste and see that the Lord is good! His lovingkindness is embracing you.

---

Carry a note pad today with you, to write down all of the Lord's lovingkindnesses to you.

# JANUARY 14

*"We who had sweet fellowship together, walked in the house of God." Psalm 55:14*

Oh, dear friend who loves God! Have you tasted the sweet fellowship and intimacy with the Lord and then experienced it with a friend or a mate? Have you been caught up in His presence with someone you love? It is like heaven on earth! It is His kingdom! How lovely those moments of fellowship are! Precious gifts from the Lord!

But the psalmist speaks of treachery. He says that if it were an enemy against him, he could bear it. But it was his friend whom he had trusted that was against him. Not only that, but one with whom he had walked together with God. Oh, how deep the pain! Have you ever experienced it? Jesus did! He knows all about it. Judas gave Him a kiss of betrayal. Jesus understands this kind of pain. He knows. Therefore, only He can carry you through it—and He will.

---

Today, give to Jesus any pain of the present or past caused by an unfaithful friend. Let Jesus have it and receive forgiveness from His wounds.

# JANUARY 15

*"For the Lord God is a sun and a shield; the Lord gives grace and glory; no good thing does He withhold from those who walk uprightly."*
**Psalm 84:11**

He is as bright as the sunshine in full strength, warming our hearts and making us transparent and holy. Let His light shine brightly in you today. Correct what needs correcting by His Spirit and shine for Him! He will be your shield, protecting you from the onslaughts of satan, keeping you safe in His own arms. He will give you grace, sweet grace, to walk in purity with Him and do His will. His glory will shine in you. Your life will glorify Him. People will see the Lord Jesus shining in you! Give Him glory this day. Worship the God of your heart! Bless His holy name!

And what? **No** good thing will He withhold from those who walk uprightly—those who walk in integrity and love. It is His delight to give you every good thing as you walk with Him in obedience and goodness. **No** good thing will He withhold. Glorify the Lord today in your heart. Go in His grace and glory!

———————————◇———————————

Draw a bright sun. In the middle of it write all of the "good" things that He will not withhold from you and believe Psalm 84:11.

# JANUARY 16

*"The Lord will accomplish (perfect) that which concerns me." Psalm 138:8*

"That which concerns me"—Oh the things which concern me! This relationship, that task, the new turn in my work, that unsaved loved one, the unanswered prayer, my character development . . . ***STOP!***

The Lord will complete it. Not only that, but He will "perfect" it. He knows all about it, more than you do. And He knows you. He is able to bring it to pass and to perfect it—to do more than you ask or think. And He is willing. He will perfect that one thing that concerns you the most. Though the circumstances seem to be unchanged, He is mightily at work to perfect it—in His timing. He will do it. Trust Him! He will "perfect" it! He is the God who does miracles. Let Him "perfect" that which concerns you. Rejoice!

---

Begin to thank the Lord in prayer for perfecting the thing you're most concerned about. See it as perfected in Him and rejoice today!

# JANUARY 17

*"Because Thy lovingkindness is better than life, my lips will praise Thee." Psalm 63:3*

Oh, Thy precious lovingkindness! Your great mercy and love! Who can fathom it? Who can drink it in? You are full and overflowing, dear Lord, in Your lovingkindness to us! It is a treasure beyond earth. That priceless jewel! Your sweet lovingkindness!

Once we experience it, and ride on its height and go to its unending depths, we find it is better than life! So much better than life! The heavenly bliss of knowing You face to face is ***better than life!*** You are heaven itself, Lord! Today, my lips will praise You for the sweet wine of Your love! I will lift up my hands and bless You all the days of my life. You are everything! All that matters is You, sweet Lord! Your precious lovingkindness is better than life!

---

◇

Lift your hands and sing to the Lord! Tell Him that His love is better than life! Rejoice in His sweet kindnesses to you, all day long!

# JANUARY 18

*"Your eyes will see the King in His beauty; they will behold a far distant land." Isaiah 33:17*

Open your eyes and behold your King! Behold Jesus your King! Do you see Him? Do you see the One who became a cell in the womb of Mary? Do you see the One who healed the sick and cleansed the leper? Do you see the One who sweat great drops of blood for your sins? Do you see Him hanging on a cross, nailed in agony for you? Do you see Him risen from the dead and reigning in glory? He is full of majesty and splendor! Look in His eyes! Do you see His love and kindness, His purity and glory? Do you see His sweet mercy to you?

Your eyes will see His beauty! Adore Him today! He is your King and He is in love with you.

---◇---

Spend 15 minutes today worshipping the Lord in His beauty—for who He is. Make a crown for Him with your praises.

# JANUARY 19

*"You will also be a crown of beauty in the hand of the Lord, and a royal diadem in the hand of your God." Isaiah 62:3*

How the Lord honors you! He sees you for who you are in your heart and all He desires for you. You will not only be beautiful but a **crown** of beauty to the Lord. Your character of beauty will crown Him. Glorify Him. You are as royal to Him. Can you imagine it? You are royal to the living God! He has chosen you!

Fall to your knees and worship Him today! He is the Sovereign King, the Lord of Lords, your glory and your God forever. He is **your** Royal One, yet He honors you. Bow down to your King today, the only true God who humbles Himself to lift you up and make you fit for heaven—for royalty! Bless His holy name!

Glory to You, Lord! Glory, glory, glory! You are our royal diadem. You are our sacred crown of beauty! How we love and adore you! Glory, glory, glory!

———————◇———————

Make a crown of paper and write words of praise and worship to Jesus, the King of Kings!

# JANUARY 20

*"And as the bridegroom rejoices over the bride, so your God will rejoice over you." Isaiah 62:5*

How does the bridegroom rejoice? He waits in glorious expectation of his wedding day. As he sees his bride coming down the aisle to give her life to him, his joy overflows greatly. Sometimes he even has slight tears of joy. His deep desires are being met and all that he is and has are hers. With every breath he pours his love out to her and his heart beats faster as they meet at the altar.

Can you imagine that the Lord rejoices over you in this way? He is beside Himself with love for you! He looks at you and is so totally in love with you! Will you receive that love today, with your whole heart? Open your heart and arms to your heavenly Bridegroom! He is pure and holy and He rejoices over you! Jesus, your heavenly Bridegroom, rejoices over you!

———————————◇———————————

Bake a wedding cake today in honor of your Bridegroom the Messiah. Tell Him you love Him and rejoice over Him!

# JANUARY 21

## *"Behold, I have inscribed you on the palms of My hands" Isaiah 49:16*

Do you know that Jesus, the Lord, the King of Kings, has inscribed you on the palms of His hands? Those hands that worshipped, those hands that blessed, those hands that healed and raised the dead carry your name. When you pray, when you worship, when you heal the sick, those holy hands of Jesus are upon you!

When you are weary or down, those precious hands reach out to you. His hands are in prayer for you, blessing you, holding you. His hands reach to heaven for you and call you "His."

Look closer at those hands! What? Scars? Yes, the nail prints forever engraved in heaven for you are the very proof of His love. Those loving, holy hands. Look at your Lord! See His hands. You are inscribed there. Take His hands.

---

Trace around your hands on paper and cut them out. Draw a nail and blood drops on each one and write Isaiah 49:16 on them. Put them in a place you can see them daily and worship Jesus.

# JANUARY 22

*"I have loved you with an everlasting love;*
*therefore I have drawn you with lovingkindness."*
*Jeremiah 31:3*

Therefore I have drawn you with lovingkindness. He loved, so He gave His Son. His love is active. He has drawn you to Himself. Maybe you weren't even aware of Him drawing you. He is so gentle, so pure. He draws you with lovingkindness. He delights to show you His love, His everlasting love. He shows you in a million kindnesses, many of which you don't notice. If you could see in the unseen realm of the spirit, you would fall on your knees and thank the Lord for all of His tender mercies toward you.

When you love someone, you want to show them your love in all different ways. It's the same with the Lord. His love for you is everlasting. He draws you with lovingkindness. Receive His love anew today!

———————————◇———————————

Make a list of all the big and small ways the Lord has shown you His love this week. Find a unique way to show your gratitude.

# JANUARY 23

*"And forgive us our debts as we also forgive our debtors." Matthew 6:12*

Do you live a life of forgiveness and love? Is there anyone you need to forgive? Be tenderhearted to one another, forgiving as the Messiah has forgiven you. What is the message of the cross? It is forgiveness. The One whose face was spit on forgives you. The Holy One, who was beaten beyond recognition has died for your sins. He who is pure and spotless was tortured to death so that He could forgive you. Yes, He willingly took up His cross for you, saying, "Father forgive them, for they don't know what they are doing."

Forgive whoever has wronged you. They don't know what they're doing. Our petty offenses to one another are nothing compared to our sins against Jesus. His hand of mercy is stretched out to you in forgiveness. Keep short accounts with people. Determine to forgive and love over and over and over again. Let your heart be free to love with His love.

---◇---

Go to anyone you need to forgive, or write a letter or make a phone call. Pray for that person. Pray and be filled with the love and forgiveness of Jesus in all of your relationships.

# JANUARY 24

*"And you shall receive power when the Holy Spirit has come upon you; and you shall be My witnesses both in Jerusalem, and Judea and Samaria and the remotest part of the earth"*
*Acts 1:8*

Blessed be the sweet Holy Spirit who desires to come to you and to fill you up to the overflow, moment by moment. Let Him pour His power into you so you can be His witness everywhere you go—at home, at work, across the world—to take the most remote place—and wherever He calls you. Not, "you will go witnessing" but, "you shall **be** My witness." Are you His witness? Do you commune with Him moment by moment? Are you obedient to do His will? Do you love Him more than anything or anyone? Do you walk in His will and not your own? Oh, commit yourself to Him again today. Let His Holy Spirit and glory fall upon you today. Receive His love and Spirit. Let Him breathe on you and be filled. Go in peace with the God of your heart. Go into the world and preach the gospel and show His love.

---

Set aside special time today to wait on the Lord, worshipping Him, just for Himself. Let Him fill you with His love and power. He will do it. Now go preach the gospel.

# JANUARY 25

*"So shall My word be which goes forth from My mouth. It shall not return to Me empty, without accomplishing what I desire." Isaiah 55:11*

Oh, the glorious power of God's word. He spoke and the universe was created. Can He not speak into your life today to create new things? His word brings life. It always brings life. When you speak His words to someone, sharing the precious gospel, the seeds of life are planted in the person's heart. In due season it will be watered and grow and spring into new life. His word **never** returns void, but **always** accomplishes His purpose. His written word does the same. It is planted and it grows according to His will.

Trust that you carry the treasure of life—His word. Use it in your prayers, use it in your conversations, use it when you write. Let the Lord's words bring life through you. Trust Him. It will never return void, but will accomplish His purpose.

---

Make a little gospel tract today, telling of the love and death and resurrection of Jesus. Use God's words in it and pray about who to give it to.

# JANUARY 26

*"Love never fails." 1 Corinthians 13:8*

Which love? GOD'S LOVE! It never ever fails. Never! No never! It always accomplishes His purpose to draw near to His heart. For Scripture says that GOD is LOVE! His very essence is pure and infinite love. Our own love only goes so far, but the Messiah's love has no end. Its depth and width and height is eternal. He wants to lavish it on you—His ocean of love. He wants to submerge you in His love—to fill you up until you're overflowing with His holy and unconditional love. All the world looks for this love—even the most evil are looking (in a wrong way in the wrong place) for this jewel of sacred love. Where is it found? In the very eyes of Jesus! In His heart as He gave his life. As you are filled with it, you go bearing His costly love. As you pour it out on others, it will never ever fail.

————————◇————————

Ask the Lord to fill you full of His love today. Receive it by faith and share it with someone today. It will never fail no matter what their response is. It will be divinely planted in their hearts.

*"But Peter and the apostles answered and said,
'We must obey God rather than men.'" Acts 5:29*

If you love Me, you will obey My commandments. Yes, to obey Jesus is to love Him. To obey Him is to walk in holiness with Him. Is it not a true joy to obey Him *just because* you love Him? "Yes," a thousand times, "yes!"

And what about when it is difficult? When it costs something? What about when it costs your very life? Oh, there is the test of all tests. Will we then obey Him? Again, "yes!" We will obey Him because we don't want to compromise our faith. We will obey Him because we refuse to have His name blasphemed or let evil reign. We will obey Him at the cost of being made a fool or losing friends. He has given us the "fear of the Lord" to help us, and His grace is entirely sufficient for the most difficult moment. Do not give in to fear. Stand firm. Look into His face, and you will be like an angel in appearance, even at the threat of your life. Obey God!

———————————————◇———————————————

Think today of the ways society is against Jesus. Pray about one of those things and choose a way that you can openly stand for Him. Overcome evil with good.

# JANUARY 28

*"But I do not consider my life of any account as dear to myself, in order that I may finish my course and the ministry which I received from the Lord Jesus, to testify solemnly of the gospel of the grace of God." Acts 20:24*

How dear is your life to you? What is it worth? What or who are you pouring your life into? May you be found this day, pouring your life into Jesus and His will for you. For your life is dear to **Him**, so dear to Him.

Are you ready to do His will with all of your heart? To finish the course He has for you? Many start but not all finish. It takes perseverance. You must overcome all obstacles and keep running the race! Run as if to win! Run for Jesus, with His fiery love in your heart!

And what **is** your ministry but to solemnly testify in word and action of the gospel of the grace of God? Shout it from the housetops! Shout it with your life! Do not consider your life dear to yourself. It's dear to Him! Give your all, even if you lose your life. Give your all for Jesus, who gave His all for you.

───────────◇───────────

Set aside some time to reorganize your priorities today. Put Jesus at the top of the list. Next, write His will and ministry for you.

# JANUARY 29

*"That if you confess with your mouth Jesus as Lord, and believe in your heart that God raised Him from the dead, you shall be saved."*
*Romans 10:9*

There's something about our words. The tongue is like a rudder of our life. In it is the power of life and death. In it is the fear of the Lord and blessing. In it is the flame of hell and cursing. For the mouth speaks what is in the heart.

When two people get married, they publicly confess before witnesses what is already in their hearts. This confession seals their commitment to one another. It is the same with salvation. We believe with our hearts that Jesus suffered and died for our sins and that He rose from the dead, being fully God and fully man. Then we confess it with our lips as we commit our lives to Him, and we are saved.

Is it not also true that in all issues of life, we believe in our hearts, and speak that which is there already, confirming it. Lord, have mercy on us. Let us have Your Spirit in our hearts and Your words on our lips. Let the words of my mouth and the meditation of my heart be acceptable to You, dear Lord.

◇

Ask Jesus to be the Lord of your heart and lips today. Find a verse about the tongue to memorize today. Determine to speak His words and His will today, and always.

# JANUARY 30

*"Every man serves the good wine first, and when men have drunk freely, then that which is poorer; you have kept the good wine until now."*
*John 2:10*

Thank You, Lord, that Your ways are above our ways. The world says that we must not spend too much time together or we will ruin the relationship. You say that we must be "one" (i.e., spend much time together). The world says that after the honeymoon the marriage gets worse, naturally. You say that after 50 years the marital love will far, far surpass the honeymoon stage.

And what about the spiritual life? How does our life with You go, Lord? Is it not a spiritual lesson that You saved the best for the last? Yes, it is shown in Your first miracle. The dry rituals of religion were brought to sparkling life in You, dear Jesus. As we grow in depth with You, the path gets brighter and brighter. As the MORNING STAR appears, the sky lights up, and we go from glory to glory now and throughout eternity. One day we will taste the fresh new wine as we see You face to face.

---

Have a time of communion with Jesus. As you prepare your heart and partake of the wine and bread, let the new wine of His love and covenant fill you up!

# JANUARY 31

*"Whom have I in heaven but Thee? And besides Thee, I desire nothing on earth." Psalm 73:25*

Oh, the sweet face to face relationship with the Lord! Whom do we have in heaven but the Lord Himself? It is He, our heavenly Bridegroom who waits for us with gentle love in His eyes! We have **Him**!

Do you love Him with all your heart? Do you cherish your times with Him? Do you look forward to more time with Him and the things He is doing in your life? Is He the very Lord of your life in a way that you feel so very bonded together with Him? Do you desire Him?

Or are there other things, other people, other delights that pull you away from Him? Are you easily distracted even by good things, godly people, ministry?

Get alone with Him and renew your love and commitment to Jesus. Spend precious time in the arms of your Lord until you can say, "Besides Thee I desire nothing on earth."

———————————◇———————————

Just by yourself, draw a picture of Jesus in Heaven with His arms open to you, waiting for you. Memorize Psalm 73:25 and keep that picture with you all day long.

# FEBRUARY 1

*"For I know the plans that I have for you,"
declares the Lord, "plans for welfare and not for
calamity to give you a future and a hope."
Jeremiah 29:11*

He knows! Yes, He knows the plans He has for you, for He designed them long ago. At your birth He saw you, was with you, and thought of the plans and calling upon your life. Again, at your second birth when you were born into His kingdom through Jesus' blood, He saw you getting closer to His plans. As you made Him "Lord" of your life He began to reveal some of His good plans to you! Even when you were afraid of His plans, or when things went wrong, He tried to remind you of His good plans for you. He wants you to know that they are **good plans**, not for calamity! They are to give you a future and a hope! Even in the broken areas of your life, there is hope and goodness from the Lord! His plans for you come from His heart of total love for you!

———————————◇———————————

Make a little map of where the Lord has brought you from. Leave a space for the future and write in big, fancy letters: *GOD HAS GOOD PLANS FOR ME!*

# FEBRUARY 2

*"My mouth is filled with Thy praise, and with Thy glory all day long." Psalm 71:8*

Open wide your heart to God this day, precious servant of the Lord! Let Him fill you up to the overflow. Hold out your cup to Him and let it run over. He will fill you to the fullest if you will allow Him. It is His sweet delight to do so.

Do not try to be ready, just begin worshipping Him. Let Him wash your heart clean. Take His mercy which is fresh and new each day and live in it. Do not look back. Do not look forward. **Concentrate on Jesus!** Look into His piercing eyes full of love for you. Do you see His kindness? Bless Him today!

Be filled and praise Him all day long. Give Him the glory due His name. Keep a song of love to Him in your heart all day. Worship and adore Him with all your heart. He is so worthy of your praise! Open wide your heart and your mouth to praise Him all day long!

---

If you have trouble with distractions, take a travel alarm with you today. Set it every 30 minutes. When it goes off, turn it off and sing to the Lord, either out loud or silently. Praise Him all day long!

# FEBRUARY 3

*"Enter His gates with thanksgiving, and His courts with praise. Give thanks to Him; bless His name. For the Lord is good; His lovingkindness is everlasting, and His faithfulness to all generations." Psalm 100:4-5*

Do you long for the Lord's sweet presence to be upon you? To carry it with you all the time? Not just to know that He's with you but to be dwelling in intimacy with Him? Would you like to not only go in and out but to live there in the holy of holies with Him? To see His face continually?

You must go through the gates first—the gates of thanksgiving. Don't be a clanging cymbal—be full of thankfulness. You cannot get through the gates without it. Then go through the outer courts, the courts of praise! Praise is becoming to you! It heals your heart, defeats the enemy and blesses the Lord! Now, enter into the holy of holies, to that sacred intimate place and bless Him! He is good! His lovingkindness is upon you. He is faithful! Love Him, bow down to Him! Give yourself to Him! Bless His holy name!

---

Get alone with the Lord and tell Him how thankful you are for Him. Then get some instrument (or make an instrument) and sing praises to Him. Then quietly enter into worship and bow down to Him. Stay in that secret place of stillness before Him until it fades.

# FEBRUARY 4

*"And they overcame him because of the blood of the Lamb and because of the word of their testimony, and they did not love their life even to death."*
*Revelation 12:11*

Oh how we need an overcoming spirit, for the enemy is about us on every side, ready to devour us. "And they overcame him" . . . by the BLOOD OF THE LAMB!" Yes, there is power over all in the blood of Jesus. *He* has overcome death and satan. He holds the keys of death and hell. Jesus, the spotless Lamb of God, has taken away your sins and overcome satan. You are in *Him!* You are an overcomer! You overcome because of the word of your testimony. Your testimony of Jesus in you has power against all evil. And what? "And they did not love their life even to death." Why? Because their lives belonged totally to Him! Do we love Jesus enough to give our lives? If we do, then we will overcome!

———————————◇———————————

Draw teardrops of blood. Thank Jesus for dying for you and overcoming satan. Be bold today and tell your testimony to someone you've prayed for. Ask the Lord to help you be able to give your life for Him.

# FEBRUARY 5

*"He who loves father or mother more than Me is not worthy of Me; and he who loves son or daughter more than Me is not worthy of Me."*
*Matthew 10:37*

What was Jesus talking about? Why does He speak in such strong ways when we know how important it is to Him that we honor our parents and love them? What do the previous verses say?

He was speaking of those who are ashamed to confess Him before others. Those who deny Him. Yes, it is difficult in the work place, in the unbelieving family—these days, believers are mocked and verbally persecuted (or more). But will you deny Him?

Jesus even warned us that His presence will not bring peace in some families—they will separate from you because you love Him. Still, we must choose. He said our enemies will be in our own households. We love them now with a greater love, His love—but we choose Jesus first! He is the Lord! He gave the answer—follow Him. Live for ***His*** sake.

He is working in their lives. If they receive you, they are welcoming Him. If they give you even a drink of water, they will be rewarded.

———————————◇———————————

Pray for your family today (or people you work with). Pray with all your heart. Ask the Lord what to do. Go to them, in His love and tell them of Jesus' love and salvation for them.

# FEBRUARY 6

*"I AM the Resurrection and the Life; he who believes in Me shall live even if he dies."*
*John 11:25*

Notice Jesus said, "I am" the resurrection! In fact, He was (and is) the great "I AM" walking about loving, saving, healing and teaching. God Himself! Doesn't it make our world holy in a way—that God came and lived with us in a human body? Yet, sadly, the world is still rampant with evil and sin, even increasingly.

Jesus is fully the Resurrection! No one ever died in His presence! He is fully Life! Whoever believes (commits their life to Him) shall live even if he dies. Live forever with the Lord in total bliss!

But there's more. For those who love Him, who make Him their Lord—He lives in them! His spirit dwells in them—that resurrection spirit! They will *always* rise again! Yes, physically, emotionally and spiritually, in this life, they will rise again! Never stay down but rise again! Rise up, O child of God! *He is risen!*

———————————◇———————————

Say to your soul today—"Rise up to the living God!" Say to your spirit, "Rise and sing to your Lord!" Say to your body, "Rise and be healed in the name of Jesus!"

# FEBRUARY 7

*"Yet Thou art holy, O Thou who art enthroned upon the praises of Israel." Psalm 22:3*

Do you long for more of the Lord? To be fully His? Not a going in and coming out, but a continual dwelling in that secret, intimate place with Him? Have you been around people who seem to carry the manifestation of His presence with them? You feel as if He has visited you when they are near?

How do they do it? What can we do? One answer is in this Psalm. It was the secret of Israel. How much more with those of us who have Him living in our hearts. And here is the secret: He is enthroned in our praises! Yes, that's where He dwells. That is His delight! He loves to come to us in our praises and all the more when we gather in unity and oneness of heart and mind. Let His stillness fill your heart and your praises to Him well up from the deepest part of your heart. Begin to praise your sweet Lord, as often as possible. Keep a song in your heart and rise above your circumstances into the arms of your Lord. Love Him! Praise Him! Experience Him!

———————◇———————

Set aside a week in which you do nothing but praise Him! Fill your home, work place and car with praises to Him! Honor Him! Exalt Him! He is worthy!

# FEBRUARY 8

*"The Lord God is my strength, and He has made my feet like hinds' feet, and makes me walk on my high places." Habakkuk 3:19*

Yes, the Lord is your strength, for in Him you live and move and have your being. He's the very strength of your life forever! And He will make your feet (your beautiful feet bringing the gospel), like hinds' feet—able to climb in difficult places, to climb on rocks and even in dangerous places. You will glide over these places and go high—up to the mountain of the Lord! To the top, where the air is clean and there's beauty all around. Up, up over the circumstances and trials. Strong feet, going up at all times. Sometimes with bruises, but going up.

The Lord is calling you up. He wants you to be in a higher place with Him. Don't stay down on a comfortable plateau. Don't take the easy way. Be strong. Climb up. Up to the Lord. See! He is waiting for you there, to speak new things, to show you new places, and new depths of His love for you.

———————————◇———————————

Make a new commitment today to grow stronger in Jesus. Ask Him to give you hunger and begin to seek Him with all your heart. Ask for new revelations. Study His word in depth.

# FEBRUARY 9

*"But for you who fear My name the Sun of Righteousness will rise with healing in its wings."*
*Malachi 4:2*

What does it mean to "fear" the Lord? It means to be in "awe" of Him! On your face before Him! How do you honor this King of glory—Jesus? By loving what He loves and hating what He hates. He loves your heart and He hates sin. Bow down before His holy face.

Have you given yourself to Him? Offered yourself as a living sacrifice of worship? Is He sanctifying you and teaching you to walk in holiness? Then you must keep a guard over your heart for out of it flow the real issues of life?

Are your eyes seeing as He sees? Looking at things that are godly? Are you listening to the things that glorify Him? Are you speaking as He would speak? What about your motives? Are you letting the Holy Spirit check your motives and priorities? Is the Lord having His way with you? Are you His? Is your attitude full of thankfulness and love?

Then the Sun of Righteousness, the bright glow and warmth of His presence will rise upon you with His healing love!

---

Consecrate yourself fresh and new to the Lord today. Be His—all that you are and all that you're not yet. Let His love fill you and ask Him that you may fear Him always!

# FEBRUARY 10

*"And the cooking pots in the Lord's house will be like the bowls before the altar. Every cooking pot will be Holy Unto the Lord." Zechariah 14:20*

Do you know that you have an anointing from the Holy One? Yes, an anointing greater and deeper than you know. All that you are and all that you do is anointed of the Lord—if you are in Him, with a clean heart. Are you walking in intimacy with Him? Then, all that you touch is anointed. The Spirit of the Lord is in you and goes through you.

And what is devotion to Jesus? Is it time with Him alone each day? Yes, and more. You can do all in devotion to Him. If you're washing dishes, do it unto the Lord. If you're writing letters, do it unto the Lord. Do your work at the office as a devotion to Him. Take care of your family as unto the Lord. Lift all of your activities unto Him and do it with Him and for Him. Only then will *all* be sweet! Yes, even the cooking pots will be as bowls before the altar, holy to the Lord!

---

Today, consecrate all of your belongings and activities unto the Lord. All utensils as items of worship. Do everything as unto Jesus! He is with you!

# FEBRUARY 11

*"And if you extract the precious from the worthless, you will become My spokesman."*
*Jeremiah 15:19B*

This is the way of Jesus—to extract the precious from the worthless. We must make it our aim to find the precious, the hidden jewel of glory in each person. Jesus was a friend of sinners and outcasts. He went to the lame and poor and needy and rejected. He found the hidden jewel in each and renewed their hope. He was a Master at loving the unlovely. He even loved those who killed Him.

Even in times of revival, the Lord uses the most unlikely person to start it, to be anointed. He uses the foolish to confound the wise. He loves. Yes, He really loves. All were created in the image of God. The image has been so marred and twisted, it is often unrecognizable. But if you extract the precious, you will become His spokesman.

Resist judging as the world does and embrace the light of glory falling on that unlikely person—that one who feels worthless. Love the unlovable and be a spokesman, anointed for Jesus!

---

Think of someone you know or have met that is an outcast or feels unworthy. Ask the Lord how you can bless and love that person with His love today. Look for the preciousness God has given to that person.

# FEBRUARY 12

*"For the eyes of the Lord move to and fro throughout the earth that He may strongly support those whose heart is completely His."*
*2 Corinthians 16:9 A*

Oh dear lover of God! His eyes are upon you, steadfast upon you. Do you feel His loving gaze? He is so in love with you. You are His treasured possession, so precious to Him.

His eyes move all over the earth searching for that one person, so valued, because their heart is completely His. He longs for you to be completely His. That is His great desire. He is searching all the time for that one. Are you completely His? Have you given yourself to Him in abandonment? Is all that you are and all that you love—His?

Then He is well pleased with you! He will **fully support you** in all you do and say. His efforts and power are upon you and His love will flow out of you as a river of refreshing to all around you! You are His, and He is yours! The living God, full of lovingkindness, is yours.

———————————◇———————————

Be still in His presence and ask the Lord to make you completely His—and to reveal any part of your life that is not His. Give that part to Him today and back it up with an action. Thank Him for His support.

# FEBRUARY 13

*"And I will make you like a signet ring, for
I have chosen you." Haggai 2:23*

I give thanks for you, beloved one, for I know His choice of you! You are chosen of God to bear His image, to walk in the glory of the Messiah! Yes, His light is upon you. It is in your eyes. You shine, for you are His choice.

He has made a covenant with you—an everlasting covenant, closer than any relationship on earth, even marriage. He has chosen you and given His holy blood for you. As a ring is round, representing eternal love, He will make you full of eternal love. As a signet ring is used for approval and to make decrees, His approval and favor of you will enable you to decree His gospel to every creature. As a king is given a ring of royalty, so your God will make you a royal priesthood, a chosen person. You are His royal bride. No one can take your place. You are His choice. ***His choice!*** Glory to God! You are His choice!

———————————◇———————————

Make a ring out of foil and put it in a place to remind you that you are chosen of the Lord and carry His authority and love!

# FEBRUARY 14

*"And you will seek Me and find Me, when you*
*search for Me with all your heart."*
*Jeremiah 29:13*

And here is a key to all eternity for throughout the Bible, from Genesis to Revelation, this is one of God's greatest promises to mankind—"If you **seek Me with all your heart**, you will find Me." If you search for Him with your heart, He will indeed be found by you.

Were you hungry for the Lord when He saved you? Was He your whole life? Your every thought? Yes, and even more! He would not let you go hungry. He is a good Shepherd, a loving Father! He fed you until you were full and overflowing. He is the same yesterday, today and tomorrow. If you seek Him now, you will have more depth with Him than you ever dreamed possible. Don't stop at a plateau. Run the race with Jesus! Taste of the Lord and His goodness. Now drink from the wells of His Spirit! Swim in it! Let Him fill you to the overflow again, only this time deeper and deeper! Ask for this thirst and hunger for the Lord! Ask and receive!

---◆---

Set aside special time or a few days to seek the Lord! Enjoy Him! Worship Him! Pray to Him and pour out your heart! Give Him your burdens and seek to know Him better! Study His word and rejoice!

# FEBRUARY 15

*"They looked to Him and were radiant."*
*Psalm 34:5*

Look into the blessed eyes of your Savior, your Lord! Jesus! Look into that radiant shine! What do you see? Do you see the power of His love and kindness for you? Do those holy eyes melt your heart? Those majestic eyes, so full of grace and glory!

Do you know that those eyes are for you? He is so in love with you! He waits for the wedding banquet with you, His bride! Those loving, majestic, fiery eyes—those eyes that see through you with perfect love—they are for you! Jesus longs for you! Do you see that longing in His eyes?

And what about your eyes? Does it amaze you that He loves to look into your eyes too? Your eyes are blessed and pure because you behold Him. That gaze can last forever. His eternal love captivates you. Be lost in His gaze! Look to Him and be radiant!

---

Add into your daily time with the Lord, time to just look at Him! Be still and let His gaze of love fill you. It will change you. It will heal you and bless you and you will go from glory to glory.

# FEBRUARY 16

*"Things which the eye has not seen, and ear has not heard, and which have not entered the heart of man, all that God has prepared for those who love Him." 1 Corinthians 2:9*

Dear beloved lover of God, your eyes have not begun to see all that Jesus has prepared for you. Your ears have not yet heard His tender and glorious voice as it really is. It has not yet come to your heart the greatness of God's plans for eternity with you! It is far beyond your imagination. It is eternal and heavenly.

This world can never satisfy your soul. As time goes on it becomes more and more strange and distant, as the powers of darkness line up for battle against the Son of God who lives in you. You have His peace which passes understanding to guard your heart and mind. His everlasting arms hold you.

But there is that trumpet ring from heaven that calls you closer and closer, until the full day. Yes, your call is upward—better and better, strength to strength, glory to glory! For the everlasting God of the Universe is planning to spend eternity showing you His deep lovingkindness and valiant, shining glory! It is beyond your understanding!

---

Meditate today on what it will be like to step into eternity and the everlasting full presence of God! Worship Him! Glorify Him!

# FEBRUARY 17

*"Be still and know that I am God; I will be exalted among the nations."* Psalm 46:10

Oh, the sweetness of being still before God! There are special times of quiet before the Lord that minister to the depths of the heart. Even nature itself discloses this truth. In the quietness of a forest or alone at the ocean, the soul feels a certain link to our Creator automatically. How much more for the seeking heart, the one who loves the Lord and only wants ***more of Him***.

Be still before Him and hear the still small voice speaking to you. Dwell in that peaceful, holy moment with your Lord. Yes, wait before Him and renew your strength, so you can run and not be weary. Drink in those still, holy moments. Even in a crowd or in busy moments you can close your eyes and be instantly in His blessed presence! And what? Know your God! Know Him! And He will be exalted among the nations! Be still and know that I AM God!

---

Clear your mind of everything but Jesus. Be still before Him and listen for His still small voice. Let Him fill you with His stillness and peace!

# FEBRUARY 18

*"But let those who love Him be like the rising of the sun in its might." Judges 5:31B*

O come, beloved believer, you who love God! Come and be strong in the power of His might. For the world around you is decaying. But you will rise up and renew your strength, mounting up with wings as an eagle. The path of the righteous shines brighter and brighter. You are getting stronger and brighter in the Lord each day, each moment—if you really love Him! You are like the sun as it rises— first just a little light, but still lighting all around everywhere. Then, more light until the shadows can be seen—the black and white, sin and holiness. Finally, the full strength which warms hearts all around you with His love. This might of His Spirit will fill you and overflow out of you. When it's hot out, people purposely go out and sit in the sun. When you are filled with Jesus, people will come to you, longing for Him. You will sit together, basking in His light, warmth and strength. Bask in the Son today!

———————————◇———————————

Today, bask in the light of God's love and power. Let it fill you and let the light fall upon your face. Then go spread that light to someone today. Pour it onto them.

# FEBRUARY 19

*"And I will betroth you to Me forever; Yes, I will betroth you to Me in righteousness, and in justice, in lovingkindness and in compassion, and I will betroth you to Me in faithfulness. Then you will <u>know</u> the Lord." Hosea 2:19-20*

Dear sweet Lord—thank You that it is Your supreme purpose to be married to Your people in oneness and intimacy! Thank You that You wait for the marriage supper of the Lamb in heaven! Thank You that You give us Your own precious righteousness so that we can be as near as we like to You. Thank You that Your blood (Your agony over our sins) has made us just in Your sight forever! Thank You that Your greatest desire is to lavish Your lovingkindness upon us now and forever—to spend eternity showing us Your compassion and great mercy. Thank You for Your absolute faithfulness to us in spite of our unfaithfulness. Let us embrace You, precious Jesus, in a new way today. Let us dwell with You as Your bride—a sacred dwelling together with You! You have chosen the highest relationship for us. Let us adore You today! For You are our holy Bridegroom!

---

Find a token of bridal love for the Lord today (a ring, a verse, a bookmark, anything). Ask Jesus to reveal Himself to your heart as your bridegroom now and forever!

# FEBRUARY 20

*"Joy and gladness will be found in her,*
*thanksgiving and a sound of melody."*
*Isaiah 51:3 B*

Dear lover of God, let this verse be a picture of your relationship with the Lord! The joy of the Lord is your strength. A merry heart doeth good like medicine. Enter into the inner courts of His presence today with thanksgiving. Do not let your emotions or circumstances lead you. Let the Holy Spirit lead you. Make melody in your heart to one another, sing psalms and hymns to the Lord. Be filled with the joy of the Lord. Let it flow out of you. He wants to give it to you. Ask and you shall receive. He is your praise and your God.

Do you want to praise Him or do you want to *be* a praise to Him? Be a praise today! Let His song fill your heart all day long. Be glad in the Lord! Let Him look and see you there, shining and sparkling for Him! A joy to Him! Make His heart glad over you today!

---◇---

Make a joyful **noise** unto the Lord! No matter what you think of your voice, make up a song for Him today. Write it down and sing it over and over! Rejoice in the Lord!

# FEBRUARY 21

*"Who is like Thee, majestic in holiness, awesome in praises, working wonders?" Exodus 15:11*

Who is like this God of ours, the King of Kings and Lords of Lords? Who is so mighty? He is the Creator of the Universe! He simply spoke it into existence. Our little minds cannot comprehend its size, nor His greatness. We do not understand eternity. We are so limited and finite. But *He* is infinite and beyond comprehension. So He became a Man and dwelt among us! A simple carpenter. He healed the sick, comforted the lonely, taught those who were seeking Him, fed the hungry and even raised the dead. Then after untold suffering, He Himself died for our sins and rose again. He lives interceding for us. Our salvation is forever, if we are really His.

His mercy is upon the smallest, the most unlovely, the outcasts. He cares for the smallest detail of our lives. *He* is love! This majestic, holy Lord of ours is pure love! He is still awesome in praises and daily working wonders in us. Greater love has no man. Who is this God? There is none like Him! He is majestic in holiness, awesome in praises, working wonders.

---◇---

Tell the Lord today all of the ways that He is like no other in your life. Mention all the ways that He is special and why He has first place forever in your heart!

# FEBRUARY 22

*"Then you will see and be radiant and your heart will thrill and rejoice." Isaiah 60:5A*

Have you seen Jesus? Did your salvation and new life with Him thrill you? Did it make you radiant and full of joy to all around you? Dear precious believer, that was only the beginning, the morning dawn. That was when He passed by and you touched the hem of His garment. You were made whole. He spoke to you, and He has been alive in you since that moment. You have loved Jesus more and more deeply and you would give your life for Him. He is your dearest relative and you love Him with all your heart. You know you do. But there is a new day coming. A day when you will see Him face to face physically as well as spiritually. You will look into His eyes and your heart will beat faster. You will see His kindness, His love, His innocence and your heart will thrill! You will rejoice over Him with songs and praises. With your whole being you will worship Him. Your heart will thrill and rejoice over the love of your life—Jesus! Bless Him! Love Him! Worship Him today!

---◆---

Write a love letter to Jesus today! Tell Him all that you see in Him and how your heart is thrilled over Him. Find a new way to rejoice over Him today!

# FEBRUARY 23

*"But we all with unveiled face beholding as in a mirror the glory of the Lord, are being transformed into the same image from glory to glory, just as from the Lord, the Spirit."*
**2 Corinthians 3:18**

Oh dear precious one, look to Jesus! He has the love and power to heal your heart, anoint you and direct you. He will do it over and over as you come to Him. The ray of the light of His face will do these things. But He wants to give you **fullness!** He wants to sweep you off your feet! He wants to give you depth and sweet communion with Himself in a way that you've never known before.

Look into His face! Behold Him! Stay there, beholding your Lord! This is where He wants you! Stay in His arms. Behold Him! Look into His eyes continually! You will not have a ray of light, you will have the full light of His gaze upon you! His own countenance will light you up. You will see Him in His glory and be transformed. You yourself will be dazzling white. You will be like Him, and you will go from glory to glory! Keep beholding Jesus!

---

Write this verse on every mirror in your home. Learn to practice God's continual presence by beholding Him as often as possible throughout the day.

# FEBRUARY 24

*"And He is the radiance of His glory and the exact representation of His nature, and upholds all things by the word of His power." Hebrews 1:3*

How glorious is our Lord! Precious Jesus! He came as a baby, being cared for by sinful mankind, growing in all the stages of childhood, adolescence, youth and adulthood so that He could show us face to face who God is and how deeply He loves us. The Messiah is the exact, the very exact representation of God's nature. If you have seen Him, you have seen the Father, for they are one. The Messiah is the very radiance of His glory! He is the *face of God* shining upon us! He is the fullness of God! The beautiful glory of God! Oh the depth of the riches of the wisdom and knowledge of God! His ways are excellent! His ways are pure!

The Messiah upholds all things by the word of His power! Jesus is the living word! The Messiah is full of power! In Him all the fullness of deity dwells. The Messiah is Lord!

———————————◇———————————

Make a list of the ways that you see Jesus upholding all things in your life, your family, your congregation, city, country. Thank Him for it! Pray for His glory there!

# FEBRUARY 25

*"And to know the love of the Messiah which surpasses knowledge, that you may be filled up to all the fulness of God." Ephesians 3:19*

Oh, to know the love of the Messiah! To plummet its depths, to rocket to its heights! To be still and know! To dwell and bask in His sweet presence! His glorious presence! That love that is way beyond our knowledge and understanding! The weight of the glory of God! Oh dear precious one, rest in it! Let His love fill you like new wine! Let it saturate your heart with peace and joy! The precious Son of God is shining on you! The light of His countenance is resting on you! Let Him fill you and fill you. Drink in the living water of the Holy Spirit until you thirst no more. Let it overflow in you like a fountain! Open your heart and receive *all* He has for you! All! Filled up to the fulness of God! Yes, filled with His rich, infinite love and glory! Never ending! The fulness of God! The bliss of the fulness of God!

---

Put a glass inside of a bowl and fill it with water until it overflows! Remember the precious fulness of God when you look at it. Bask in His presence!

# FEBRUARY 26

*"Because I am doing something in your days you would not believe even if you were told."*
*Habakkuk 1:5*

Isn't that just the way the Lord is? He is always at work in every situation doing more than we could ever imagine or think. There is always hope, always faith, always love that never fails. But that is only a taste of what He has. Just a mere glimpse.

Expand your horizons, move out your tent pegs, for the Lord Almighty is desiring to do a great work in you and through you! His plans are out of reach of your own expectations. Nothing is impossible with Him, for those that believe. Take His fresh new mercy, His gift of faith today.

Dare to believe for the impossible. Take His hand. Step out in faith and begin to take risks for the kingdom of heaven, for Jesus' sake. Determine to do His will and to believe that He is doing something incredibly great and you are part of it. Then reach out with instant obedience—strengthening your faith!

———————————◇———————————

Make a "mega faith" list today. Write down things you will believe by faith. Stretch your faith to new levels. Believe for the impossible and thank Him by faith ahead of time!

# FEBRUARY 27

*"I urge you therefore, brethren, by the mercies of God, to present your bodies a living and holy sacrifice, acceptable to God, which is your spiritual service of worship."* Romans 12:1

Paul urges us, with deep desperation in the mercy of God Himself, to present our bodies as living and holy sacrifices which are acceptable, to God. This is our worship! It is humbling ourselves before God daily and offering ourselves upon the altar, saying—"Do as You want, O Lord, with me. I am Yours." This is worship! Are you a living sacrifice to the Lord! Is the Holy Spirit purging you and fine tuning you? Is He making you a living and holy sacrifice unto Himself? Often we must not only give Him our weaknesses and sins, but also those good things (even gifts from Him, or serving Him) that get in the way of pure and holy fellowship with Him. Rid yourself of all but Him today and offer yourself as a living and holy sacrifice of worship to Him! You are a worship to Him!

---◆---

Find a place to make an altar to God. Write on a paper all that you are in Him, and all that you're not yet. Leave it on the altar and say, "I'm Yours, Lord! Take me. Use me."

# FEBRUARY 28

*"Now unto Him who is able to keep you from stumbling; and to make you stand in the presence of His glory, blameless, with great joy." Jude 24*

Now unto Him be glory! Yes, unto Jesus be glory forever and ever. One day we will stand before You, precious Lord! What a day it will be! A day of trembling, a day of the full awe of Your physical presence. Silence in heaven.

Jesus! Sweet Jesus! Thank You for keeping us from falling. Thank You for holding us up, for picking us up, for fresh new mercy and grace, for trusting us though we be unworthy. Thank You for Your faithful love, for Your kind patience. Thank you for never giving up on us when others would, when we ourselves would. Thank You dear, dear Jesus, love of our lives! Thank You, that You not only present us before the Father as Yours, but You and You alone present us as *blameless* with *great joy*, full of Your own glory! Hallelujah! Glory to Your holy name!

---◇---

Imagine yourself right now before the throne of God, blameless and holy, full of joy! Rejoice before Him! Sing with an instrument! Dance for joy!

# FEBRUARY 29

*"Blessed are the pure in heart for they shall see God." Matthew 5:8*

Oh dear, sweet lover of Jesus! Have you called out to God for a pure heart? Have you longed to walk in greater holiness? Have you encountered trials along the way and at times felt shattered into pieces? Has the Lord often spoken to you about your motives and priorities?

Rejoice, dear lovely one of God! His precious Holy Spirit is hard at work in you, answering your prayer for a pure heart! He is doing it! Oh, satan would desire to sift you and accuse you, to say that you are getting worse. No, you are drawing near to the Lord if you love Him daily and walk with a clean heart. Yes, you are getting closer and closer to the Holy One, being transformed into His image and character. That is why you see your own blemishes so much. The light is brighter upon you. Let it be! Rejoice in the Holy One of Israel! He is making you pure and beautiful so that He can look at you, and that look will reflect Him in you! You will have a shining, clear, pure, beautiful reflection of Jesus in your eyes!

---

Wear some kind of a heart today to remind yourself that Jesus is perfecting a pure heart in you!

# MARCH 1

*"And you shall set aside what is full."* **2 Kings 4:4**

Dear beloved one, have you given the very core of your being, that deepest place of your heart, your very life itself to the Holy One of Israel? To Jesus, your King, the One who loves you way beyond your comprehension?

And have you determined to follow Him with all your heart, to do His will alone, and to bring His kingdom to this earth? Do you long to leave a mark on this earth which will draw people to Jesus, to eternal life? Has the enemy often made you feel inadequate or unworthy? Resist his lies in the name of Jesus and the power of His Spirit.

Jesus said if you give a cup of water to a disciple in His name you will receive a reward!

The widow in 2 Kings had but a jar of oil. She was ready to die. By faith she obeyed and got many jars. She began to pour and as she did, the oil multiplied! She set aside what was full. Set aside yourself, by faith, to be fully used of the Lord! A full vessel of His love, mercy and salvation.

————————◇————————

Think of what you need to honor Jesus. What do you need more of? Pour it out. Use it for Him—all of it and He will meet you there and fill you and multiply you. Glorify Him.

# MARCH 2

*"But a cheerful heart has a continual feast."*
*Proverb 15:15 B*

Open your heart wide, dear precious believer! Open your heart this day and receive greatly from the Love of your life—Jesus! Let Him pour new joy into you today! He longs to do it! He will fill your mouth with laughter and your lips with shouts of joy!

You know it already—the joy of the Lord is your strength! A merry heart is medicine to your soul! Rejoice before the Lord today! Shout for joy! Tell Him of your love! Sing for joy! Dance for joy! Clap your hands for joy! *Squeal* for joy! *Let joy get a hold of you* this day! Bring pleasure to Him with joy!

Then let your heart feast in delighting in Him! Keep that continual feast of His delights in your heart all day! Your God is full of light and joy and He is radiating joy over you today!

————————————◇————————————

Find a new way to express joy to the Lord today! Bless Him and love Him! He is worthy to be praised! Rejoice! Make a feast of praises to Him!

# MARCH 3

*"Therefore, holy brethren, partakers of a heavenly calling, consider Jesus." Hebrews 3:1*

Do you know that you are holy in His sight because He became sin for you on the cross? He gave you His own righteousness because you have none of your own. His blood is holy. His righteousness is a breastplate to protect you from the evil one. You are His brother (or sister) bonded to Him by the covenant of His blood and suffering.

So also you are a partaker of a heavenly calling. He calls you to the heights with Himself. He gives you His own divine nature.

He makes you holy, for He is holy. Dwell in the heights with Him today—up on the mountain tops in the heavenly air, clean and pure.

Consider Jesus! Jesus! Name above all names. Set your heart and mind on Him. Be with Him in holiness today. Refresh your heavenly calling. Partake of Him! Consider Jesus! Lovely, precious Jesus! Lord of all!

———————————◇———————————

Write the name JESUS in huge letters and keep it with you all day. Meditate on Him with just a glance at His name over and over throughout the day!

# MARCH 4

*"Now to Him who is able to do exceeding,
abundantly beyond all that we ask or think."
Ephesians 3:20*

What a great comfort this is! What a strengthening of faith to know that Jesus is well able not to just answer our prayers, but to do exceeding, abundantly more than all we have asked or even thought of. He works in another realm. His ways are higher than ours. Nothing, absolutely nothing is impossible for the Lord.

Have you ever believed something when all circumstances were the opposite? That is nothing for the Lord. Believe you have received it, for He is faithful. Stir up the gift of faith that is in you! Your God will never let you down. Believe for that mountain to go into the sea. He will do beyond your imagination. Wait on Him, trust Him, though the answer lingers. It will come as a shining moonbeam and when it does, it will bless you way beyond your dreams. Ask, according to His perfect will and see Him lavish the answer upon you!

---◇---

Write in big letters "BEYOND" and put it somewhere special to remind you of Ephesians 3:20!

# MARCH 5

*"Arise, shine; for your light has come, and the glory of the Lord has risen upon you."*
*Isaiah 60:1*

Rise up and shine, beloved believer! It's your move, to rise! The Lord wants to shine in you. He has lit up your soul and given life to your heart. He is building His own divine character into you. The Light of the world, the Creator of the universe has come to you. Your light has come. Don't miss this moment. His light has come to you now. Rise up and give Him the chance to shine through you. The glory of the Lord is rising upon you! You are a light and a glory! You are His! Shine now and glorify Him! Bring life and light and love to the world around you. Light the dark! Glorify Jesus! In everything give thanks. Let the joy of the Lord flow out of you for that is your strength. Be a blinding light to the darkness, revealing the light of the glorious Son of God!

---

Light a candle as your worship today! With all your heart rise up and shine for Jesus today! Give Him glory in every occasion.

# MARCH 6

*"We will rejoice in You and be glad; we will extol Your love more than wine."*
*Song of Solomon 1:4 B*

Come this day, sweet godly one, and rejoice in your Lord! Close your eyes and dwell in His presence! Drink in His love as sweet wine! Then rise up and rejoice in Him! Sing to Him! Shout for joy because of Him! Jump up and down for Him! Tell Him of your love! Exalt His name! Let Him fill you with gladness! Magnify the Lord! Bless His holy name! Fall in love with Him all over again! For the Lord is a great King, a mighty refuge. He is the Rock of your salvation. He is your song of peace in the night and your bright joy in the morning! He is all you could ever want or need, the very love of your life. All that matters is Him! Rejoice! Give Him praise! Glorify Jesus! Adorn Him with your whole heart today for His love is sweeter than wine! He is your song of all songs and your joy of all joys! The King of glory is in love with you!

---◇---

*Get a tambourine or some form of instrument and dance around to the Lord! Exalt Him! Honor Him! Bless Him! Rejoice in Him!*

# MARCH 7

*"And day and night they do not cease to say, 'Holy, Holy, Holy is the Lord God, the Almighty, who was and who is and who is to come.'"*
**Revelation 4:8**

Can you imagine what it must be like in heaven? Constant worship! Constant praise and adoration! Constant prayer and glory all around! The physical presence of the living God! The King of the universe! If we could peek into heaven now, we would fall on our faces because of the awesome power of His glorious presence! Without Jesus in our hearts, we would die in His presence! But the resurrection spirit in us longs for His glorious presence and splendor and majesty.

Day and night, 24 hours a day "Holy, Holy, Holy!"—He is worshipped and adored every second—just as He should be. "Holy" is the quality that is called out. "Holy!" Holy is He that calls to you, dear one. The Holy One wants the closest of intimacy with you. He loves you.

Will you join this heavenly worship? You can, right now! Add to it—just for Him! "Holy, Holy, Holy!"

———————————————◇———————————————

Pin onto your clothes today a heart that says, "Holy unto the Lord!" Worship Him all through the day for His holiness!

# MARCH 8

*"Let the high praises of God be in their mouth,*
*and a two-edged sword in their hand."*
*Psalm 149:6*

Begin to worship and praise the Lord today. As you do, wait for a moment and ask Him to put high praises into your heart for Him today! He is worthy of all praise and honor forever!

Lord, You are my Creator, my High Priest, my costly anointing, the apple of my eye. You are all wisdom and depth, the sweet singer of Israel, the Rose of Sharon, Lily of the valley, Prince of Peace! You are my King of Kings, Lord of Lords, poured-out Spirit, eternal Kingdom, MORNING STAR. You are my Good Shepherd, Immanuel, Servant Heart, blessed Hope. Your blood is holy. You are my healer, my faith giver, the love of my life. You are the Giver of all good gifts, the glory of my heart, the jewel above price. You are my Best Friend, my Brother, my Everlasting Father, my wonderful counselor, my eternal peace forever. You are my broken bread of life, my poured out wine on the altar, the glorious Son! The glorious Son of God in all radiance, power and majesty! You are my Bridegroom, all glorious and full of splendor. You are the Resurrection and Life forever!

———————◇———————

Write or sing a new song (one you make up yourself) and praise the Lord in honor and truth and power! Give Him glory!

# MARCH 9

*"And who knows whether you have attained royalty for such a time as this." Esther 4:14*

Dear precious lover of Jesus, where are you right now? What are your circumstances? Can you see the face of Jesus in them? Is He working all things for good in you? Do you see what He is doing, or are you having to trust without seeing?

Lean your head on His chest. Rest in Him. Be yoked with Him today. Let Him hold your face and look into your eyes. Let Him renew your love! Drink in the fresh well of His depth and joy today! Rejoice in your Lord! His thoughts of you are as the stars! He has a great and mighty plan for you! You only see dimly, as in a glass, but He sees the clear, bright new day! He knows the new song of your heart! He is gentle and caring, for you are His jewel.

You are right in place if you are loving Him wholeheartedly, if you are devoted to Him. His timing is perfect and He has called you to this place for such a time as this—a time to do His will, His way, in His history!

---◇---

Make a list of front line headlines today. Now add your own headline of what you are doing for God! You are His history, His important news! **You** bring Him glory!

# MARCH 10

*"And let the peace of the Messiah rule in your hearts, to which indeed you were called in one body; and be thankful." Colossians 3:15*

Oh, precious lover of God, what a glorious verse this is! What is better than to dwell in the peace of God? It is truly heaven on earth! It is there for us, continually. And it is God's will for us.

We must be one to "let" the peace rule in our hearts. We must take it and keep it all day long, everyday of our lives. It is the peace that passes understanding. It only comes through the Holy Spirit. *Let* it reign in your heart and mind today. Be still in His presence each morning. Give Him time to fill you up. Don't be in a rush and quench His Spirit. The more often you let Him do this throughout the day, the more quickly His manifest presence will come to you. Cast your cares upon Jesus. He is your burden bearer. Keep priorities right—not too busy. Get rid of distractions. Concentrate on Him. He is first. He is your love. Love Him! Sing to Him! Let Him fill you. Receive His peace. You were called to it. *Let* it rule your decisions and actions. Be thankful and bless Him! Dwell in His peace today and always.

---------------◇---------------

Throughout the day, stop and be still and receive His peace again. Be filled and refilled. Let His peace (not your own) rule you and guide you in all you say and do today!

# MARCH 11

*"I thank my God in all remembrance of you, always offering prayer with joy in my every prayer for you." Philippians 1:3-4*

What a joy, what a privilege to be clothed with a thankful heart—to give thanks in everything. Thankfulness should dominate our attitudes. If it isn't there, take time with the Lord to enter into His gates with thanksgiving—to get a fresh revelation from Him—to be filled up again! Are you predominantly and continually thankful? If not, let Jesus heal your wounds. Let Him give you fresh new joy!

Do you see Jesus in your relationships? Are those closest to you a reflection of Him? If not, let Him show you how He sees them and you see them that way too.

Does prayer flow out of you in faithfulness for those closest to your heart? It should be a natural reaction of your love—always offering prayer with joy for them!

Be a channel of His blessings! Forget yourself. Concentrate on Jesus and those who are a gift from Him!

---◇---

Make a list of all you are thankful for (ten things) to the Lord! Then make a list of those closest to you that you are thankful for (two or three) and thank the Lord with all your heart!

# MARCH 12

## *"Hallelujah! For the Lord our God, the Almighty reigns." Revelation 19:6*

Though we see in a glass darkly, one day we will see Him face to face! The mustard seed will be a full tree. The sun will rise to its fulness!

In these days as troubles on earth get darker, the veil is about to be torn between us and heaven. The light of His countenance is about to shine its first streams of glory! The veil is lifting and we shall see the Son of Man coming in the clouds with His holy angels. We will see Him whom we have pierced, the Holy One of Israel. All anger, fear, hatred and death will begin to fade and the peace of His presence will fill the air. His song will be heard by those who love Him. The trumpet will sound and we will see Him as He is. We shall be like Him and He will take His stand on earth. Hallelujah! For the Lord our God, the Almighty reigns! Hallelujah! Hallelujah!

---

Rejoice today that soon your King will come! Draw a bright sun, covering a black background to remind you of His coming!

# MARCH 13

*"And I saw the holy city, new Jerusalem, coming down out of heaven from God, made ready as a bride adorned for her husband." Revelation 21:2*

The holy city! The city of God, full of His glory forever! The new Jerusalem coming down out of heaven. God's own city is sent from heaven, coming down from Him—a new city, not stained by the earth. This city will be made ready by God Himself. He has been preparing these mansions and streets of gold and gates of pearls for 2,000 years.

Even the street will be pure. And there will be no sea—no division of peoples. Jewels there, will be as nothing compared to the pure radiance of the Son of God! Oh, bless your holy name, Lord! How we love You!   You, Lord have made the holy city ready, as a bride—as a pure, chaste virgin. She will be adorned for You—clothed in Your salvation—the blood of the precious Lamb of God! Wrapped in Your righteousness—a royal diadem in the hand of the Lord! Adorned for You, Lord—in You, through You and for You! Glory to the Lamb!

———————————⬦———————————

Find a piece of jewelry to wear today to remind you of the holy city and that you are the bride of the Messiah!

# MARCH 14

*"And they shall see His face." Revelation 22:4*

Oh dear Lord, what blessed and holy words these are! The sound of them causes all hope and joy and peace to rise up in us. For all we long for in the end is to see Your beautiful, beautiful face! We serve You, Lord and we love so much doing Your will. We joy in You! You are our very life! Without Your grace, Your words, Your Spirit, we would surely perish. You are our source of life and the very love of our hearts.

We run the race with gladness, proclaiming Your love. We work while it is day, for the night is coming when we cannot work.

But when that final day dawns and we see the beginning of the light of Your countenance, our hearts will beat faster, for You, our Bridegroom stand at the door. Today, in the Spirit, let us catch just a glimpse of the glow of Your face upon us, knowing that soon we will see, fully, Your glorious face!

———————————◇———————————

All alone, without inferiority, sketch a word picture of Jesus (a description of His character in words. Don't show anyone but offer it to Him as a child would do to you. It will be precious to Him. Let the time spent remind you of Revelation 22:4.

# MARCH 15

*"Thou hast crowned the year with Thy bounty, and Thy paths drip with fatness." Psalm 65:11*

What a blessing that our Lord desires to crown our year with His abundance and fullness. He came to give us life in its fullness. He is the Life giver, the Joy giver, the very Lover of our souls. He is concerned with every big thing in our lives and even with the smallest detail. He knows our frame. He knows when we stand or sit. He knows every hair on our head—and He loves us in spite of all. He is faithful and full of goodness—always ready to forgive, to uplift, to encourage and bless. He has more confidence in us than we do. He even trusts us! The Son of God entrusting humans.

What a kind giver He is—always looking for a way if we will only receive. He wants to pour anointing (fat) upon our paths so that we drip with His very presence. Let us live in the overflow with Him today! Receive all He has for you. Open your heart to Him and give Him glory!

---

Get some olive oil (or any kind of oil) and consecrate it to the Lord and anoint yourself and your home and family today, as a sign that you will let Him crown you and fill you for this year!

# MARCH 16

*"But He knows the way I take. When He has tried me, I shall come forth as gold." Job 23:10*

Oh, trust in the Lord, dear saint of God. Trust in Him and don't try to lean on your own understanding. He knows. Oh yes, He knows. Resist the temptation to figure things out. Let it go. If you never know why you are in such a fiery trial, it won't matter. He knows. Give your devastation to Him. Oh, pour your heart out to Him, for He is your loving Father. But do not blame Him. He is the Giver of good gifts, of everlasting love and kindness. Resist the enemy—satan—and he will flee from you. Know that this trial will pass. The Lord will turn it to good. Praise Him even in the heat of battle. Worship the Lord! He is nearer than your own breath. Your faith is more precious than gold. Be faithful to Jesus and come forth as gold! The refiner will turn up the heat until every impurity is gone. He will look in you and see His own reflection shining back. Pure gold!

---◇---

If you have anything gold or imitation gold, take it with you today to remember that you will be like gold with a pure heart. Worship God!

# MARCH 17

*"For this is My blood of the covenant, which is to be shed on behalf of many for forgiveness of sins."*
*Matthew 26:28*

That holy, holy blood of Jesus! Oh, the precious blood of Jesus that washes us clean from our sins. Do we know how terrible the smallest sin is? That it causes death—first death to thousands and thousands of animals as sacrifices—to be substitutes until the real sacrifice came—the Holy Son of God? That innocent, pure, sweet Lamb! The Lamb that takes away the sins of the world! Do we really understand the terrible pain that Jesus went through for us because of the depth of His love for us? How far His love reaches? The extent He has gone to? Why? Because He wants a covenant with us! A covenant with us! A covenant relationship is even beyond marital closeness. It is the most intimate of all! He is so in love with us! He desires communion with us throughout eternity. In a covenant exchange, you give all you have to each other. God has given us Himself and all that He is, in Jesus! Have you given Him all you have and all you are? Give yourself to Him today, all of yourself and let Him give Himself to you. Receive all He is and all He has for you today.

———————◇———————

Wear something red today to remind you of His blood covenant with you and that He has given Himself to you. All He has is yours.

# MARCH 18

*"For you will go out with joy and be led forth with peace." Isaiah 55:12*

The Lord will guard your going out and your coming in, from this time forth and forever. He will not allow your foot to slip for He is your keeper. He will protect you from all evil. He is your shade from the heat of the trial. He is your sunshine in the dark of the night. He is your Good Shepherd. His eye is upon you. Where can you go from His Spirit? He is your very heartbeat and life! His lovingkindness is better than life!

Take His hand. Fix your eyes on Jesus, the Author and Perfecter of your faith, the Alpha and Omega. He is your security, your life giver, your faith, your peace, your joy! Every time you go out, let Him fill you with His joy! It is His delight to do so! Open your heart—let His joy and laughter be poured into you today. He will faithfully lead you in peace—peace that the world does not know. Be led by it. Do nothing without His strong, secure peace. All around you will clap for joy! Bless Him today!

———————————◇———————————

As you go out today, rejoice—sing, dance, clap for the Lord! Then as you go—rest in peace—deep peace. Rejoice in God!

# MARCH 19

*"How lovely (beautiful) on the mountains are the feet of him who brings good news (the gospel)."*
*Isaiah 52:7*

Dear saint of God, you have beautiful, lovely feet! They were designed in secret, in the womb, to carry the Good News all over, to every place. They were predestined to proclaim that "our God reigns!" To announce peace with God through the Messiah. To say, "Blessed are the pure in heart for they shall see God."

Every day put on the shoes of the gospel of peace. Let His peace and His word dwell in you richly. Be ready always to give an answer to those who ask about the hope that is in you. Be ready in season and out of season. You have the medicine of life that heals the world of death. Fill your heart and mind and words with Jesus. Let His strong peace and joy and love overflow out of you to believer and unbeliever, to Jew and Gentile. Be filled with the fullness of God. Let nothing, absolutely nothing stop the gospel (in word and deed) from going out of your life to others daily. You have beautiful feet! The Lord loves your feet that go swiftly to tell His news!

---

Trace around your feet onto paper and cut them out. Write out Isaiah 52:7 on one foot and Mark 16:15 on the other. Pin them up somewhere to remind you to preach the gospel daily and have beautiful feet!

# MARCH 20

*"Fixing our eyes on Jesus, the author and perfecter of faith, who for the joy set before Him endured the cross." Hebrews 12:2*

Oh, how often we need to hear these words, "Fixing our eyes on Jesus." Over and over we need to refocus and keep our eyes on our Beloved! As we behold *Him* alone, we stay in His presence and dwell in Him. As we look at Him and let His light shine on us, we are changed in ways that would take years normally. He is committed to conforming us into His image! That is His main purpose. Out of that will flow ministry. *He* is the One who changes us if we will submit our will to His will daily with fresh surrender of love and praise. He is committed to perfecting our faith. Not strengthening only, but *perfecting* our faith.

Jesus considered crucifixion a joy because He knew that after He endured it He would have joy eternally with us! How deep His love is! How strong His commitment and faithfulness! How caring He is and devoted to every detail if we will just keep our eyes fixed on Him! A divine secret!

---

Put this verse in every room of your house and in your car or pocket. Memorize it and begin practicing keeping your eyes on Jesus! Beholding Him!

# MARCH 21

*"... and she who was called barren is now in her sixth month. For nothing is impossible with God"*
*Luke 1:36-37*

The Hebrew word for compassion is built on the word "RECHEM" which means "womb." It seems to be God's very precious specialty to bring life from death, despair to hope, dark to light. It is in the wilderness places that we learn who He is and how to follow Him and love Him. Suddenly, we're on the mountain top! He gives us several examples of barren women—impossible situations. But nothing is impossible with God for those who believe! They believed the Lord and gave birth to miracle babies—each one with a strong calling from the Lord! It is in that seemingly hopeless place that we cry out to Him and He brings us the miracle. Nothing is impossible with God! He carries us in the womb of His love and then births us into His anointing—into that glorious intimacy with Him! Are you believing for something that seems impossible? Do not be weary, faithful soldier of God—He will come to you in compassion. Be steadfast and immovable, always abounding in the work of the Lord. Believe Him.

---

Find a picture of a newborn baby and write Luke 1:36-37 by it. Believe the Lord with all your heart!

# MARCH 22

*"For as the heavens are higher than the earth, so are My ways higher than your ways, and My thoughts than your thoughts." Isaiah 55:9*

Oh, what a comforting verse! Bless You, Lord! Thank You that Your ways are so much higher than ours. You are our Good Shepherd! You lead us when we cannot see what's ahead. You are our eternal Father. You hold us and comfort us as we go through dark valleys. You are our Wonderful Counselor! You advise us and command us in every situation. You are our Prince of Peace (shalom)! You bring still waters to us when all around us is a raging storm. You are our Almighty God—fully trustworthy because Your ways are high. You are full of strength and power and You are sweet and kind. Your thoughts are precious towards us, as the grains of sand in number. You have high thoughts of us and for us. Your loving thoughts are for our best—they are beyond our thoughts. We love Your ways and Your thoughts today.

---

Call out from the shores of earth to the throne of heaven today, thanking the Lord for His high thoughts and high ways for you and for your life. Bless Him!

# MARCH 23

*"In repentance and rest you shall be saved, in quietness and trust is your strength."*
*Isaiah 30:15*

Let us all keep our hearts open and transparent so that the Holy Spirit can be free to work as He desires. How often are we blind to even know we have a certain problem or sin, until the light of the Holy Spirit shines upon us. Let us be open to continual workings of repentance in our lives. Like salvation, the initial repentance is only the first step. True, it is the door to heaven if it is deep and penetrating, but there is the process of sanctification and holiness that comes through continual repentance. And so, our hearts are changed. We are His, citizens of heaven and only pilgrims on this earth. We bear His likeness increasingly as we do His will.

Yet it is in rest and quietness and trust that is your strength. Rest in Jesus today. Let His quiet gentleness be your trust. Give Him all your cares. Trust Him for He is trustworthy. He is your salvation and your strength. He is a Mighty Warrior going before you. Walk on His holy highway today in peace and rest. Enter into His peace and rest!

---

Open your heart and let the Lord search you to see if there is any sin or wrong thing. If there is, confess it to Him and repent. Get all things right with the Lord and with others. Keep your heart open to His correction in the next weeks. Then rest in Him, clean and pure!

# MARCH 24

*"Therefore the Lord longs to be gracious to you, and therefore He waits on high to have compassion on you." Isaiah 30:18*

What a wonderful Father He is! What a Good and Kind Shepherd! The Lord is faithful and loving, full of tender compassion for you!

Have you ever been devoted to someone or had someone be that way to you? Well, God is even more **devoted and true**, much more than you can imagine. He **longs** to be gracious to you. It's His chief desire to pour out His kind grace upon you. He favors you! He waits on high! Can you imagine it? The King of the entire universe waits in the highest place to bend and have compassion on you. He is looking for every opportunity to show you His great love and passion for you. He waits!

There are plenty of opportunities on His side, but we often pass them by, blindly. We need to respond to His love as we would to a devoted relative or friend. Today, run to the Lord with open arms. Let Him embrace you and hold you tight. Let Him express His love for you!

———————————◇———————————

Wait on the Lord in silence. Now sing softly to Him. Picture Jesus coming to you and holding you. Stay in His arms awhile. Let Him speak tenderly to you. Be still. Now write it down.

# MARCH 25

*"Then you will take delight in the Lord, and I will make you ride on the heights of the earth."*
*Isaiah 58:14*

Precious saint of the Lord, delight yourself in the Lord! Delight in His rivers of joy and deep peace. Enter into that holy dwelling place where the Son shines! Drink in His love today. Let it nourish you from head to foot. Open your heart, open your spirit. Open your mind and emotions and bathe in His sweet love. Be submerged in His precious Spirit. Enjoy your Lord today! He created you to enjoy His presence and His moving in your life. He gave His life for these intimate moments with you. He knows you. He loves you. He delights in you and understands you! He is your chief joy! All that matters is Him! Be His today. Dwell in Him!

How He longs to scoop you up to the heights with Him, to keep you in that most holy and blessed place with Him above all else. He will make you ride on the heights of the earth. Cast your cares on Jesus, for He cares for you. His attention and affection is upon you. You are His love and joy! Ride on the heights with God today!

———————◇———————

Make a quick sketch of the earth and you and Jesus next to it! Put musical notes of joy all around and write Isaiah 58:14. Sing to the Lord in the heights today!

# MARCH 26

*"Seek the Lord while He may be found; call upon Him while He is near." Isaiah 55:6*

Dear one, keep a searching heart for the Lord! Ask for divine hunger to be poured down on you from heaven. The more you hunger and thirst for the Lord, and set yourself aside for Him, the greater your anointing will be in pouring out your life to those around you. They will sense His presence in you! "Seek the Lord while He may be found." Proclaim this to all of the unsaved people around you—those you know and those you don't know, those who receive and those who reject, the lovable and the unlovable, those popular and those outcasts, the rich, the poor, the needy, the educated, those in high positions, those in trouble, those who are healthy, those who are sick, the old and the young. Find ways to help people seek Him while He may be found; call upon Him while He is near. Let them take His hand of mercy now so they won't have to take His hand of judgment later. For a day will come when the grace is stopped and the door is shut. It will be too late to seek Him. Judgment Day will be here.

---

Draw a big, life size door and write Isaiah 55:6 on it to remind you that Judgment Day is coming and we must work while it is still day to help people seek the Lord!

# MARCH 27

*"And we know that God causes all things to work together for good to those who love God, to those who are called according to His purpose."*
*Romans 8:28*

What blessed, blessed words of encouragement from the Lord! How often it warms our hearts in every situation of life. Our sweet God will cause all things, both good and bad, to work together for good. The condition is . . . to those who love God and are called for His purpose. Are you living for His purposes? Is the Lord everything to you? Is He the love of your life? Then *all* is in His blessed hands, to work for your good! How fully He supports us, just for loving Him and living for Him! God is so good!

Romans 8:28 was fully demonstrated to all of heaven and earth and even hell below when Jesus was crucified. Throughout eternity man's destiny was changed from the pit of hell to the ecstasy of heaven when Jesus cried out, "It is finished!" The cruelest, most evil act to ever take place was turned to pure glory when Jesus rose from the dead! Forevermore satan's work was overcome and defeated. All evil on earth will be stopped and all the goodness of God revealed one day when the trumpet sounds and Judgment Day comes! Alleluia!

---

Write down any problems you have and next to each one write, "It will be turned to good!" Consecrate yourself anew to the Lord, knowing that you too will be turned to good!

# MARCH 28

*"The Lord will command His lovingkindness in the daytime; and His song will be with me in the night." Psalm 42:8*

Have you thought about the word "command?" It is not optional. We are His and He will **command** His lovingkindness upon us in the daytime. Have you allowed the command of the Lord to grace your life today? Let it rest upon you as a crown! Let His lovingkindness be yours this day! Receive it!

What is the rest of this promise? His song will be with you at night! Are you troubled or weighed down from the pressures of the day? Cast them off unto your burden bearer—Jesus, and let His song be with you at night. Lay your weary head down to rest in His sweet song! Let the melody of His love fill you this evening, full of His peace and tenderness! His song will be with you in the night, not at night. It will stay in your spirit all night long. When you wake up you will still hear that sweet sound! This is heaven on earth, to be full of His lovingkindness in the day and His song in the night! It's His command!

---

Open your arms to Jesus and receive His lovingkindness for this day. Let it be your refuge and weapon against the evil one. Fill your heart with His song tonight. Wait. Be still. Let His melody flood your heart!

# MARCH 29

*"Nevertheless he would not drink it, but poured it out to the Lord." 2 Samuel 23:16*

Oh, that we would have sacrificial love for God, honoring Him as David did! In the heat of the battle, amidst terrible discomfort and disappointments—when his life was even in danger, David came to the basic need of terrible thirst. And how his men loved him! They loved him enough to risk their lives and get for him the life-saving water. They had proven faithful in character! And were they offended when David poured out that blessed water? No! They knew their leader and his devoted heart after the Lord. They had learned from him that sacrificial love! They knew!

David denied himself to follow the Lord! He deliberately chose (even in his desperate need to satisfy his thirst) to honor the Lord! To him that water was sacred and therefore must go to the Lord rather than himself. Have you given that which is sacred to you, even needy for you, to the Lord? Will you honor Him in this way? What will you give to Jesus today in sacrificial love?

———————————◇———————————

Meditate on 2 Samuel 23:16 and offer in prayer that which you cherish most (or need most) up to the Lord! Bless His heart today!

# MARCH 30

*"And everyone who has this hope fixed on Him, purifies himself just as He is pure." 1 John 3:3*

Oh, what blessed and holy words! "Everyone who has their hope fixed on Jesus . . . ." What is your hope fixed on? A position, a person, a thing, a recognition? Maybe a certain skill, or reputation? No! Fix it immediately on Jesus. We must keep our eyes on Him alone. The world and the devil will bring many "good" things to distract us from Jesus. Business or even godly activities can do this. Let us bring every thought captive to Him this morning. Put on the mind of the Messiah, your helmet of salvation and go forth, holy unto the Lord! Let your hope, all of it, be on Jesus continually. He alone is your hope. Only He can satisfy your soul. Fix your hope on Him and He will purify you! What a wonderful miracle! Merely our hope and desire to see Jesus, to be with Him . . . purifies us! Why? Because He is pure. That hope is like a mirror. His reflection flashes back on us and makes us pure! The glorious stream that comes from dwelling in Him with all your heart, mind and strength will bring the power of His own purity upon you! Praise Him!

---◇---

Right now lift your heart and hands to the Lord and let Him be your total hope. Tell Him. Rest in Him. Let His light and warmth purify you. Write 1 John 3:3 on a small paper and tape it onto your mirror.

# MARCH 31

*"My flesh and my heart may fail; but God is the strength of my heart."* Psalm 73:26

Yes, how very often my flesh fails me. It doesn't want to die. It still lifts a hand out from the grave. The flesh and the spirit are at war within me. And yes, even my heart fails me for often my motives are wrong or my thoughts of another are critical. Lord, have mercy on me. Who can save me from this, for I often do that which I hate and not that which I long to do? Only Jesus can save me from the sin that is in me. It lingers and follows after me even though I've been washed in the blood of the Messiah.

But God, . . . yes, God . . . is the strength of my heart! Our merciful loving God comes to us in those dark times and says, "Let Me do it for you. My grace is sufficient. My way is above your way. Be yoked to Me. Take rest for your soul, for I am gentle. Learn of Me. Let Me lead you. I have overcome the world. Do not be troubled. I give you My peace. *I AM* the strength of your heart!" God is the very strength of my heart. Bless His holy name forever!

———————————◇———————————

Open your heart to the Lord today. Let Him carry your burdens and take control. Ask Him to be the strength of your heart. Receive that strength. Cut out a big heart and write, "God is the strength of my heart" on it.

# APRIL 1

*"For momentary, light affliction is producing for us, an eternal weight of glory far beyond all comparison."* 2 Corinthians 4:17

Oh dear lover of God, are you in the fiery trial today? Remember that your brothers and sisters all over the world are also. Are you suffering in some way? Pray and the Lord will comfort you. Are you weary? Persevere and you will reap a harvest with joy. Put on a merry heart which doeth good like medicine. Drink in the sweetness of His love! But why does it say "momentary" when it lasts so long? Why does it say "light" affliction when it feels so heavy? Because it is producing for you an eternal weight, a weight of glory far beyond all comparison. It will be light and the scale will drop the other direction when you look upon Jesus and see Him in all His glory! The light of the glory of His countenance will cause all to fade and you will only remember a "moment" of trial, a "light" affliction. His glory will be a weight. The weight of God will be upon you! The weight of God's glory! You will have unspeakable joy forever! An eternal weight of glory!

———————————◇———————————

Find a feather and label it "trials." Find a rock and label it "God's glory." Put them in a place where you can see them all day long. Rejoice in the middle of your trial and the Son will set you free!

# APRIL 2

*"For where your treasure is, there will your heart be also." Luke 12:34*

What heavenly wisdom these words hold. Where your treasure is, your heart will be. What do you treasure today? Where is your heart? Wherever it is, your speech will reflect it. Is it in your work, your family, a certain hobby? You will speak about that which you love the most. Is it in yourself? Where is your heart?

God asked Adam, "Where are you?", after the fall into sin. Where is your heart, Adam? Where is our sweet fellowship? Where is your heart?

Your money too, will be where your heart is. Is it in possessions? Are you holding onto it? Did not God give all He had when He gave His only Son? Can we give less? The Lord is a giver! He so loved the world, that He gave. His nature is to constantly give. Should we give our all? Shouldn't we give our money and our possessions and all we have for Him? For His kingdom? Shouldn't we give our best? Our families and ourselves? Shouldn't our thoughts and our speech be of Jesus, our Lord, our very Love? Where is your heart today?

———————————◇———————————

Consecrate yourself to the Lord anew today. Give Him all you have in prayer and in practical ways. Determine to be a "giver." Let your treasure show that you are His!

# APRIL 3

*"And when they saw Him, they worshipped Him."*
*Matthew 28:17*

Over and over it happened. From the moment of Jesus' birth when kings in their majesty bowed down prostrate, to the glory in heaven where cherubim and seraphim never cease to cry out, "Holy, Holy, Holy!" All of heaven bows down to worship Jesus, the King of Kings and Lord of Lords! All authority in heaven and earth has been given to Him. Every knee will bow and every tongue confess that *Jesus is Lord*, to the glory of the Father!

When they saw Him, they worshipped Him! Shouldn't that be our immediate response to the Lord? To worship Him? Shouldn't our hearts burn with love for Him? When we see Him in the Spirit, let us bow down and worship Him! Never be in too much of a hurry to worship the Lord! Practice loving Him and worshipping Him in words during moments all through the day. In songs in the night, in the early morning! Lift your heart to Jesus as a continual worship! Find times to fall on your face before Him in adoration! Even silently you can adore Him deep in your heart! A continual feast!

---

Look for special times alone to worship the Lord this week, even if it's only a few minutes. Steal time away with your Beloved! Worship Him!

# APRIL 4

*"Jesus also was immersed (baptized), and while He was praying heaven was opened." Luke 3:21*

"Jesus also was immersed (baptized)." Is there any more humble than Jesus? Letting a sinful human being immerse (baptize) Him? God, our God has humbled Himself and become a man, born in the lowest estate, and now stooping to be immersed (baptized) by man. Although God, He knew it couldn't be grasped, He became fully man.

And while He was praying, heaven itself opened up. What it must have been like to see the sky roll back and heaven revealed! It will be like that when He comes again! The very voice of Jesus in prayer caused heaven to open and the Holy Spirit to land on Him and the Father's affirmation of Him out loud, so all could hear. Who could not have been changed that day? The Trinity displaying honor to One another. Heaven opened! "This is My beloved Son in whom I am well pleased!" Let heaven open your heart today! Rejoice!

---◇---

Take time to praise the Father, Son and Holy Spirit. Wait until your heart is open and heaven fills it! Rejoice in God!

# APRIL 5

*"Follow Me, and I will make you become fishers of men." Mark 1:17*

Keep your eyes on the Fisherman to see how He catches the fish! Where does He go? What kind of bait does He use? Does He catch them with poles, one at a time, or a with a big net, 100's or 1,000's at a time? When does He pull the fish in?

Do you want to bring people to Jesus? Then do it! Do you feel afraid? Just do it! Do you feel inadequate? Go ahead and do it! The more you do it the more the fear and inadequacy will go away. He is with you to anoint you fully. Keep your heart clean and fill yourself with prayer. Go where He says, speak to the ones He points out. Keep your eyes open at all times, in season and out of season. Minister to hearts, not just their minds. Show them the very love of Jesus! Pour out your life to them. When love is felt the message is heard.

You will be successful because His love **never** fails and His word **never** returns empty. Plant the seeds, water them, reap the harvest. God is faithful! He will do it! And you will be His joy! Complete the work of Jesus! Tell them! Sow in tears and reap in joy! Be a fisherman for Jesus and bring Him the fruit He deserves!

---

Draw a ⌢⌢ with Mark 1:17 on it. Let Jesus Himself teach you to witness. Pray to share with someone everyday this week (or more)!

# APRIL 6

*"Then those who feared the Lord spoke to one another, and the Lord gave attention and heard it, and a book of remembrance was written before Him for those who fear the Lord and esteem His name." Malachi 3:16*

Do you fear the Lord? Do you honor Him in all you do and say and think? Is He your every thought? The very love of your life? And how is it when you meet with your closet friends? Is Jesus the topic of your conversations? Are you thrilled and excited about all He does in your life daily? Or has that all faded? Can you remember when it was like that? Have your friends begun to talk of other things now?

Oh, beloved one, stir up the gift of God that is in you! Do you know Jesus stands at the door of your heart and knocks? He longs to be your only love, the center of your life and heart. He rejoices over you when He is your central theme! He is in your midst! He writes it in a book of remembrance in eternity . . . for those who esteem Him, who lift up His name! Bless the Lord today! Tell of His love everywhere you go—to everyone!

———————————◇———————————

Today you start a book of Remembrance and write down all the beautiful things the Lord does for you! Share it with a friend!

# APRIL 7

*"And those who have insight will shine brightly like the brightness of the expanse of heaven, and those who lead the many to righteousness, like the stars forever and ever." Daniel 12:3*

Those who have insight, wisdom, and discernment from on high will shine brightly. Daniel had God's wisdom and after fasting his face shone brightly. Those who are wise win souls. It is a wise thing to build up heaven while you are on earth, before the final curtain is drawn and it is too late. Jesus' last words were to go into all the world and make disciples, preaching the gospel to all creation. Where your treasure is your heart will be. Store up your treasure in heaven and bring people to Jesus. Add to the glorious worship in heaven. Bring glory to His name and surely His glorious face will shine on you. You will bring a smile to His face and your own joy will light the expanse of heaven. Lead many, many to righteousness and you will shine like the stars forever and ever. Our faithful and loving God will shine on you and bless you throughout eternity. His purpose, His way!

---

With glitter or with foil make some stars to remind you of Daniel 12:3. Pray for someone different to witness to each week. Make evangelism a lifestyle.

# APRIL 8

*"Do not come near here; remove your sandals from your feet, for the place on which you are standing is holy ground." Exodus 3:5*

Do we fear the Lord when on holy ground? How do we tread the congregation grounds, in our mannerisms, in our dress and words and actions? Is there an awe of God's presence? "Do not come near here; remove your shoes." Do we reverence God's house?

What about the temple of the Holy Spirit? Do we honor it? Are we careful to make it clean for Him? How do we honor our places of prayer—home, car, street? Do we honor these places because Jesus is in us?

We know that any place is His, but do we keep it sacred when we pray or read His word? Is it a quiet, holy place where we can be still and know that He is God? Do we fill that place with praises and worship, thanksgiving and glory? Let our walls be of praise and our gates of salvation! Determine to fill your home, your car (or mode of transportation), your working place full of praises and worship and prayer! Take off your shoes, for they are holy places! Honor Jesus!

———————————◇———————————

Consecrate today, your place of morning and evening worship! Take off your shoes for it is holy ground. Fall on your face and worship the Lord there in that holy place!

# APRIL 9

*"Give thanks to the Lord, for He is good; for His lovingkindness is everlasting." Psalm 136:1*

Dear precious believer, do you need a touch from the Lord today? Are you longing for some answer or direction or encouragement?

Begin to give thanks to the Lord! Enter His lovely courts with a thankful heart! Thank Him for His goodness. Oh, He is so good! He is so good! Bless Him for His lovingkindness for it is everlasting! It never stops! It is there even when you don't feel it. Receive His precious lovingkindness and new mercy today! Start the day with a new song!

Now turn to Psalm 136. How many times does it say "His lovingkindness is everlasting?" If I say something twice in a row to you, it's because I really mean it. If I say it three times, it's extremely important! How many times does your Lord say to you that His love for you is everlasting? Over and over and over! It's because He is completely in love with you! Bless His holy name! Receive His love today!

———————————◇———————————

Write a Psalm back to the Lord in the same style as Psalm 136, expressing your love to Him! Rejoice today in His love! He is good!

# APRIL 10

*"Let everything that has breath praise the Lord."*
*Psalm 150:6*

Do you realize the full impact that you were created to praise the Lord? You can bring glory to Him in all you do, say and think. Everything can be a praise to Jesus!

Psalm 150:6 says let ***everything*** that has breath praise Him! Not just everyone, but everything. Every bird, every animal, every single thing that breathes was created to praise Jesus and glorify Him. All of creation!

But you are so unique that no one else can glorify Him the way you do! God is totally self-sufficient but He still needs you to receive love and praise from you! You can fill His heart! Do you know that your praises join into the heavenly worship? You can add to heaven's praises day and night!

Let your very ***life*** be a continual praise to the Lord! He is so worthy! Let everything that has breath praise the Lord!

---

Choose a beautiful place and go on a praise walk. Praise the Lord for everything that has breath and worship Him!

# APRIL 11

*"Render to Caesar the things that are Caesar's
and to God the things that are God's."*
*Mark 12:17*

The Lord Jesus told us to pay our taxes. Certainly governments often use our money for unrighteous deeds, even things which we oppose deep in our hearts. The balance is that we use our freedom to make the truth known and preach the gospel fearlessly in high places of government, praying and fasting and believing the Lord to turn things around as He did with David and the giant. We must stand firm and render unto God what belongs to Him. The nations are but a drop in the bucket for Him. He deserves for every knee to bow and every tongue confess that He is indeed Lord!

Romans 13 tells us to obey leaders over us, and we must, unless they go against the One we love—Jesus. Acts 5:29 says we must obey God rather than men. Yes, we stand for Jesus, above all, at any cost. *All* people have a right to hear of His salvation and own a Bible. Every person must have the freedom to choose. The bloody imprisonment of countless martyrs before us has brought us His word and salvation. Can we do less? Render to God what is His.

———————————————◇———————————————

Today, pray for kings, presidents, prime ministers of all countries. Pray in detail for your own government. Ask the Lord to show you how to use your freedom to reach them with the gospel.

# APRIL 12

*"For it is only right for me to feel this way about you all, because I have you in my heart."*
*Philippians 1:7*

Oh, dear one, have you experienced that sweet fellowship of oneness with the Lord and with another? Is it not the most precious time as the oil of anointing falls from the Father onto you and to each other? Isn't it glorious that the face of the Lord is revealed in times like this?

That is why we must "Rejoice always; pray without ceasing; and in everything give thanks." This is the will of God. Let us not quench the Holy Spirit, for He longs to be poured out on you so that you might have sweet and heavenly communion together!

And are those you love in the Lord so very dear? Yes, they are as your very own heart. Whatever is done to them is done to you. Such a deep love you feel for one another—that unconditional love of the Messiah flowing, filling and being poured out! Indeed His own fragrance fills the entire room!

---

Rejoice in the Lord today with a friend. Pray together and spend a good amount of time together giving thanks to the Lord. Enjoy Him together. Let your friend know how dear he/she is to you!

# APRIL 13

*"And you shall love the Lord your God with all your heart, and with all your soul, and with all your mind, and with all your strength. You shall love your neighbor as yourself. There is no other commandment greater than these."*
*Mark 12:30-31*

Yes, if we fulfill these two commandments, by the Spirit of grace from Jesus, Yeshua, the Messiah, we will fulfill all others, for love covers transgressions. If we love the Lord with all of our hearts we will cry out, "Not my will but Thine be done." We will desire His purity and His motives in the depths of our hearts. We will long for His kingdom on earth, for all to be saved and discipled, glorifying Him. Our whole life will be pointed this way and Jesus will **be** our life and our love, beyond all. With our emotions we will love Him fully and even those times without feelings we will remain His. With our intellect and choices we will love and praise Him. Our mind will be on Him and our energy for Him.

And we will truly love our neighbors as ourselves. We will have sacrificial love for people, as Jesus does. Our life's purpose and fulfillment will be in pouring our lives out for Jesus first, and also for our neighbor.

---

◇

Today ask the Lord to purify your desires and motives, to fill your heart full with love that glorifies Him and reaches to those around you. Pray for five people to pour your life into.

# APRIL 14

*"Thou hast loved righteousness and hated wickedness; therefore God, Thy God, has anointed Thee, with the oil of joy above Thy fellows." Psalm 45:7*

Oh Lord, set our hearts on You, our Righteous One. It cost You Your life dear Jesus, to give us righteousness—Your blessed, holy life. Let us be full of Your righteousness for we have none of our own. Cause us to hate with the utmost hatred, wickedness, for it tortured You in the Garden and in Your death. Let us hate our sins which drove nails into Your blessed hands and feet, which crowned Your head with bloody thorns and broke Your heart.

Precious Lord, please anoint us with Your sacred oil of joy! Give us dancing in place of sorrow. Let us rejoice always in You! Let Your joy be our greatest strength. Yes, anoint us Lord, even above our fellows—not to be better, but to have that secret holy place of intimacy with You that we choose. Let us have that "bridal" place of sweet communion with You—filled up to overflowing with Your fullness.

---

Consecrate yourself unto the Lord today anew. With all you are, love His righteousness, hate evil and rejoice with new anointing and intimacy unto your Lord!

# APRIL 15

*"How precious is Thy lovingkindness, O God."*
*Psalm 36:7*

Oh how precious, how very, very precious is Thy loving-kindness, Oh Lord! If you should remove the tiniest drop of it we would indeed feel the pain of it missing.

Is there anything on earth or in heaven more precious than His love? No, nothing! It is the jewel beyond cost. It is that for which we give up all. It is what we long for and would gladly become a bondslave for.

Oh the depth of the riches of the love of the Messiah. The endless worth. If we offered up all we have, our homes, our lands and even those we love, it would be yet a small way to say thank You, Jesus, for giving Your life.

His love is incomparable, unspeakable, beyond our comprehension for sure. We know not how to even begin to describe its worth.

Therefore, let us fall on our faces and cry, "Holy, Holy, Holy." Let us cry, "Glory to the Righteous One." Let us whisper tenderly in His ear, "How precious is Thy lovingkindness, O God!"

---

On your face today, meditate in silence on the precious loving-kindness of the Lord. Be still without distractions. See His face. Love and adore Him.

# APRIL 16

*"Having thus a fond affection for you, we were well-pleased to impart to you not only the gospel of God but also our own lives, because you had become very dear to us."* 1 Thessalonians 2:8

Oh, isn't this the very precious love of the Messiah in us? He is in our hearts and we also bear each other in our hearts because of Him. We have a fond, even a great affection for those we love in the Messiah—especially those we disciple. We carry them as babies and nurse them and feed them until they are strong adults reproducing their own babies.

Is it not the very nature of the Messiah's sweet love, to impart? Yes, it is an all consuming, sacrificial, giving love! It pours out like a gushing fountain. The Holy Spirit in us, longs to pour out that costly, precious love, lavishing it on those who are thirsty. To impart the gospel, that is our goal in life, and to do it full of His love. When it is done in Jesus' love, His way—it causes us to impart and give our very own lives. We give our lives as Jesus did—to those who are so dear. May He be glorified in our giving!

———————————⬦———————————

On your knees today, thank the Lord for one in whom you can pour out your life in the love of the Messiah. Glorify Him in this relationship. Give this verse to that person who is so dear to you.

# APRIL 17

*"Your eyes will see the King in His beauty."*
*Isaiah 33:17*

How blessed are your eyes because they see! Do we have eyes to see? Do we see as God sees? Do we see Him in each other? Do we **see God?** Oh yes! If we seek Him, if we love Him, we will see Him! Our eyes will be blessed, and we will see Him.

We know Jesus and we see Him in all we do, in all we are—but soon our holy eyes will see the King! Yes, we will see Jesus as our King of Kings, our Risen Savior! Our Lord of Lords! We will see Him as He really is—in all of His beauty!

Lift your blessed eyes to the throne of grace today. See Jesus in all His majesty, in all of His splendor! Our human eyes can only see Him for short times in all His glory and radiance! But, gaze upon Him now, as long as you can bear that holy sight. Now keep that sight in your heart all day. Soon, we will not only see Him but dwell with Him in His glory and splendor forever! Blessed be His holy name.

————————◇————————

Make a king's hat and put it in the place where you pray to remind you of that holy gaze up to Him in all His beauty and majesty.

# APRIL 18

*"Thou hast turned for me my mourning into dancing." Psalm 30:11*

Are you downcast and full of sorrow? Has some circumstance or person broken your heart? Turn to the Man of Sorrows—the One crowned with thorns, dripping with holy blood out of love for you. Surely the Son of Man who trod the bitter pain of the winepress, the One who was crushed beyond recognition and nailed to death can understand your deepest sorrow. Only He has sunk lower than you and even tasted of hell for your soul. Have you resisted sin to the point of shedding blood? Consider Jesus, the Author and Perfecter of your faith. He is the everlasting arm for you. Embrace Him. Let Him fill up His bottle with your tears and make them His jewels! Arise, precious one—for He is the **Resurrection!** He is your hope! He is your joy! Only He can turn your sorrows to joy, your mourning to dancing! The One who raises the dead lives in your heart! Rise up and sing! Rise up and dance! Yes, dance to the Holy One who loves you and gave His life for you! He is worthy of praise and honor! Dance! Dance! Dance! The joy of the Lord is your strength! Dance!

---◇---

Determine to sing and dance when your heart is sad. Have a tambourine or a song to dance to each time you feel down. Rise to victory and dance with your heart before the Lord of glory!

# APRIL 19

*"Thou didst make me bold with strength in my soul." Psalm 138:3*

The Lord is your strength and your shield. He goes before you. He is your protection and your victory. He is your refuge. He gives strength to the weary and He Himself is like the sun shining in its strength.

They were all filled with the Holy Spirit and began to speak the word of God with boldness. We have boldness and confidence through faith in Him. Therefore, do not throw away your confidence, which has a great reward. For you have need of endurance, so that when you have done the will of God, you will receive what was promised.

We, the children of His light, the very apple of His eye, are able to walk in all boldness for His namesake, yet remain humble in heart. He can make the weakest saint strong and bold as a lion.

Do you love Jesus? Will you be as bold as a lion for Him and let Him support you? Put your full trust in Him. Let His perfect love cast out all your fears. With all boldness let the Messiah be always exalted in your body, whether by life or death. He has made you bold with strength.

---

Pray about the most difficult situation or person who causes you to shrink back. Determine to be bold for the Lord. Ask for His strength to carry you. He will fully support you!

# APRIL 20

*"Is not your fear of God your confidence, and the integrity of your ways your hope?" Job 4:6*

Do you fear God? Are you in awe of His presence? Do you fall on your face before His holiness? Do you fear Him in the things your eyes see, your ears hear, your tongue speaks? Do you fear God in your thoughts? Do you speak and act as you would in His physical presence? Do you fear and tremble before Him? In the fear of the Lord there is strong confidence and a fountain of life.

Oh beloved, let us repent and return to the Lord. Let Him sanctify us in mind, heart and motives. Let His sweet Holy Spirit flow through us like a clean fountain, making a way for the Lord. He who walks in integrity walks securely. No good thing will He withhold from the upright.

Let the potter mold you as clay. Let His light shine on your ways and direct your path. Let repentance be a lifestyle so that the Son of God may rise up in you and bless those around you with hope. Fear God and keep His commandments. Let Him be your confidence, your hope and your glory!

---

Pray today and let the Holy Spirit wash you and cleanse you and bring you to the kindness of repentance in every area, large and small. Be holy for He is holy!

# APRIL 21

*"For I am confident of this very thing, that He who began a good work in you will perfect it until the day of the Messiah, Jesus.' Philippians 1:6*

Oh, faithful God! How lovely You are! How patient and kind and encouraging You are. You save us and allow us to come near You. You even dwell in us in the deepest way! Glory to You, Lord! You are the Author and the Finisher of our faith. Thank You that You never tire of us as we do of ourselves. You never give up but believe the best in us. Peter, the most unstable, You called a "Rock." Rahab, the harlot, you made a saint. You said David, who fell into adultery, was a man after Your own heart. Moses, who killed, saw Your glory pass by him. You never give up but keep on conforming us to Your own image—that is Your desire and goal—to form Your own self in us! Oh, Lord, how we long to be like You! Thank You, dear sweet Jesus, that You will not only complete, but You will perfect our faith. You've begun a good work in us and will perfect it until we see You face to face! Let us be a reflection of You, Lord!

---

Make a chart of character and spiritual growth that the Lord has brought you through. Thank Him and worship Him! Glorify Him by telling someone or sharing at your congregation!

# APRIL 22

*"For I could wish that I myself were accursed, separated from the Messiah, for the sake of my brethren, my kinsmen." Romans 9:3*

What kind of deep love is this? Is it hard to imagine? Hard to understand? It is the very love of the Messiah—that unfathomable, all consuming, sacrificial, selfless love of the Messiah. Who can give as the Messiah gives? He who said, "Father forgive them," as they nailed His hands and feet? What is intercession but the laying down of one's life for another? Did not Moses do the same in asking God to take his life instead of the children of Israel? That unexplainable, unconditional, all giving love.

Yes, the Apostle Paul wished himself accursed for the sake of the Jews' salvation, even though he was called to the Gentiles. What heartache and love he had! What "pouring out" love he had—for the sake of his brethren! Yet, he was not required to do this. The Lord is full of mercy. Jesus went further in going into hell itself to save us and then raising up to glory! Holy God accursed on a tree—for you!

———————————◇———————————

Today, ask the Lord to give you His own sacrificial love for someone. Keep it as a sweet prayer to Him in secret and put it in His blessed nail-scarred hands.

# APRIL 23

*"My frame was not hidden from Thee, when I was made in secret." Psalm 139:5*

A blessed and holy mystery of God's love—He knows our frame. Our blessed Creator knew us even before our creation. He was the first to know us and love us at the moment of conception! No matter whether we were loved or not, wanted or not by our parents—we were **loved by our Lord** at the moment of creation and of conception. He knew and He loved us even before our mothers knew. Why is it so? Why is it that a mother cannot know the moment of conception of her baby? Maybe because a new life is so sacred to the Lord—such a gift to be grasped! Maybe because we are really His! It is His life, His child, given to us as a gift. He is the Creator, not us. Even conception itself is a miracle. No one can plan it exactly. We depend on God.

God's ways are above our ways. His mysteries are holy and beyond our understanding. Let us rejoice that He is full of lovingkindness in all of His divine mysteries.

———————————◇———————————

Thank the Lord today for your own birth and that you were loved at the moment of conception, even before. Thank the Lord for the birth of people you love today. Rejoice in the Life giver!

# APRIL 24

*"I have heard of Thee by the hearing of the ear; but now my eye sees Thee." Job 42:5*

Bless the Lord! He gives us ears to hear Him and eyes to see Him!

We go from strength to strength and glory to glory. We have seasons of wilderness and seasons of abundance and overflow.

All too often we grow and grow and Jesus is our every thought, then we settle at a plateau and don't know that if we stay there, our light will grow dim.

All through the Scriptures it says to seek the Lord! Seek the Lord while He may be found. Seek Him, hear Him, do His will. If you fall, get up and run the race. Run the race to win and He will be everything to you.

When you are in the depths of a catastrophe or a tragedy, you will still hear His voice. The light shines even brighter in the dark. You will hear Him with your ears and when you come out into the resurrection light, you will see Him! You will see Him as you have never seen Him! Your eyes will behold Jesus in His glory!

---◇---

Concentrate today on hearing the Lord in every situation, on seeing Him as He really is. Write what He tells you. Look into His beautiful eyes!

# APRIL 25

*"And the Lord restored the fortunes of Job when he prayed for his friends; and the Lord increased all that Job had twofold." Job 42:10*

Oh sweet saint of God, will you take on the nature of Jesus? Will you be committed to always, always love and forgive? Will you be wronged for His sake? Will you bear up under it for Him? There is often "friendly fire" upon those who serve Him. Instead of hitting the enemy, one of our own is wounded. Then there are also the wolves in sheep's clothing.

How was it with Job, our example of patient suffering? Truly in the depth of his pain and sorrow, when he needed human comfort the most, his "friends" condemned him and scorned him. Did the same not happen with our Lord? Denied and betrayed? Yet those blessed words—"Father forgive them, they ***don't*** know what they're doing." They really don't know what they are doing. Jesus said to pray for our enemies. Job's friends acted like enemies. When he forgave them and prayed for them he was restored and his blessings were doubled. Be like Jesus—love your enemies. Bless as your Heavenly Father does.

---

Check your heart to see if there's anyone you need to forgive or love more. Pray for that person and look for practical ways to love them.

# APRIL 26

*"Then Moses said, 'O pray Thee, show me Thy glory.'" Exodus 33:18*

Oh to be caught up and lost in the very presence of God! "Come up higher," says the Lord. "Come up to Me." Moses was on the mountaintop. He had come as high as he could, to dwell with the Lord, to do His will, to be obedient. He was there in His midst. He stood on behalf of the people, yet he hungered for more.

Do you have that divine hunger? The more hunger, the more anointing. Do you long to be in the inner courts, in the holy of holies with the Lord? You may have as deep intimacy as you want with Him. Ask and receive. Knock and go in. Seek and you will have a face to face relationship with Him. His love never ceases. It is steadfast and new and abundant. Moses said, "Show me Thy glory." It was the deepest desire in his heart. The Lord heard him and answered. Moses' face shone with the glory of the Lord. Be His faithful bride. Dwell in Him in the inner courts. Know Him. Love Him. See His gory! The Lord Thy God is in your midst. He is mighty. Make His praise glorious!

---

Take some time to close yourself off in a quiet place. Lay on your face in His deep and quiet presence. Be silent. Drink in His love.

# APRIL 27

*"And it will come about while My glory is passing by, that I will put you in the cleft of the rock and cover you with My hand until I have passed by."*
*Exodus 33:22*

The woman with the issue of blood saw Jesus passing by. Though timid in her ways, she reached out and touched the hem of His garment and was instantly healed after 12 long years. Her faith made her well. She had to reach out to Him as He passed by. While Jesus is passing by, reach out and touch the hem of His garment and be healed. Let His healing virtue flow into you. Touch Him! Do not let this moment go by. Touch Him!

While the glory of the Lord was passing by Moses, the Lord put him into the cleft of the rock and covered him with His blessed hand. He could not behold the glory of the Lord and still live. He was thirsty for the Lord, so the Lord gave as much as he could stand.

Because of the Lord's death, we can come boldly into the throne of grace to behold His glory! Come today! Come into the holy of holies. Bow before His throne. ***Behold His glory!*** See Him face to face! Dwell in the glorious presence of the Lord. Stay there until you are filled up to the fullness of God. Let your face shine today with His glory!

---

Bow down to His holiness today. Worship the Lord in holy array. Give Him honor and glory all day long. Stay in His presence. Love Him! Find a robe and make it a garment of praise holy unto the Lord!

# APRIL 28

*"O my dove, in the clefts of the rock, in the secret place of the steep pathway, let me see your beauty, let me hear your voice."*
*Song of Solomon 2:14*

You are His precious dove, His pure and lovely one. You are an exquisite and rare flower in His garden. Your fragrance brings Him pleasure! You are His dove. Go into the clefts of the rock, into the secret place with Him. It may be a steep pathway leading to the heights. The way may be rough. Your feet may be cut, your heart may be weary. Go into the cleft, under the shadow of His wings. Dwell in the Almighty. Delight in Him! He wants to see your beauty. He wants to hear your voice. He has made you beautiful and He wants to gaze upon you in love. He is in love with you. He loves to hear your voice. No matter how many millions or billions may sing and worship Him, He is listening for your voice. You have a place in His heart that no one else has. You bring Him joy! You are His precious one, His dove!

---

Draw a dove to remind you of the sweet Holy Spirit today—also to remind you that you are His special dove. Let Him see your beauty!

*"The Lord bless you, and keep you; the Lord make His face shine upon you, and be gracious unto you; the Lord lift up His countenance on you, and give you peace (shalom)."*
*Numbers 6:24-26*

Is there anything greater than to have the Lord's blessings upon your head? The holy weight of the blessings of God. He is your provider, protector, creator, comforter, sovereign Master, healer of sickness and sorrow, victor in conflicts, peace (shalom) giver, righteous judge, shepherd of your soul, discipliner, guide, Savior, and Lord. He is everything to you. He will surely bless you as you give yourself to Him and walk with Him. He is the keeper of your soul. He who has begun a good work will perfect it. He is your righteousness. He will set you apart for holy service, He is the God who reveals Himself to you. He is always with you—a faithful God! He will make His face shine upon you. As you look into the glow of His face you will be healed of heartache. You will be transformed into His image. He is the God of grace and glory. He will be gracious to you. Without His grace we would surely die. He Himself will look upon you and give you great peace (shalom)! Bless the Lord, O my soul, and all that is within me bless His holy, holy name.

---

Write out Numbers 6:24–26 on nice paper. Pray and give it to someone today. Walk with His blessings upon you all day.

# APRIL 30

*"And David was dancing before the Lord with all his might." 2 Samuel 6:14*

Do you feel free in your heart, dear lover of God? Are you free to worship Jesus? To love and adore Him? Do you rejoice deep inside because of His love for you? Is your closeness with Him alive and shining?

Cast your cares upon Him today and be free, for He cares for you! Rejoice in the Lord always! Always! For this is the will of God for you!

He changes your mourning to dancing! Praise Him with dancing! There is a time to dance! Dance before the Lord! Let your whole self be a living sacrifice of worship to Him! David was beside himself with joy in the Lord! He expressed it with all of his heart. His heart was after God alone.

Come into His presence today in resurrection joy, with a shout of joy! You shall be radiant over the goodness of the Lord! Sorrow shall flee away. You shall rejoice in the dance! You will be satisfied with the goodness of the Lord! Rejoice! Dance! Give Him all you are! Dance with all your might! Be a dance of joy to Him!

---

◇

---

Get alone with the Lord and dance! Make up a dance to express holy love to the Lord! He is your joy!

# MAY 1

*"Do all that is in your heart for God is with you."* **1 Chronicles 17:2**

Beloved of the Lord, what has God put in your heart? Has He given you dreams to fulfill for His kingdom? Nothing is impossible with God! Have you dared to step out in faith and believe the impossible? Without faith it is impossible to please Him. He is pleased with your faith. You have favor with your Heavenly Father. His eyes are ever upon the faithful in the land! Are you believing for the Lord to transform you, to do miracles, to save family and friends? Are you believing for your city or country to be touched by the Lord? Has He put a distant land or a certain ministry in your heart? Do you have a desire to reach out to the poor and needy, the orphan, the widow, those in hospitals and prisons? Do you know for certain what He has called you to? If not, ask Him. He will show you. He will support you. He will send you and care for you. He will anoint you and use you mightily! Do all that is in your heart for God is with you!

———————————◇———————————

Draw a big heart and write in it what your calling is. Hang it up. Now kneel down and ask the Lord what steps to take. Do it for God is with you!

# MAY 2

*"My sons (daughters) do not neglect now, for the Lord has chosen you to stand before Him, to minister to Him." 2 Chronicles 29:11*

Neglect. Is it not the most crushing thing? How many families are broken and scarred forever because of this one sin? It creeps in subtlety. It can even come in what appears to be good. A family can be neglected because of ministry. A needy person can be neglected because of busyness. The Lord says affectionately, "My sons (or daughters) do not neglect now." Do not neglect. How is it that we who are devoted to the Lord could neglect Him? It is possible. We can be so busy serving Him that we neglect Him.

His way is different. His way is that we would do *all* things as unto Him—devoted to Him. In Him.

Still, there is that personal quiet time with Him, a time for intimate communion. Has it become routine? Or an obligation? Then stop! Stop neglecting Him. Renew your love in Him.

He has chosen you to stand before Him, to minister *to Him!* He lets Himself be ministered to by us! What an awesome privilege! We can minister to God Almighty! Give Him your love and your heart today!

---

Find a quiet and sacred place. Stand before the Lord. Open your heart and mouth and minister to Him. Do not ask anything. Only bless Him.

# MAY 3

*"He is your praise and He is your God who has done these great and awesome things for you."*
*Deuteronomy 10:21*

Oh, the very loveliness and glory of the ability to praise and worship the Lord! The awesome privilege that He lets us get so near to Him, that He wishes intimacy with us, that He receives our kiss upward as we praise Him. What a gift to have breath to praise His blessed name and exalt Him. Do we dare not use this gift? If we do not, it will be lost in all of eternity.

But what does this verse say? It says that ***He is*** your praise—He Himself is your very praise! There is no one like Him. He's the object of your praise and He is your praise! He is your God, your Lord, your life and He has done great and awesome things for you!

Today, praise Him for His mighty works in your life. Speak out praises to Him for the great things He has done. Praise Him for the daily small things He does. Praise Him with your lips, praise Him with your hands, praise Him with your feet (dance). Praise Him with your work. Praise Him with your relationships. Praise Him in your quiet time alone with Him. You be a praise to Him for He is your God and He is your praise!

———————————◇———————————

Write a praise book for a week. Write all things for which you can praise the Lord. At the end of the week, share it with a person or group as a blessing, to glorify Him!

# MAY 4

*"But only a few things are necessary, really only one."* Luke 10:42

Oh, how we try to please the Lord—running busily from one activity to another. It's all for Him! Then suddenly we find our hearts to be shallow and no longer overflowing with His grace and glory! Yes, we must be doers of the word—but only one thing is necessary! Yes, we have many needs, but only one thing is necessary! But Lord, I need a healing, my family needs to be saved, I need a spouse, I need a child, a friend, a ministry, a job, a home, help when sad. So many, many needs—but are they really needs? Only one thing is necessary! Does not your Heavenly Father care for the sparrows? Hasn't He promised to provide for you, to protect you? But, what about your needs? Only one thing is needful! What about those heroes of faith who were martyred for the Lord? Did they have needs? Do those in prison for the gospel today have needs? Only one thing is needful! One thing! To sit at Jesus' feet, receiving from Him and giving Him your love! One thing. Sweet, continual communion with Him!

---

Pray and rearrange priorities this week to allow time to minister to Jesus, to soak in His love. Wait on Him, at His feet today. Just love Him!

# MAY 5

*"And there shall no longer be any night; and they shall not have need of the light of a lamp nor the light of the sun, because the Lord God shall illumine them; and they shall reign forever and ever." Revelation 22:5*

Can you imagine no night, or living without lamps and candles? Halleluiah—the darkness will be gone forever! We are the children of the light! We walk in the brightness of the Son of God! Not even the sunlight will be needed because the Lord God, He Himself will illumine us! We will thrill and rejoice! We will look to Him and be radiant! The radiance of the face of Jesus in His glory will fill our hearts and illuminate all of heaven!

What about today? Today, we look to Him with unveiled faces, as in a mirror. We see the glory of God in the face of Jesus and we are changed instantly into more of His precious image, from glory to glory! For God has shone in our hearts to give the light of the knowledge of the glory of God in the face of the Messiah! Now we see in part, but then fully! But we must look! Look and keep looking!

---◇---

Determine to behold Jesus each day, steadfastly. Make it a lifestyle. Adore Him. Worship Him! Then serve Him all day long.

# MAY 6

*"But the path of the righteous is like the light of dawn, that shines brighter and brighter until the full day." Proverbs 4:18*

Do you sometimes feel that things have gotten worse? Do you feel you can't conquer certain weaknesses in your life? Are you sometimes tired and weary? Do you often feel attacked by satan, the enemy of our souls? Are you dry spiritually, waiting for a touch from the Master? These things may be very real for many are the afflictions of the righteous. But the path of the righteous—the path of the righteous, is like the light of dawn! We are children of the MORNING STAR! Our path shines brighter and brighter until the full day—when we see Jesus face to face! As we become more intimate with Him, the brightness of His countenance shows us our hideous faults and blemishes. Still the path of the righteous is like the light of dawn, shining brighter and brighter. He will perfect that which He has begun in you, making you able to stand before the Father, blameless and full of joy! He is committed to you. You are shining more and more in the image of Jesus!

---

Decide to get up at sunrise tomorrow morning. As the sun rises and brings greater and greater light, worship the Lord! Dance unto Him! Your path shines bright!

# MAY 7

*"The lamp of your body is your eye; when your eye is clear, your whole body is also full of light."*
*Luke 11:34*

Oh, those eyes! What a glorious thing that the Lord has created in us, beautiful eyes as the window of our soul. Jesus said, "Blessed are your eyes because they see." Do your eyes see? Do they really see Jesus? Blessed are your eyes!

What stories the eyes can tell. Some tell of sorrow, some of anger, some of violence, some of demonic forces. It's there in the eyes, without a word spoken.

Blessed are your eyes—so full of peace, dancing with joy, overflowing with hope and faith! Blessed are your eyes when you see Jesus in those who love Him! Blessed are your eyes because they are clear, reflecting His purity in your heart! You shall see God!

What about those beautiful eyes of Jesus? Have they captivated you yet with His holy, loving, piercing look? Do you behold Him and look into His eyes so full of eternal glory? That look! That love! His face shining in strength and radiance! Those majestic eyes! Have you been under His awesome gaze of love? Blessed are your eyes! They see!

————————————◇————————————

Ask the Lord to make you pure through and through and to give you clear eyes. Now look upon Jesus! Be still under His gaze. Receive all that He wants to give you today. Love Him! Adore Him!

# MAY 8

*"For everyone who exalts himself shall be humbled, and he who humbles himself shall be exalted." Luke 18:14*

It's not the outward exalting of self that's shocking because it's blatant enough to be dealt with quickly. It's the inner, secret exalting of self that is so subtle. Isn't that what satan does? Exalting himself arrogantly against Almighty God? But with us, it's so subtle. It's in the little things that we must catch ourselves. We need to ask the Holy Spirit to sound an alarm in us when we do it. It's especially prominent in areas of skills or talents—all which is God given. We want to glorify ourselves and get praise from man—which is the opposite of Jesus.

Are you going through trials of fire? Praise God because it will keep you humbly clinging to Him. *He* is the One to be exalted. If you lift *Him* up, He will be exalted and draw all men unto Himself. *All* men! Do you want salvation on earth? Then exalt and glorify Jesus! Let your life be a praise to Him. Love one another and the world will see Him. Be a humble love slave like Jesus. He humbled Himself more than any other and now He is exalted higher than any other!

———————————◇———————————

Ask the Lord to show you whose feet you can humbly wash today! Be His love slave!

# MAY 9

## *"But there is a friend who sticks closer than a brother." Proverb 18:24*

At times the Spirit is thicker than blood. There is a knitting of hearts together in the deepest way, quickly, with those who love the Lord. It sometimes goes beyond the flesh and blood of relatives. How blessed we are when there is both—doubly blessed. Oh, the joy of reaching the throne of heaven in prayer together, or bringing a soul out of darkness into the glorious light, or worshipping together in the love of the Messiah.

But a real friend is also one who weeps with you as well as rejoices with you. It is only so far that another human being can go in this area. But there is a Friend who sticks closer than a brother. A Friend who knows the depths of your heart more than you do. One who feels that shout of joy in you and makes it your strength. One who is called the Man of Sorrows and felt your pains on the cross. He is the Resurrection and the Life, the Alpha and Omega, the BRIGHT MORNING STAR, the Light of the World, the Son of God. He is your Friend. He sticks closer than a brother.

———————————————◇———————————————

Write down all the ways that Jesus has stuck closer than a brother to you. Rejoice in Him! Give a shout of joy! Thank Him!

# MAY 10

*"For from Him and through Him and to Him are all things. To Him be the glory forever. Amen." Romans 11:36*

All things are **from Him**. Every heartbeat, every breath, the gift of each new day. Without His unlimited grace we would be dead. It is His kind grace that keeps the world going. All of life and every good gift is from Jesus. Are you talented? It's from Him! Do you have good character? It's from Him! Do you have a loving person in your life? It's from Him! All things are from Him!

All things are **through Him**. Apart from Him we can do nothing, but with Him we can do all things for nothing is impossible with God. The gifts and the calling of God are irrevocable. He has called us out of darkness into the glorious light of His beloved Son.

Our lives are *to Him*. All things in our lives are unto Him. Our thoughts, words, and deeds are unto Him. For from Him and through Him and to Him are all things. Let all things in us glorify His holy name forever. Let us *be* a worship unto Him!

---

Fold a paper into three parts. Thank Him for all in your life that is *from Him*, all that is *through Him* and all that is *to Him.*

# MAY 11

*"For if we live, we live for the Lord, or if we die, we die for the Lord. Therefore, we are the Lord's." Romans 14:8*

In Him we live and move and have our being. He is nearer than our own breath. Jesus is our life. Only Jesus. There is no life in anything or anyone else. He is our life and He is our love. He is our everything, our all in all. He is our Creator who breathed His precious Spirit into us and gave us life. He us our continual fountain of life, the very Bread of Life. But our Good Shepherd laid down His life for us. No greater love has any man than this—that he lays down his life for his friends. He came that He might give us eternal life. The Prince of Life gave His life for us. Can we do any less? Isn't He worthy of our lives? Yes, every moment of every day we must give our lives to Him—deny ourselves and follow Him, the Life giver! We live for Him. We also die for Him. We are His. While we live let's praise the Lord. When we die let's praise Him. The Messiah in us is the hope of glory. Let us be willing to lay down our very lives for the Lord who is so precious and dear to us. Praise Him!

---

*Go before the Lord today and make a commitment to live and die for Him—that your life is completely His. Bless Him today!*

# MAY 12

*"Around God is awesome majesty." Job 37:22*

He is a great and awesome God, awesome above all those around Him. He is as awesome as an army with banners. He is awesome in praises! Stand in awe of Him, in awe of His mighty works and miracles! Bless the Lord, oh my soul, bless His holy, holy name. He is awesome in praises!

How majestic is His name. The name above all names! He is clothed with majesty, enthroned above the cherubim, above the mercy seat! Yet, as He walked this earth, He had no stately form or majesty. He was like us, so that He could make us like Him. He humbled Himself, putting aside His awesome majesty, to the point of crucifixion. Now, in glory, He sits on the right hand of majesty on high! To the only God, our Savior, through the Messiah our Lord, be glory, majesty, domination and authority forever. Worship His majesty today! Stand in awe before Him!

---

Today, do a word study on the majesty of the Lord! Worship Him in awe of His glorious majesty!

# MAY 13

*"How precious also are Thy thoughts to me, O God! If I should count them, they would outnumber the sand." Psalm 139:17-18*

Yes, how precious! How precious are His thoughts of you, dear one. Isn't it true that we think all the time of the one we love the most? His thoughts of you are constant. You are always before His eyes. He knows your inmost thoughts, your sorrows, your weariness, your delights, your ways. He knows. His thoughts of you are always tender, loving, wise and pure. They are heavenly thoughts. He is your Eternal Father, your Good Shepherd, your Comforter, your peace. He is your Lord of Love forever. He is with you always, until the end of the age. He will never let you down, not for one fraction of a second. He longs to encourage you, to hold you, to delight in you!

If you were to count His thoughts, they would outnumber the sands on the shores. How devoted He is to you! How faithful! He is yours!

Sweet friend of God, set your thoughts on Him! Return His love and affection to Him. Fix your heart and mind on Him. Be devoted to Him, in season and out of season. In the wilderness and in times of great joy. Receive His perfect peace!

———————————◇———————————

Today, get some sand or soil and put it in a glass jar to remind yourself of His thoughts to you. If you have trouble keeping your mind on Him because of distractions, take an alarm clock in your bag or pocket. Set it every half hour and praise Jesus when it rings.

# MAY 14

## *"Rejoice always."* 1 Thessalonians 5:16

Are you searching for the perfect will of God in your life? Then rejoice! Rejoice always—this is the will of God! Delight yourself in the Lord and He will give you the desires of your heart.

A joyful heart doeth good like medicine. For the joy of the Lord is your strength. Rejoice in your faithful God. Rejoice!

Rejoice exceedingly and be glad of the works of the Lord! Proclaim His salvation day to day! Sing to the Lord! Rejoice! Rejoice with joy inexpressible and full of glory over the One you love! He is worthy of all your joy! Let your mouth be filled with holy laughter and your lips with joy! Shouts of joy! The outcome of your faith brings the salvation of souls! Rejoice! Rejoice with those who rejoice! Be an overcomer and rejoice in the Lord always. How often? Always, always. Again I say always! Isn't this a divine secret in the life of God to walk in His blessing and light? Rejoice always!

---

Get a tambourine or some type of instrument and rejoice in the Lord! Shouts of joy to Him! Bless Him today and commit to being a rejoicer over Him! Shine and glory in Him! Rejoice!

# MAY 15

*"Pray without ceasing."* 1 Thessalonians 5:17

And this is where the battle begins, for the enemy will not only fight us *in* prayer but bring obstacles before we begin praying. Therefore we are told to pray without ceasing so that the enemy has no place, so that we may continually dwell in His presence, so that we may be transformed and go from glory to glory, honoring Him. Let us obey the Lord and do His will. Let us live in worship and prayer, in the heavenlies. Let us pray what is on His heart. His sheep hear His voice. Be still and know that He is God. Pray for His will to be done. Open your heart to carry His burdens. Be available to feel His heart and emotions for people and nations. Lay aside yourself and give yourself to Him, to those He gives you. Be in His army and do His spiritual warfare against the powers of darkness. The name of Jesus is above all—above sin, above sickness, above sorrow, above principalities in high places. Nothing can separate us from the love of God. Stand in the gap, dear soldier of God. Pray without ceasing. Pray for the kingdom of heaven on earth, for His will to be done. Bless His heart. Pray without ceasing.

———————————◇———————————

Ask the Lord for the discipline to pray without ceasing, in the Spirit and in your language. Interpret. Prophesy. Hear His voice and speak. Let it be a lifestyle. Honor the Lord. Pray without ceasing.

# MAY 16

*"In everything give thanks; for this is God's will for you in the Messiah, Jesus. Do not quench the Spirit." 1 Thessalonians 5:18-19*

Not **for** everything because some things come from satan, the accuser and deceiver—but **in** everything. In every situation, in spite of all, give thanks. Your citizenship is in heaven. You are only a pilgrim of light here. In Jesus, give thanks, for He has blessed you with **every** spiritual blessing under heaven. He works **all** things for good to you who love Him and are called to His purpose. He is able to do exceedingly, abundantly more than we ask or think. He will never leave you or forsake you but is with you until the end of the age. In everything give thanks. You cannot enter into His presence without a thankful heart. It's your choice. Thank Him even when it's difficult, when your heart is breaking. You will have His glorious presence and light, His everlasting arms, His embrace, His deep piercing gaze. Are you distraught or discouraged? Give thanks to Him, rejoice, pray without ceasing. This is His will and you will have peace. Do not quench the Holy Spirit. Give thanks. Bless Him today. He is worthy all the time. Give thanks.

---

◇

Make a list of all the things you are thankful for in the Lord, in yourself, in the world around you, in every situation. Do it everyday for two weeks. Cultivate thankfulness and He will flow through you by His Spirit.

# MAY 17

*"Faithfulness is He who calls you, and He also will bring it to pass." 1 Thessalonians 5:24*

The precious faithfulness of God. Who is like Him? He is a God of faithfulness and promises. He, Jesus, was faithful unto death. The Father faithfully sent His Son. The Holy Spirit faithfully brings us to Him! Faithful is He who calls you! A God of faithfulness without injustice, righteous and upright is He. He answers His own faithfulness. Faithful is He who calls you! The One you love is full of unending faithfulness and goodness. He is the only trustworthy one. How faithful the Father was when Jesus said, "Not My will but Thine be done." How faithful Jesus was when He bore the cross and the nails and crown of thorns. How faithful His raising from the dead on the third day. How faithful was the Holy Spirit on Pentecost. How faithful He was to save you! Faithful, faithful God! Will He not freely give you all things? What is that special thing you are entrusting Him with? Have you waited a long time? He will bring it to pass! What is that immediate need that can't wait? He will bring it to pass. I know whom I have believed and I am convinced that He is able to guard what I have entrusted to Him until that day! Faithful God! He who calls you will also bring it to pass.

---◇---

Make a little booklet for the week. Each day write all the ways the Lord is faithful. Present it to Him at the end of the week. Entrust that important thing to the Faithful One.

# MAY 18

*"Let all who seek Thee rejoice and be glad in Thee; and let those who love Thy salvation say continually, 'Let God be magnified.'" Psalm 70:4*

Isn't it a natural result of seeking the Lord, to rejoice and be glad? Let us always seek the Lord. If you haven't done it regularly, do it now. Pursue Him! Do not be complacent. Do not lose your joy because of the cares of this world. Rejoice and be glad in your salvation! Rejoice and be glad! Do you love His salvation? Is it the very joy of your heart? Is it your life? Are you caught up in telling others of His love? We always talk about the One we love the most! He is your salvation and your song! Bless His holy name.

Does your heart say continually, "Let God be magnified?" Is your heart burning to have more of His love to reveal to others? Does your life constantly magnify the Lord? Oh, bless the Lord at all times. Let His praise be always in your mouth. Seek Him at all times. Magnify the Lord with me! Let us exalt His name together. Let everything that has breath praise the Lord! Let those who love His salvation magnify Him with all their hearts. Let God be magnified!

---------------◇---------------

Find a magnifying glass and place it over the name JESUS to remind yourself to keep magnifying Him daily.

# MAY 19

*"Your name is like purified oil."*
*Song of Solomon 1:3*

Oh, the sweet, sweet name of Jesus (Yeshua)! That name above all names. The name to whom all the hosts of heaven fall on their faces! The name which lights our hearts bringing salvation. The name which deserves all glory and honor and praise forever! His precious name. The name of Jesus!

*"Jesus, Jesus, Jesus!"* Oh, how Your name fills and warms our hearts. How it brings a song of peace and joy that is everlasting. Your name, Jesus, has melted my heart. It truly is poured out like purified oil! Holy is Your lovely name! How majestic is Your name, which endures forever. Nations will bow to Your name! It is hallowed forever! Every knee will bow and tongue confess that You are Lord—Jesus. All will bow before Your name. Your name is holy and awesome—it is like poured out perfume! Miracles arise because of Your name! The sick are healed by Your name. The oppressed are set free in You name. Our souls are saved to eternal life in the *name of Jesus!* Your name fills our hearts to the overflow with joy and peace and fullness. The rich, pure oil poured out unto glory forever. *The precious name of Jesus!*

---

◇

---

Dwell on His name today. Let it comfort your heart and fill you. Say His sweet name over and over all day. Tell Him you love Him all day. Say the name of Jesus. Write it in big letters and hang it over your room!

# MAY 20

*"But with all boldness, the Messiah shall even now, as always, be exalted in my body, whether by life or by death." Philippians 1:20*

. . . with all boldness. The Lord has humbled Himself and with boldness He wants to be exalted in you. The Messiah in you! The Messiah in you, the hope of glory! How He wants to exalt Himself in your body. Let us be a living sacrifice unto the Lord so that He may be boldly seen in us. Offer yourself as a sacrifice to Him so that He may do what He wants with you. There is nothing as precious as a person abandoned to Jesus—one who is so surrendered that they are able to say, "I will do anything for You, Lord. Have Your way with me." And He will do just that. He will reveal Himself boldly in such a person, even if they are unaware of it. Have you said to the Lord, "Let my life **and** my death count for You, Lord!" Will He reign in you in life and also in death? Will He be exalted and glorified? If we live, we'll praise the Lord. If we die, we'll praise the Lord. Let our first and our last breath cry out, "The Messiah in me!"

———————————————◇———————————————

Meditate on your commitment to Jesus in life and in death. Rejoice that He is alive in you forever!

# MAY 21

*"'Bring the whole tithe into the storehouse, so that there may be food in My house, and test Me now in this," says the Lord of hosts, "if I will not open for you the windows of heaven and pour out for you a blessing until there is no more need. Then I will rebuke the devourer for you. And all the nations will call you blessed, for you shall be a delightful land.'" Malachi 3:10-12*

Oh that we would learn that **every** good gift comes from the Father of Lights. All we have is His. He asks for only a tenth back—not because He needs it, but so that we honor Him and thank Him and keep our hearts soft, not letting the snare of the love of money get a small place in us. For where your treasure is so your heart will be. Where is your treasure? Is it not Jesus Himself? Yes, and should we not give Him great offerings also? Just to show our love and thankfulness to Him? He is the great Giver! No one will ever come close to giving as He does. If we gave all—homes, lands, and even those we love, it would not be enough to thank Him for giving His life for us. Is not giving the sure sign of love in the heart? God loved, so **He gave**. Let us give to Him with a cheerful heart, in great measure! This is the only place where the Lord says—"Test Me!" Let us trust Him. Give and it will be given to you in full measure, flowing over. Sow and you will reap. Let His full blessing be upon you—give, give, give! He will rebuke the devourer and nations will call you blessed and delightful! Give to Him!

---◇---

Pray and ask the Lord to give you large faith in tithing and giving offerings. Ask Him to show you where to give and how often. Step out in faith and give big amounts. Have one secret offering, anonymously given—just between you and the Lord!

# MAY 22

*"For I," declares the Lord, "will be a wall of fire around her, and I will be the glory in her midst." Zechariah 2:5*

Oh, that the Lord Himself would be a wall of fire around us—that out hearts would burn with love for Him! May it be that He has the freedom to surround us with His holy fire and take us into the holy of holies for sweet communion with Himself! May our hunger and thirst for more of Him burn as a blaze and be satisfied with a waterfall of His fresh, pure, living water! Oh, fill us up, Lord! Give us more of You! We need You so desperately! Come Lord, be as the glory in our midst! Let Your cloud of glory fall on us until we cannot stand up! Let our songs be as a trumpet call ushering in Your glorious presence! Let the light of Your shining glory be evident in us. Protect us. Go before us and behind us. The radiance of Your face is before us, the glory of Your countenance is our rear guard. Thank You for the glory of Your holy fire! Glory, glory, glory to You, oh Lord! You are pure light and holy glory! We adore You!

———————◇———————

Fall on your face before Him and cry, "glory, glory, glory!" Bless Him!

# MAY 23

*"But the things that proceed out of the mouth come from the heart, and those defile the man."*
*Matthew 15:18*

Oh, the tongue! Like our free will, it can be the greatest blessing or the worst curse. May God have mercy on us all. It is so true that what comes out of our mouths reflects our hearts. Depending on the spiritual condition of the heart, the man (and those he speaks to or about) is either blessed or defiled. Wars and violence and terrible crime, causing untold suffering have begun with words. Yet the words of Jesus, the word of God brings cleansing and life and eternal bliss to the heart and soul. What defiles us more than our own words? What can the enemy use more against us? Isn't it his job to lie, deceive and falsely accuse us, even to the point of death? Our words should be transformed just as our hearts are. We need to ask for the fear of God to fall on us and make us trustworthy in our thoughts and speech. The tongue reveals the trustworthiness of a person, his integrity. The tongue can be set on fire by hell unless it is tamed by the Holy Spirit. Our tongues were created first to bless our Lord, our Redeemer, also to bless those around us. Only His discernment and knowledge has the right to correct and rebuke. Bless the Lord!

---

Ask for the fear of God to come and the Holy Spirit to check your words. Make a covenant with the Lord to think on things praiseworthy and to speak His praise and His encouragement and His gospel of salvation.

# MAY 24

*"Come, you children, listen to me; I will teach you the fear of the Lord. Keep your tongue from evil and your lips from speaking deceit. Depart from evil and do good; seek peace and pursue it."*
**Psalm 34:11, 13-14**

Oh, Lord, teach us! Teach us Your precious holiness. Let us walk in Your grace and purity. Give us humble hearts to honor You, to lift up Your name so that all may be drawn to You!

Help us listen when Your Holy Spirit speaks to us. Let us not quench Your gentle promptings but let us obey. Cause us to fear You, full of reverence, allowing You to have Your way. Let us live before You as we would face to face, every moment. What would we look at? What would we listen to? What would we think and do? Let us live like that. You are with us every moment, in every place, in every thought and conversation. Is it pleasing to You? Do we honor You? Lord, put a guard over our lips. Let the angels bring a cleansing coal to our lips. Let us speak as You would speak and live as You would live. Let us speak the truth, with no exaggerations, no pretense. Let us do good and seek peace. Give us Your grace, Lord, to walk in the fear of You always.

—————————◇—————————

Use your Bible to do a small Bible study on the "fear of the Lord." Pray over it and do it!

# MAY 25

*"With it we bless our Lord and Father; and with it we curse men, who have been make in the likeness of God." James 3:9*

Oh, that precious tongue! So designed by our Creator and Father to praise and bless! The riches for all of eternity that can come through our tongues. How beautiful that the Lord made it so we can sing songs to Him and to each other bringing healing and joy to hearts! How wonderful that we can use it to communicate our deepest feelings and desires. We can powerfully proclaim the glories of the gospel of God and see lives changed for all eternity through the Messiah! We can join into heavenly worship! We can pray in the Holy Spirit!

But the awful side is that the war of the flesh, selfishness and the devil get in the way and we break down—then we sin with this small weapon, the tongue. Instead of blessing each other, we curse each other even though we are truly made in His image. Instead of edifying and encouraging, we slander and gossip. Come brothers and sisters, it should not be! Rise up! Overcome! Let the Holy Spirit be in control of your tongue. Bless God!

———————————◇———————————

Consecrate your tongue to the Lord! Ask Him to wash your heart and mind and words clean. Set yourself on blessing the Lord and everyone around you with your tongue.

# MAY 26

*"The harvest is plentiful but the workers are few. Therefore, beseech the Lord of the harvest to send out workers into His harvest."*
*Matthew 9:37-38*

Oh, taste and see that the Lord is good! He sends us as co-workers with Himself to reap the harvest! He shares His deepest joys with us! For the rocks could praise Him and witness of Him, but He desires to share with us His purpose and kingdom work. He plows up the hard ground of people's hearts with our earnest prayers. As we seek God on our faces, He plows the ground and makes it soft. He sends prophets to declare the word of God and the truth to the people. He avoids judgment if they begin to repent, but He sends adversity to wake them up and turn them unto Himself, snatching them out of the fire of hell. Then He plants seeds of the gospel as the evangelists and faithful witnesses proclaim His good news. He plants and weeds out the strongholds of darkness. Then comes the rich and gracious harvest. When it comes, it is plentiful. But the workers are few. Oh, it is written in scripture because it is always true—few workers. Will the fruit rot on the vine with no one to pick it? Where are the harvesters? Get on your knees and ask the Lord urgently for workers, for the sake of Jesus' wounds, to bring the harvest. Ask Him if you should go, or give or pray or do all three! Bless the Lord for this honor and privilege.

---

◇

Ask the Lord what your part is in the harvest. Commit it to Him and obey without fear or reserve. Bless Him today!

# MAY 27

*"If anyone wishes to come after Me, let him deny himself, take up his cross and follow Me."*
*Matthew 16:24*

First, we need to have the desire to come after Him. If anyone wishes. Do you wish to follow hard after Jesus? If not, ask Him for the desire. The next step is to seek Him earnestly—to hear and obey and walk in His Spirit—His way. Is your life His? Are your desires His desires? Is He your priority over all else? Is your time His? Is all you have His? All? We must have our priorities right, daily, to go after Him. Next . . . are you willing to deny yourself? Are there things in your life that you will give up (good things) for the sake of Jesus and establishing His kingdom on earth? Are there sacrifices you will deliberately make for Him concerning those ones that you hold most dear? Will you also give up some of your deepest desires? Will you entrust them into His hands completely, to do as He wishes? Will you surrender all to Jesus and let that freedom of His peace invade your heart and soul? You will know sweet intimacy, as you have never known, with Him. There is no loss in His kingdom. Only gain. When you give all for Him, then you have all in Him! Take up your cross and follow Jesus!

———————————◇———————————

Write down all that you need to give Him to really be His. Keep it in a special place. Rejoice in Him!

# MAY 28

*"But lay up for yourselves treasures in heaven, where neither moth nor rust destroys, and where thieves do not break in and steal; for where your treasure is, there will your heart be also."*
*Matthew 6:20-21*

Not only are we to give everything including ourselves for the Kingdom of God, but we are to lay up for ourselves treasures in heaven. How do we do it? We live our lives in the light of eternity and God's will. Do you have heaven in your eyes? Is your life counting for eternity? Is it influencing people for God's kingdom? Is your heart with Jesus? And all that you do, is it for Him in your attitude? When you must do something difficult or painful, say these three precious words: "For You, Jesus!" and your soul will soar to heaven. What about all you are? Are you His? Can you say, "I'm Yours, Lord, all I am and all I am not yet"? Are you growing in Him and sanctified? These are glorious jewels to store up in heaven. Is Jesus your life? Are you free of idols (anything that you love too much)? Where is your treasure? Is it in heaven? Wherever it is, that is where your heart is. Is your treasure Jesus?

---------------------◇---------------------

Find a small jewelry box and empty it. Inside, write out jewels for Jesus (i.e., "Jesus, You are my pearl of great price. You are more precious than silver," etc.).

# MAY 29

*"In those days ten men from the nations of every language will grasp the garment of a Jew saying, 'Let us go with you, for we have heard that God is with you.'" Zechariah 8:23*

Oh, Israel, My beloved! Didn't I deliver you out of slavery and bondage? Didn't I take you unto Myself as a holy nation? Didn't I even betroth You unto Myself in the wilderness? Yes, and I carried you as on the wings of an eagle! I wept over you, Jerusalem, for you missed your time of visitation. Was it not your sins too, that I died for when I, **your Messiah**, hung on the cross? Yes, I came to **you** first—the lost sheep of Israel! It was through you that the message came for the whole world! **You** had the calling first to be a holy nation and draw all nations unto your God! **You** are the natural branches, the others are grafted in. I am your peace (shalom), oh Jew, oh Gentile! I have broken down the wall between you. I, the Messiah of Israel, the Savior of the world, the Passover Lamb, your Lord and God, I am calling you again. Together you shall go proclaiming the gospel. For I will pour out My Spirit in these end times. You shall have a double anointing to reach the world. They will say, "Let us go with you, for **God is with you!** " They will grasp you in every nation. They will come to Me and you will worship together! I, Yeshua (Jesus) am your Lord!

---◇---

Pray for Messianic Jews today and ask the Lord how to be involved in reaching out with them! Let God's blessing fill you! Shalom!

# MAY 30

*"'Return to Me,' declares the Lord of hosts, "that I may return to you.'" Zechariah 1:3*

What precious words: "Return to Me!" Our God is the God of second chances—of mercy and kindness without compromising His holiness and righteousness. His love triumphs over judgment. When we fall, He catches us. The only requirement is a willing and repentant heart. He's there. He still longs for us. He hasn't given up on us. Oh, if we only knew the strength of His everlasting grace! Without it, we would be dead. For we cannot take a breath without Him. He gives us each heartbeat. He loves us. How precious His voice—"Return to Me; that I may return to you." He is the God of reconciliation. Return to your first love—that awesome "bridal love" for Jesus! Repent and do your first works. Cling to Him! Let Him be your every thought—your life! Speak to Him and of Him constantly! Rejoice in Him with an overflowing, thankful heart! "Return to Me," says our sweet God. He longs for you. Return! Return! Return to the lovingkindness of your heavenly Father! He loves you! Return!

---

Ask the Lord to show you if you've slipped away from Him in any way—large or big. Run to His arms. Embrace Him. Love Him. Let Him return to you and correct yourself. Repent deeply and be reconciled to the Lord.

# MAY 31

*"Cry aloud and shout for joy, O inhabitants of Zion, for great in your midst is the Holy One of Israel." Isaiah 12:6*

Let us learn to shout for joy! Shout! Shout for joy—for great in your midst is the Holy One! Great in your midst!

Oh Israel, daughter of Zion! Shout because the Holy One, the Lord **your** God has not forsaken you. He was with you in the wilderness. He even called Himself your husband. You are the apple of His eye! And He is the perfection of beauty coming out of Zion! Shout! Rejoice! For He, the Holy One is great within your midst. He was in the cloud of glory, in the blazing fire of holiness. But now . . . now He is great in your midst—face to face. Do you see Him? **He is your Messiah, Yeshua, your Lord!** He is in your heart!

Shout, "Glory to the Lord," all inhabitants of the earth—for God has made Himself known to you! God has become a man—Yeshua (Jesus). He has taken away your sins. Embrace Him! Receive Him! Belong to Him! Cling to Him! For great in your midst is the Holy One! Cry for joy! Our God reigns! He is high and lifted up, yet He dwells in our hearts. Shout for joy!

---◇---

Shout for joy! Pour out your thanksgiving and adoration for the Lord in your midst. Pray for Israel today—that the veil would be lifted and they would see their Messiah in their midst!

# JUNE 1

*"For they all put in out of their surplus, but she, out of her poverty, put in all she owned, all she had to live on." Mark 12:44*

Oh, blessed woman of God, saint! You are forever written in scripture for your loving, giving heart. Let us learn from you. Let us learn to give what is of value to God—not the surplus or the left over. Yes, we can give our 10% and our faithful, loving Father will gladly open the windows of heaven and pour out blessings too great to contain. But do we want to give Him the minimum? Could we give a big offering besides? Could we give 30%, or 50%? Could we give 80%? This woman gave **all**, in her poverty. She trusted the Lord as her provider. He was her life. Out of all the multitudes giving, **she** caught His eye and He saw her heart. Should we give clothing and food that we no longer want or should we give our best? That is giving to God. He gave His **Best**. He gave His **All**. He gave **Jesus**. Isn't it the attitude of our hearts that He looks at, not the gift itself? In your heart, does everything belong to God? Are you totally His? Where your treasure is, your heart will be. Will you be a big giver? A channel of His blessing to others? Can He trust you as you trust Him? God so loved, that He **_gave_**! Will you?

---◇---

Pray and ask the Lord how you can give money and possessions, also your time and love to Him! You will bring Him joy as you give cheerfully. In giving you will receive heavenly treasure!

# JUNE 2

*"Truly, truly I say to you, unless a grain of wheat falls into the earth and dies, it remains by itself alone; but if it dies it bears much fruit." John 12:24*

Let us learn to die to ourselves and follow Jesus. All of nature tells of His death and resurrection. The seeds are buried in the earth. The sun shines on them and they are raised to new life! Let us forget ourselves and live for God, magnifying Him! Let us take the low seat and not exalt self or compete with others. Let us honor Him first and our brothers and sisters second. Let us learn to wait on His timing and trust in Him **without** leaning on our own understanding. We want to glorify Jesus with our hearts and lives, loving Him and each other, but we have to die to do it. Have we bowed down and offered ourselves as a living sacrifice—for His purposes? Death is not easy. The natural life fights it—we must be crucified with the Messiah so that He can live in us. He gave His life for us—and He will do the miracle of raising us up so we can bear much fruit. His fruit. His way. And it will last forever.

---◇---

Ask the Lord to do whatever He needs to do to cause you to die to yourself, live for Him and bear much fruit.

# JUNE 3

*"And I, if I be lifted up from the earth, will draw all men to Myself." John 12:32*

All men! Draw all men! Isn't that the very heart of God—to draw **all** men unto Himself? He's not wishing for any to perish but for all to come to repentance! Isn't it also our very desire? Yes! We want to see cities and nations come to the Lord Jesus!

Here, Jesus gives us a key—"If I be lifted up." How do we lift Him up? It is in our hearts. It's keeping Him on the throne of our lives, as our King in all things, big and small. It is standing for Him in adversity, yes, even when loved ones are against Him. It is purposely preaching in the market place. It is honoring Him in worship and prayer continually, moment by moment. It is pointing the way to Him in a dying world. It is preaching the Messiah and Him crucified and not a mediocre message. It is singing a new song to Him, living by every word from His mouth. It is forsaking all for the love of the Messiah. Lift Him up! Lift Him up today so that He may draw **all** men to Himself.

---

Write in big letters John 12:32 and put it on the wall for the week.

# JUNE 4

*"He loved them to the end." John 13:1*

Blessed, blessed words! "He loved them to the end!" Jesus, precious Jesus, only You are truly faithful. The human heart is not ever faithful, except for the grace and character You give it. Yes, we may be faithful in character or in a situation or relationship—but we are never completely faithful in all things—thoughts, words, and deeds—toward You or each other. But how we long to be. Lord, divinely grant that we may truly be "faithful unto death." Give us the grace to be faithful in small things so that we may be faithful in all things. Let us be trustworthy to You—faithful until You come for us, faithful unto our death unto You, faithful under persecution, torture and martyrdom. For if we love You with a whole heart but do not finish the race, then we have run in vain. You loved Your blessed disciples unto the end—to the point of crucifixion, for us all. Give us faithful hearts, dear Faithful Jesus!

———————————◆———————————

Pray and make a list of ways you've been faithful to the Lord. Receive His affirmation with joy. Make a list of small ways you can grow in faithfulness and do it.

# JUNE 5

*"First of all, then, I urge that entreaties and prayers, petitions and thanksgivings, be made on behalf of all men, for kings and all who are in authority, in order that we may lead a tranquil and quiet life in all godliness and dignity."*
1 Timothy 2:1-2

First of all . . . let us count our Kings and Presidents and Prime Ministers of countries as a "first of all." Let us regularly lift them to the throne of God for we are all Ambassadors of the Messiah! We have even a higher position and duty as God's children. These leaders, and "all who are in authority," are on the heart of God. Notice too, that it says, "on behalf of *all* men"— for God is not wishing for any to perish but for all to come to repentance. So often we pray for our family, city and country or one that is in trouble and forget the world. *All* are on His heart. Let's make an effort to lift up each continent and country with its leader during the year. Let us petition today for the salvation of Kings and Presidents in all lands. Pray for the one He puts on your heart during this time—also for all. He exalts and cuts down—He puts them there for blessing or judgment and correction. His desire is a great outpouring of His Spirit and revival in every place. Let us thank the Lord for what He is doing in each place. Bless His holy name. His mercy endures forever.

———————————————◇———————————————

Find a world map or globe and lay hands on it—pray for all countries and leaders. Ask for one country a week to pray for. Get a map of that country. Stand or kneel on it and worship the Lord. Pray for its leader. Bless that nation.

# JUNE 6

*"Of two of you agree on earth about anything that they may ask, it shall be done for them by My Father who is in heaven. For where two or three have gathered together in My name, there I am in their midst." Matthew 18:19-20*

Isn't it something how the Lord honors our very smallest efforts in the smallest groups possible and makes it full of His love and power to change for His kingdom in prayer? If only two—husband and wife, parent and child, siblings, friends—only two—agree in unity—(oh, what a precious commodity is that oneness), our Father will hear and it will be done for us—according to His will. For where only two or three are gathered in the sweet name of Jesus—only two—"there I AM in their midst"—God will be with us. How He loves to be in our midst and inhabit our praises! He looks for every opportunity. He's in love with us. When you love someone, you love to be with that person. Do you love Jesus? Do you love to be with Him every moment? Do you expect Him when you are with just one other believer? Do you go to a congregation or Bible studies to meet with *Him*? Is He the topic of your conversation? Do you love to worship and pray with your friends? He does. He's in love with you!

---

Today, call your dearest believing friend to get together and pray and be with the Lord. Reveal your love for Him and each other in some special way.

# JUNE 7

*"These men who have upset the world
have come here also." Acts 17:6*

"Have upset the world"—oh, that we who love Jesus, would be like those men who upset the world with the very power and glory and love of the Messiah! "They have come here also." Have they come to your city, your town? Who are they? **YOU** are one of them! Do you feel too small, too insignificant, too overwhelmed for the task? You are not! You are the seed of the resurrection of the Messiah that God wants to use to plant His life and love into people's hearts.

Rise up and walk by faith for you are an ambassador of the Messiah! Nothing is too difficult for Him. What is impossible with man is possible with God. The very nations are only a drop in the bucket for Him! He will use every word you speak, every act of love, for His word accomplishes His purpose through you and His love never ever fails. Your life **CAN** upset the world! Be strong and courageous in the Lord—let Him lead you. Be full of His love. Do not shrink back for you have need of endurance. You are more than a conqueror through Jesus. Be steadfast and wholehearted—fully His. He will fully support you. You will upset the world with the love and power of the Messiah! Amen!

---

Do a prayer walk around your neighborhood praying for each home. Then pray for the Mayor and all city officials. Pray for those co-workers or students around you all day.

# JUNE 8

*"Believe in the Lord Jesus, and you shall be saved, you and your household." Acts 16:31*

"Believe"—(commit totally) in the Lord Jesus and you shall be saved. You must put your life completely into His hands forever. Trust Him. This is life. We must trust God or die. And when we find this eternal, glorious life and love of the Messiah, it so radically changes us that we instantly want all people around us, especially family, to also know Him and love Him! But Jesus said a prophet is not honored in his own home. It is true. Even He could do no miracles in His hometown because of the unbelief. But God has not left us without a promise. If we believe in Jesus, we will be saved, we and our households. It is His promise and comfort to our hearts that He is faithfully working in those we love so much. The blood of the Messiah has washed away our sins and in us it is on the doorpost of the house so that the death angel may pass over. We are the first fruits. A little holiness will make the whole lump holy. We know whom we have entrusted and He is able to bring it to pass. Bless His holy name.

---◇---

Today, concentrate all your prayers on family members. Ask the Lord to give you His heartfelt prayers for each one. And thank the Lord ahead of time for their salvation!

# JUNE 9

*"Have this attitude in yourselves which was also in the Messiah, Jesus. He humbled Himself by becoming obedient to the point of death, even death on a cross." Philippians 2:5, 8*

How can we put our attitude to death when it's so fleshly at times, so wrong, so unlike Jesus. Our criticism, our smoldering anger and stubbornness or wanting to always be right—it all needs to be nailed to the cross. But here the Lord tells us—"Let *this* attitude be in you . . . ." Which attitude? That of Jesus—who humbled Himself. He, Almighty God, Creator of the Universe, humbled Himself and became a man, one of us. Really, He became a microscopic cell in the womb of a woman, Mary. Then a helpless baby who had to be cared for by those with a sinful nature. He went through all the stages of childhood, youth, adulthood, going to school, working—identifying with us at every point—fully God and fully man. Even . . . to the point of torture and death on a cross, for our sins—His holy blood poured out, His body broken for us. Pierced for our iniquities. Our Lord, so sacrificial in His endless love for us. God have mercy on us, prideful sinners. Help us, Lord, to truly have Your attitude—to humble ourselves under Your mighty hand, to be *Your* servants, not self servants. To love with sacrificial love, like You.

---◆---

Have a time of repentance before the Lord. Surrender all to Him. Write Philippians 2:5-8 out and carry it in your pocket all day.

# JUNE 10

*"If you are reviled for the name of the Messiah, you are blessed, because the Spirit of glory and of God rests upon you." 1 Peter 4:14*

Are you misunderstood for your love for Jesus? Are you mocked and called a fanatic? Are you falsely accused and discriminated against, even arrested or beaten for your faith? Then rejoice! Rejoice for so are all who truly walk with the Lord. Jesus said we would be hated by *all*. *All* who live godly will be persecuted —some in small ways, some in big ways— but *all* will be persecuted. Prepare yourself oh soldier of God. Prepare for persecution. Be faithful to Jesus in small things and you will be faithful to Him in big things.

Stand up for Him in every way with every person. Do not let fear paralyze you. Pray that you will be faithful to Him unto death no matter how you are treated. Watch and pray. Do not sleep. Be alert, for the enemy, satan, prowls as a lion, looking for someone to devour. Dwell in Jesus. Stay in His presence. Look into His face continually. You are blessed. The glory of God rests upon you all the stronger in moments when you are reviled for His name. His light shines in your eyes. Your very persecutors will see it and be changed. Rejoice and be steadfast for your reward is great. Rejoice and love your enemies.

---

Today pray for any person (every person) who has mocked you or made fun of you or been critical because of your love for Jesus! Bless them in the name of the Lord.

# JUNE 11

*"For the Lord your God is a compassionate God;*
*He will not fail you." Deuteronomy 4:31 A*
*"For God did not send the Son into the world*
*to judge the world; but that the world should be*
*saved through Him." John 3:17*

The precious and mighty mercy of God. He is our God of compassion, full of new lovingkindness for us with each new sunrise! He will never fail us! He is *the* Faithful One, never forsaking or leaving us. Faithful, loving, compassionate God. He faithfully sent His Son Jesus to us—to His own joy and also His own pain. How deep His love is that He would give His own Holy Son to be crushed for our iniquities. A divine mystery. But He did not send Him to judge us, although He would have been justified to do so—He sent Jesus to *save* us! Even His name "Jesus" means "Salvation!" He came to save, to seek and save those who are lost. He is our hope and the only way to God and eternal life. He said in the Garden, "Father, if Thou art willing, remove this cup from Me; yet not My will but Thine be done." If there be any other way but crucifixion . . . but there wasn't. He is the way, the truth and the life. Have your sins been forgiven by the blood of Jesus? Are you following Him, denying yourself and going His way . . . the way of crucifixion?

———————————————⟡———————————————

Today, write out a salvation tract and pray about what it should say. Use plenty of salvation scriptures and a prayer and give it to someone today. Or make copies and give them out!

# JUNE 12

*"But being full of the Holy Spirit, he gazed intently into heaven and saw the glory of God, and Jesus standing at the right hand of God."*
*Acts 7:55*

Stephen was full of faith and full of the Holy Spirit. He was humble, willing to serve food while others devoted themselves to prayer and the word. Yet he was the one chosen of God to be the first martyr for the glory of God. He was full of grace and power, performing miracles. God's wisdom and Spirit were so heavy upon him that his enemies could not cope with him. His face was as an angel, aglow in the Spirit. He spoke the truth in love with the fear of God and not the fear of man, even after they had falsely accused him. He confronted them about resisting the Holy Spirit. They began to gnash their teeth at him, as it will be in hell. But being full of the Holy Spirit, he gazed intently into heaven. His heart and mind were on things above. He dwelt with the Lord continually, even in the worst of circumstances. They were about to stone him to death, yet he gazed intently into heaven. What did he see? The glory of God! While all of hell was against him, he was absorbed in the glory of God. And he saw Jesus standing there to receive him. Jesus sits at the right hand of God, but He stood to receive the first martyr, for **His** sake. Oh saint of God, will you be faithful to the end for Jesus? Will you lay down your life for Him now, so that you will truly be His at the point of life and death? Will you be so filled with Him that you see His glory?

---

Ask the Lord to so fill you with His Spirit and sanctify you that you will be able to dwell in His peaceful presence continually. Ask for discipline in your heart and mind to not get distracted. Make a commitment of faithfulness to the end.

# JUNE 13

*"Whatever you do, do your work heartily, as for the Lord rather than for men; knowing that from the Lord you will receive the reward of the inheritance. It is the Lord, the Messiah whom you serve." Colossians 3:23-24*

Those sweet words—"For You, Lord." Isn't it true that we can do all things through the Messiah who strengthens us when we do it with our heart for the Lord? Whatever it is. Is it your job? Is it school? Is it housework or caring for little ones? Is it retirement years or volunteer work? Whatever—do it heartily, wholehearted and in total devotion to Him. It is the **Lord, the Messiah** whom you serve. So serve Him, rather than men and you will please both—your reward will be great. Do not look for the praises of man. Even when they come (praises), they are worth little in the light of heaven. Look for Your Master, Your loving Father who gave all for you, to say, "Well done, My good and faithful servant!" Use your menial tasks (shopping, cleaning, painting, walking, etc.) for worship and prayer. Do all things well as if Jesus were with you, watching to see how it turns out. Commit work that takes concentration, unto Him and He will be in your thoughts, hands, feet and skills. Not only in special time with Him but be **devoted** to Him in all things!

---------------◇---------------

Practice His presence today in all you do. Thank Him that you will do well because of Him. Enjoy His presence and doing all for Him.

# JUNE 14

*"To Him who sits on the throne, and the Lamb, be blessing and honor and glory and dominion forever and ever. Amen." Revelation 5:13*

To Him! To the One who sits on the throne! To our only wise God, eternal in love and strength and glory. To our High Priest who has gone ahead of us and offered Himself on the altar for us. To Him who was broken as bread to feed the hungry, whose holy blood was poured out upon the altar as a sacrifice. To the One who spoke life into existence, who called the dead up from the grave, who lives forever. To our only true God! To Him! And to the Lamb, the precious, sweet Lamb of God, who takes away the sin of the world, who is risen forever—be blessing. Let all blessing in heaven and on earth forevermore go to Him. Let everything that hath breath praise the Lord! Let there be honor. Oh, let us honor Him continually in our hearts, our words, our thoughts and actions. Honor to Him who is awesome in praises. Let us extol Him! And let there be glory. Oh, glorify the holy One. Bring glory to Him! Lift Him up! Glory to Him! And dominion. Let His Kingdom come to earth through you and rule in you. Bow down to Him who sits on the throne today. Honor Him. Bless Him.

―――――――――――――⬦―――――――――――――

Fall on your face before His throne. Let His glorious presence fill you up. Bless Him. Worship Him. Love Him. Stay until you feel released by His Spirit to get up.

# JUNE 15

*"And they came into the house and saw the Child with Mary His mother; and they fell down and worshipped Him; and opening their treasures they presented to Him gifts of gold and frankincense and myrrh." Matthew 2:11-12*

And they came, those majestic kings from the East. They had travelled so far hoping to find the King of the Jews. They had brought the finest gifts to honor Him, but what they saw, they were unprepared for—the glory of His countenance filled the room. They saw the Child! They did not see with human eyes only but they really *saw* Him. Then they humbled themselves. With their rich flowing robes with jewels, they bowed down to the floor to honor this King of all Kings. They saw! They knew. One look at His face and they could do nothing but worship. They bowed low to the ground and gave Him worship and honor. They knew they had seen the face of God and would never be the same again. They gave their finest treasures: gold, frankincense, and myrrh. It is said that the gold represented His deity and was used to pay for Mary and Joseph's escape into Egypt. The frankincense represented worship and was shown later when the alabaster of perfume was broken upon Jesus' head, anointing Him for burial as an act of worship. The myrrh represented grief and was taken to the empty tomb to be used for embalmment, although it never was used. They saw *Him* . . . and they fell down and worshipped Him. Do you see Him? Do you fall down and worship Him?

---❖---

Today, find 3 gifts you will give to Jesus as a worship, such as your time, your will, the one you hold dearest, etc. It must be costly to you so that it can be a sweet sacrifice unto Him. Worship Him in it.

# JUNE 16

*"Then the virgin shall rejoice in the dance and
the young men and old together; for I will turn
their mourning into joy, and I will comfort them,
and give them joy for their sorrow."
Jeremiah 31:13*

Oh Israel, hear the word of the Lord for you, for your time is drawing near. You will be a pure virgin as you look into the beautiful face of your Redeemer, the Messiah, Yeshua (Jesus). The veil over your eyes is lifting, your heart is softening to the sweet Holy Spirit. Your mourning and sorrow shall be changed to joy and you shall come dancing! The joy of the Lord will be your strength—young and old together! You shall see the One whom your sins pierced. The Son of Righteousness shall rise upon you and you shall be healed! You shall go about skipping as calves! The Holy One of Israel is in your midst! And you, His chosen ones, shall receive power when the Holy Spirit has come upon you and you shall be His witnesses. All of the nations shall come to you and say, "Take us to God." Your Messiah Yeshua, shall dwell in the hearts of Jews and Gentiles. He is our peace. He has broken down every wall. We shall worship Him in oneness. We shall be His glory and His light forever! Shalom!

---◇---

Pray and let the Lord change any sorrow in your life to joy! By faith, dance unto Him with joy today. Then pray for any Jewish friends to be open to the Lord and share with them.

# JUNE 17

*". . . that the proof of your faith, being more precious than gold which is perishable, even though tested by fire, may be found to result in praise and glory and honor at the revelation of Jesus, the Messiah." 1 Peter 1:7*

The proof of your faith! Glory to God for His faithfulness to refine us as silver and purify us as gold. We would never choose this crucible, but God in His commitment to conform us into His precious image, allows us to go through manifold trials and sufferings. Have you ever noticed that some of those who love Jesus the most and shine the most with His radiance, are those who have been through terrible, fiery trials? The **pure** in heart shall see God. And what makes us pure? Trials. It is during trials that we press in close to the Lord. **His** desire is for us to press in all the time—to rejoice in Him and enjoy Him in good times, but our human nature is weak and our hearts can harden quickly. More people fall away from the Lord during easy times than during trials. Our faith must be tested both times. The goldsmith must heat the liquid gold until the dross comes to the surface so he can scoop it out. When the gold is pure he can see his reflection in the gold. The Lord wants to see His reflection in us, resulting in praise and glory and honor at His own revelation. Let Jesus make your faith as pure as gold.

---

Find something like gold or the color of gold and write 1Peter 1:7 on it. Carry it with you all day. Ask the Lord for a pure heart and pure faith to result in His praise and glory.

# JUNE 18

*"Now may the God of peace Himself sanctify you entirely; and may your spirit and soul and body be preserved complete, without blame at the coming of our Lord Jesus, the Messiah."*
### 2 Thessalonians 5:23

He is our God of peace, the Prince of Peace (shalom). All true and lasting peace comes from our vital relationship and clinging to Him. Not only walking with Him, but "clinging." Cling to the Lord and take His peace. His desire and purpose is to sanctify you entirely. Entirely. Without reserve. He will sanctify you in His truth. He calls you holy. Do you walk in holiness with the Lord? Are you set apart for Him without reserve? Are you growing step by step in His ways which are so opposite of the world's ways? Are you doing His will and not your own? Is your character being changed into holy character? Cry out, dear saint. Cry out to the Lord for a pure and holy heart, for right motives and holy desires. He will do it. His purpose is to conform you into His own image—to sanctify you ***entirely***. He will preserve your spirit and soul and body and make you complete in Him. You will stand before Jesus at His coming, ***blameless***, full of praise and adoration! You will be clothed in His righteousness alone. When you hear the trumpet, you will stand before Him, pure and holy without blame, completely pure!

---◇---

Get on your knees and thank the Lord for His precious breastplate of righteousness which protects you. Thank Him for the glorious gift of His sweet, sweet Holy Spirit.

# JUNE 19

*"Above all, keep fervent in your love for one another, because love covers a multitude of sins."*
*1 Peter 4:8*

How quickly our love can die. We are weak human beings. We cannot truly love without the Holy Spirit of God. The wick of our fire goes out, or it grows dim after some time goes by. In the book of Acts the blaze of the Holy Spirit caught hold and turned the world upside down with the precious love of the Messiah! In a short time, in the book of Revelation, Jesus is having to rebuke the seven churches, all except one, because they each had fallen in some way. He says, "Return to your first love." Return to your bridal love. We can return and stir it up. Oh backslidden believer, return to your first love for Jesus. Oh, broken marriage, return to your bridal love. Severed friendship, return. Return! The best is to never leave. Keep running the race steadily. Don't look back, no matter how tired you are. Keep going. You are not far from the prize of the upward goal of the Messiah. Keep fervent in your love. Fervent, fervent! God will fill you afresh in your relationships with His love. Pray and act in faith and your feelings of love will follow. Be committed to love, to love with Jesus' love. For His love covers your mistakes and sins. He will support you. Be fervent in your love.

---◇---

Pray and ask the Lord if there are any relationships in which you need to renew your love. Submit yourself to forgiving and loving anew. Call or write that person today.

# JUNE 20

*"... knowing, brethren beloved by God, His choice of you." 1 Thessalonians 1:4*

Dear servant of God, do you know, really know how loved you are? You are God's beloved, the very apple of His eye. You are His royal priesthood, His faithful witness, His true worshipper. You are anointed with the oil of joy, His light and glory. You walk in His grace and have anointing from the Holy One. His mercy to you is new every morning. You are His beloved and you are His very choice! Not that you loved Him, but He loved you first. Wherever you were in life, He reached down and touched you and made you new. He chose you and made you His own. You are ***His choice***! You are the choice of the God of the universe. He chooses you because His heart is so filled with love for you that it aches. His great longing is for you. You are the very desire of His heart. He's so in love with you. You are His choice! Is He also yours? Is your heart beating with love for Him? Tell Him today. Show Him today—that He is your choice too!

———————————◇———————————

Show the Lord today that He is your choice by doing something special for Him or spending some special time with Him.

# JUNE 21

*"And may the Lord direct your heart into the love of God and into the steadfastness of the Messiah."*
**2 Thessalonians 3:5**

Oh, blessed be the Lord for His holy ways. All His paths are full of lovingkindness. His ways are excellent. His faithfulness surrounds Him. Those who love Him are full of His mercy and love. Oh sweet believer, let the Lord direct your heart. Let Him be Lord of your heart, mind, soul and spirit. And most of all, let Him direct you into His own precious love, so full, so rich! It is an ocean of delight and fullness of joy! Let His love fill you up to the overflow—not just a splash but go into the depths and swim in it. Let your very heart beat just for Him! Look into the face of your Redeemer—the One who went to Calvary for you—the Risen One! Look into His shining face full of love for you! You have a place that no one else on earth has, in His heart! Only you can love Him back, in His desire for your love. Only you can worship Him in the way He designed *you* to do it. Therefore, let Him also direct you into the steadfastness of Himself. Be steadfast and immovable in your total love for Jesus. Stand firm and grow strong in Him.

---

Pray today that you will always grow in your love and steadfastness for Him and not stand still, because standing still is really going backwards. Love Jesus today!

# JUNE 22

*"The joy of the Lord is your strength."*
*Nehemiah 8:10*

Rejoice! Rejoice! Because the Messiah is in you! The hope of glory lives in your heart. Divine mystery—the Messiah in you! Rejoice in the Lord always and again I say rejoice! He is your unspeakable joy! His great desire is for His joy to be made complete in you! There is great joy in the Holy Spirit. The fruit of the spirit is joy. And even in times of distress and sorrow there is still that deep joy inside your heart. It is Jesus. He is the joy of your heart, the very jewel of your life! Consider it all joy, this trial that you are going through. He will purify your heart and make you like Jesus. He will perfect your faith. A merry heart doeth good like medicine. Sing to the Lord! Offer Him a sacrifice of praise in all circumstances. He is worthy. David was beside himself with joy. He danced for joy unto the Lord. Those who sow in tears will reap with shouts of joy! Jesus is the joy of the whole earth and in Him is your strength. The joy of the Lord is your continual strength. It will overcome circumstances, it will overcome self, it will overcome the devil. Don't lose the song in your heart. Keep your mind on things above. The joy of the Lord is your strength.

―――――――――◇―――――――――

Declare a fast unto the Lord of joyful praise unto Him. Rejoice in the God of your salvation!

# JUNE 23

*"He has made everything beautiful in His time.*
*He had also set eternity in their heart."*
*Ecclesiastes 3:11*

How good the Lord is! He gives us seasons of beauty. He turns our ashes to beauty, gives us the oil for joy for mourning, and a garland of praise for the spirit of heaviness. He created all things and everyone, everywhere to be perfectly beautiful in grace and glory—in character—in the depths. But the beauty was marred to ugliness when mankind chose sin. Rebellion and pride and unbelief and stubbornness stalked the land. Even nature was affected, and all living things. But He is a Restorer of life. He is the Resurrection. He sent Jesus to take away the ugliness of sin, that awful stench that we could never get rid of, and He made all things beautiful again—to all who receive Him. In His time He did it. His timing is perfect. And He set eternity in our hearts. He has made all things beautiful because *He* is beautiful! Jesus is the most beautiful Being in the universe and He bestows it onto you. Are you going through a time of ashes? Of ugliness? Take on the beauty of the Lord Jesus. Glorify Him in the season you're in and He will turn it to beauty!

---

Look into the beautiful face of Jesus and let His beauty reflect in you! Make something beautiful for Him today!

# JUNE 24

*"For I am not ashamed of the gospel, for it is the power of God for salvation to everyone who believes, to the Jew first and also to the Gentile."*
*Romans 1:16*

Oh, my brother, my sister, please heed these words and do not be ashamed of the gospel. Let His perfect love cast out all fear. Take your stand in the front lines of His mighty army and be faithful unto death. For the gospel is the power of God for salvation to **everyone**. And what? And to the Jews first! Certainly Jesus our Lord and Savior came through the chosen people, the Jews. The Apostle Paul, who was called to the Gentiles, always went to preach to the Jews first and even said he would give up his salvation for the salvation of the Jews. They were **so** on his heart that he would go to hell for their salvation. Can we even imagine such a thing? The Lord did not require it of him but he shared God's heart for those who are the "apple of His eye." Jesus also said He had come for "the Lost Sheep of Israel." Can we do less? Wherever the gospel is preached to the Jews consistently, the city is blessed. The Jews are the key to the world's salvation. It is God's plan as He pours out His Spirit in preparation for world revival and persecution.

---◇---

Pray for the Jews in your city and state—also for Israel. Visit a Messianic fellowship and find a prayer partner there.

# JUNE 25

*"The steadfast of mind Thou wilt keep in perfect peace, because he trusts in Thee. Trust in the Lord forever, for in God the Lord, we have an everlasting Rock." Isaiah 26:3-4*

How we need to keep coming back to the very steadfastness of the Messiah. Keep your mind on things above. And **He** will keep you in peace (shalom)—but not just peace—**perfect** peace. Oh that delightful dwelling in His presence in a way that His perfect peace comes. That indwelling of the Messiah. How we need to practice the presence of God continually—to discipline our minds to concentrate on Him, so that whether we are busy or resting, whether it's an easy time or hard time—He is there with us—we are *in Him*, not just living *for Him*, but *in Him*. Let us trust in the Lord in this way, that we constantly dwell in Him. Do not dwell on circumstances or self, for the devil will torment you. Dwell in Yeshua (Jesus). Let your spirit soar into His arms. Trust the Lord totally, forever—for He truly is your everlasting Rock. In Him is a firm foundation—the Rock of your salvation. Be strong in the Lord, take courage. Fix your heart on Him, steadfastly.

---◇---

Find a rock and write "Yeshua" on it—the rock of your salvation. Ask the Lord for a disciplined mind to be steadfastly on Him— for pure and simple devotion.

# JUNE 26

*"And it will be called 'the highway of holiness.'*
*But the redeemed will walk there. And the*
*ransoms of the Lord will return, and come with*
*joyful shouting to Zion, with everlasting joy*
*upon their heads. They will find gladness and*
*joy, and sorrow and sighing will flee away."*
*Isaiah 35:8-10*

Sweet friend of God, do you walk on the highway of holiness which is for the redeemed? Have you been washed by the blood of Jesus from all of your sins? Are you ransomed by His torturous death? Are you a new creation of His? Have all things become new in your life? Is He transforming your mind? Have you given yourself to Him as a living sacrifice and said, "Not my will, but Thy will be done" in my life? Is He your praise and joy in life, the very glory of your heart? Then you shall return to Zion. You shall come with joyful shouting! Joyful, joyful shouting! Will you shout for joy in the Lord? With everlasting joy upon your head? You will find gladness and joy, and your sorrow shall be gone. Jesus is the Healer of broken hearts and the great Giver of joy! Your heart and soul and spirit shall be made new, overflowing, rejoicing for your King! For He is the gladness of your soul. He is your holiness. He is your sweet love!

---◆---

Write on a paper every sorrow you've ever had. Cast it upon the Lord! Now make a garland or crown for your head. Write all of your joys on it and come rejoicing to the Lord!

# JUNE 27

*"Exalt the Lord our God, and worship at His
holy hill; for holy is the Lord our God."*
**Psalm 99:9**

Exalt the Lord, your sweet God! Exalt Him! Praise Him continually! Worship Him with your whole heart! Enter into the holy of holies to see Him face to face—each day, each moment, commune with the One who loves you beyond your knowing—the Holy One, who has humbled Himself and been crucified for you, who has risen up from the dead. He is waiting for you. Let His praise and thanksgiving be always in your mouth and heart. Bow down to Him. Honor Him. Come to His holy hill and abide there. Dwell with Him and bring Him glory and honor. Bless Him!

And who may dwell there? He who walks in integrity and works in righteousness. He who speaks the truth in his heart and does not slander nor do evil. He who is faithful and does not reproach his friend. He who despises reprobation. He who is faithful and keeps his word even to his own hurt. He who fears and honors the Lord and honors those who fear Him. He who gives freely and does not take a bribe. He who does these things will never be shaken. Never! But he will dwell with the Most High God, exalting Him, enjoying His presence, going from glory to glory in worship and in life. Exalt the Lord today and worship at His holy hill! Enjoy Him!

---◇---

Today, worship the Lord in freedom until you enter into that holy place. Don't ask anything of Him but just enjoy Him. Enjoy being with Him.

# JUNE 28

*"Therefore thus says the Lord God, 'Behold, I am laying in Zion a stone, a tested stone, a costly cornerstone for the foundation, firmly placed. He who believes in it will not be disturbed."*
Isaiah 28:16

Behold! Look! *I am!* The Great I AM! I am laying in Zion a tested stone, a costly, costly cornerstone as a foundation, firmly placed. Oh, that beloved tried stone! Who is it but Jesus, precious Jesus, our Lord and Messiah! It is He who was tried beyond our comprehension, marred beyond recognition. It is He who sweat great drops of blood when our hideous, filthy sins came upon Him. He is so costly. Even laying down our own lives could not buy a single drop of His precious blood. Jesus is that blessed cornerstone and foundation laid for our salvation. He was firmly placed on the cross between two thieves and nailed into place, alive, for our salvation. He is the jewel of our hearts. Sweet Holy One of heaven, fill us with Your love! You are our glory. Our costly stone. One day we will see this costly cornerstone. We will see His wounds, His scars for us, proving His love. Our eyes will look upon the One we wounded with our sins. *He* alone was laid in that firm place, to save your soul, to set you free, to give you new life!

---

Find a stone and write on it "Jesus." Put a nail next to it to remind you of His death for you. Thank Him for your salvation today. Thank Him for the gift of faith and repentance. Thank Him for His security today.

# JUNE 29

*"Turn to Me, and be saved all the ends of the earth; for I am God, and there is no other. To Me every knee will bow, every tongue will swear allegiance." Isaiah 45:22-23*

**All** the ends of the earth. **Every** mountain, **every** valley, **every** sea, **every** lake, **every** desert and **every** island. **All** peoples everywhere, on **every** continent, in **every** hidden place. Turn to the Living God and be saved! Turn to the Lord while there is still time. Do not wait. For today is the day of salvation. Tomorrow will be too late. It is the Lord who calls you! He calls! Oh, He calls your name! With His tender, loving voice He calls! How long has He waited for you? Where have you been? What have you done? Have you seen His heart breaking? Oh, turn you Kings and Presidents and Prime Ministers of the lands. Turn, you who have lived in riches. Turn, you who have suffered. Turn! Do not miss His day of visitation to you. Today, if you hear His voice, do not harden your heart. Turn, you who have lived good lives without Him. Turn, you who have sinned beyond imagination. It is not too late. Turn, you who are sick and dying. Turn! It is a life or death choice! Hear His loving voice! See His blood on the cross! Turn now and give Him your heart forever! Let Him fill your heart with His love. For you will one day bow your knee and confess with your tongue that the Messiah is Lord! Do it now and belong to Him forever!

---

Today, pray for all nations and all leaders of nations and all hidden people groups, that they will turn to Jesus! Get a world map and lay your hands on it, praying for each country. Choose one country to pray for each week.

# JUNE 30

*"His eyes were like a flame of fire. His face was like the sun shining in its strength."*
*Revelation 1:14b & 16b*

It's the eyes. They truly are the windows of the soul. In them we see if there is light or darkness, joy or sadness, peace or anger, the Messiah or devil. One look and we know. Are they clear and full of the light of the Messiah, or are they dull and full of darkness? Often believers are known by the light of His love shining in their eyes. It pierces the heart. The man at the Beautiful Gate gazed at Peter and his legs were healed. Demons were cast out and people healed by one glance at Jesus. His countenance brought life and even eternal life. No one ever died in His presence but many were risen from the dead! Halleluia! His eyes! Those eyes! Glorious eyes!

Today, look into the eyes of Jesus. Look into His glorious, heavenly eyes. Do you see His kind love for you? Do you see His radiant beauty? Do His eyes pierce the depths of your heart? His eyes are full of holy fire and blazing love. Full of eternal love, of which we know nothing. Let them melt your heart. Fall in love with Him all over again. Abandoned to Him. Absolute surrender. His blessed face shines bright as the sunshine. Let His light cleanse you and fill you up to the fullness of God! Love Him!

———————————◇———————————

This morning be alone in a quiet place with Him. Fall on your face in worship. Adore Him. Then wait, in holy silence in His presence. Let Him minister to the depths of your heart. Love Him. Worship Him. Look in His eyes.

# JULY 1

*"To Him who overcomes . . . He who overcomes."*
*Revelation 2:7, 11, 17, 26*

Oh dear brothers and sisters how desperately we need to have an overcoming spirit! Lord, have mercy on us. Let us not just run the race, but let us run as if to win. Let us finish the course. Let us take up our cross and follow Jesus, denying ourselves, daily. Let us be determined not to let any weapon of the enemy be formed or cause us to fall. Where are your weak points? Do you fear, or doubt, or fall into unbelief or pride? Do you get easily hurt or fall into condemnation? Then stand strong with the armor of God—give all to Jesus. Let His everlasting arms be around you. Dwell in the shelter of His wings. Let the high praises of God be in your mouth. He will defend you. But, what were His words to the seven churches? It was "repent" and "to He who **overcomes**!" And what were their weaknesses? Loss of first love for Jesus, fear of suffering, spiritual deadness, indifference and pride. Only one congregation had no rebuke from Jesus—He told that congregation to hold fast to what they had and to conquer or overcome. It will do no good to have a heart fully for the Lord most of your life and come to ruins in the end. Repent. Hold fast. Overcome. Be fully His in your heart and will.

---◇---

Pray to the Lord to strengthen your weak areas. Ask for His grace and power. Repent in any areas necessary. Receive an overcoming spirit from the Lord!

# JULY 2

*"And the witness is this, that God has given us eternal life and this life is in His Son. He who has the Son has the life; he who does not have the Son of God does not have the life."*
*1 John 5:11-12*

God has made the message so simple—so black and white. He wants us to know for sure what salvation is, how to have eternal life. He doesn't want us to guess or to be insecure about the most important issue of all—eternal destiny. He tells us exactly where to find it. This life is in His Son. This is eternal life, that they may know Thee, the only true God, and the Messiah whom Thou hast sent. Knowing Jesus is eternal life—and this knowing Him, so personally and intimately, starts here on earth and goes into eternity. Heaven came down when Jesus was born in the manger. It was *God* in that manger. It was *God* who walked among us and loved us and healed us. It was *God* who sweat great drops of blood in the garden. It was *God* who hung on the cross and said, "Father forgive them, they don't know what they're doing." It was *God* who rose up from the dead on that glorious resurrection day! *He who has the Son, has life*. He who does not have the Son of God does not have life. Do you have the Son of God? Has he forgiven your sins by His blood on the cross? Has He radically changed your life? Are you living for Him? Is He deep in your heart? If not, repent today and give Him your life. Let Him be the Lord of your life.

---

Today write on a paper all of your thankfulness for what He has done for you and how He has changed you. Bless His holy name!

# JULY 3

*"And this is the confidence which we have before Him, that if we ask anything according to His will He hears us. And if we know that He hears us in whatever we ask, we know that we have the requests which we have asked from Him."*
*1 John 5:14-15*

Anything! Anything! Anything according to His will. **This** is the confidence we have. We have a loving Heavenly Father, who will not grant us according to our fickle desires which can often lead to destruction. No! He is caring—a Good Shepherd—a good Husband! He watches out for us. We can be confident that if we sometimes ask amiss, He will not grant it. The other side—if we ask according to His will—anything! Anything! How big is your God! How big is your faith! Don't limit Him—ask anything when you know it's His will. He is not willing for any to perish—pray for the salvation of the world. Pray for all Kings, Presidents, Prime Ministers, leaders of countries, states, cities. Pray for your congregation to grow and multiply ten times its size with firm discipleship and teaching. Pray for miracles, salvation and healings. Lift up faith in the Son of God over every seemingly impossible situation. He will do it. This is the confidence we have! Pray again and again for unsaved loved ones. He hears us! We have our request! It is done in heaven and will come about on earth in His timing—according to His perfect and sweet will! Ask and receive!

———————————————◆———————————————

Make a list of three to five things in your life that seem impossible. Be sure they are His will. Pray each one. Fold up the paper and cast it up into His care. Now unfold it and write "done in heaven" and thank Him ahead of time that He hears you and you have the request.

# JULY 4

*"Watch over your heart with all diligence; for from it flows the springs of life." Proverbs 4:23*

Dear saint of God, be wise, get understanding and knowledge. Fear the Lord and humble yourself in His sight For He is God and you are not. Be careful to honor Him and to watch over your heart at all times, with diligence. Where is your heart? In the garden God said, "Adam, where are you?" He missed the sweet fellowship with him. Does the Lord miss His closeness with you? Has anything subtly come in between you so that the springs of life do not flow? It may be something good, like a person, or even serving in His kingdom too busily, or too much to do. It may be His tangible blessings, possessions or money. It may be a burst of fame because of your service to Him. Whatever it is, it must be treated as an idol and turned away from. In life, do you have consistent quality time with the Lord—meeting with Him and not only dry routine? Do you dwell in Him? Do you also have quality time with your family? And do you put a priority on doing His will and serving Him, His way? Are your motives right? Let Him change you and correct you and fill you today with the fresh oil of anointing and a new vision. Walk with Him!

---

Today, give the Lord a chance to rearrange your life and priorities and desires. And a chance also to say to you, "Well done, my faithful servant!"

# JULY 5

*"For the Lord will be your confidence and will keep your foot from being caught. Proverbs 3:26*

Yes, the **Lord** will be your confidence. Elohim, The Triune Creator, the God who reveals Himself, all wise, all knowing is for you. Who can grasp the depth of His love? It is full of majesty and splendor. Our God is awesome and full of power. He is righteous and holy. The great *I AM!* He is mighty and sufficient, the God of all comfort. He is your sovereign Master, the provider of the sacrificial Lamb—Jesus, your Redeemer. He's the God on high, full of grace and glory. He's the Healer of sickness and sorrow. He's your victor in conflicts. He goes before you. His banner over you is love. He sets you apart for holy service. He's your peace giver, your righteous justifier. He's the Shepherd and Keeper of your soul. He is God and He is here with you always. He's your loving Father! This is the One who will be your confidence. And He will keep your foot from slipping. He is the Rock of your salvation, strong and mighty. His love for you endures forever and His mercy is new each morning. Trust Him. Rest in His arms. Let Him lead you. He will not fail you. He is trustworthy. He will never lead you astray. Cling to Him with all your heart.

---

Give to the Lord those things which are difficult to give, or to trust Him with. Break that bondage of fear. Step out in faith, according to His will and trust Him. He is your confidence. You will not fall!

# JULY 6

*"Oh the depth of the riches both of the wisdom and knowledge of God! How unsearchable are His judgments and unfathomable His ways!"*
*Romans 11:33*

Oh, the awesome depths of God! His infinite wisdom and love for you. He is wonderful and full of overflowing compassion for you. He is beyond description or words or understanding—our amazing Lord! Who can know the very depths of His love? It is endless, into eternity. Too wonderful to be understood but perfect to hold on to. His knowledge is so beyond us—oh, that we would trust Him as He deserves to be trusted. Lord, give us that pure, innocent, childlike faith and trust. Let us not trust in our own intellect or understanding. His ways are unsearchable, yet they are excellent. Do you know His ways? Do you hear and obey even when it makes no sense to you? Are you humble before Him? And His judgments. They are perfect. Even they are done in kindness and mercy. Yes, His ways are unsearchable, but how we need to know them. Let the word of God rise up in resurrected revelation knowledge to you. Let the sweet Spirit of God have His way in showing you more of Jesus!

---

Declare your inability to do things or even be His on your own. Take His Spirit of grace and faith and anointing freshly into your heart. Seek the Lord with all your heart and you will find Him!

# JULY 7

*"I am the rose of Sharon."*
*Song of Solomon 2:1*

Jesus is the most exquisite and rare of all loves. He is the fairest of ten thousand, the perfection of beauty out of Zion. He shines as the sun in full radiance. He is the best of the best. He is your very heart, altogether lovely. Heaven itself cannot possess Him, for He is the highest and holiness of all. He alone is the fullness of all love. All eternity will praise Him. Only His beauty can satisfy our soul. He is the rose of Sharon! He pours out His fragrance in beauty and grace! He is the lover of your soul, your BRIGHT MORNING STAR. Stand in His glory and strength forever. He is your fresh new wine, your oil of joy! He is your sweet rose of Sharon. Love Him forever. Praise His holiness. Praise His loveliness. Nothing can excel the sweet rose of Sharon—Jesus! Your abounding preciousness is in Him. *"I am"* the rose of Sharon. He proclaims who He is—the eternal living God! Let Jesus, your rose of Sharon bloom in your heart today!

———————————◇———————————

Either get a rose or draw a rose. Set it near you today and worship Him for who He is, not only what He does. Bless Him. Love Him. Worship Him.

# JULY 8

*"But they who seek the Lord shall not be in want of any good thing." Psalm 34:10 B*

It is a continual process, all of our lives, not just at the beginning or in times of need—seeking the Lord. How many marriages also would be put back together if people would continue to seek to know and understand each other better—not only at the beginning. Seek the Lord while He may be found. Seek the Lord and you will find Him. Do you want to know new things about the One you love? Or do you say, "I know enough." Lord, have mercy on us if we say that, if we hurt the Lord in this way. Even with a lifelong partner we can never learn enough or appreciate enough. How much more with the Son of God in whom are endless treasures! Isn't it when we seek Him that we have the most joy? Our hearts are full of Jesus and overflowing with love for Him, which spreads to others. And the Lord is not only quick to reward us with His presence, which is the best—but He promises that we won't be in need of any good thing. He will take care of us. And isn't it true also that when our hearts are full of Him we feel that we don't even want anything else?

---
◇
---

Take some time to really seek the Lord for who He is, to enjoy Him and love Him. Give Him all of your cares and rest in Him!

# JULY 9

*"The Lord is my Shepherd, I shall not want. He makes me lie down in green pastures; He leads me beside quiet waters. Surely goodness and mercy shall follow me all the days of my life, and I will dwell in the house of the Lord forever more." Psalm 23:1, 2, 6*

Holy Lamb of God. Shepherd of my soul. Oh, what a Good Shepherd You are. How caring and loving in every way. You keep us from falling. You hear us when we call and You give us ears to hear You, eyes to really see You and a heart to really love You. You are the only One who can fulfill all our needs. You are our peace. How we love Your holy presence. Kind Father, holy and true, thank You that in You—really *in* You, we need nothing. We want nothing and no one—only You. If we were to lose all but You we would still be rich. You are the very delight of our lives. You give us great peace and stillness in Your presence. Oh, how we love those quiet waters—peace that overflows. It's You, sweet Lord! The whisper of Your precious love! Let us dwell in You and enjoy the green pastures of Your nourishing love today. Let us be still and know that You are God. Our cups overflow with Your goodness. You give us mercy forever. One day we will dwell in Your house forever. Today, let us dwell in Your presence more continually—still and not busy—enjoying You!

———————————◇———————————

Cast your cares and your schedule today upon the Lord. Determine to stay still and quiet in His presence and depend on Him to give you the time you need for everything. Bless Him today!

# JULY 10

*"The Lord is near to the brokenhearted, and saves those who are crushed in spirit. Many are the afflictions of the righteous, but the Lord delivers him out of them all." Psalm 34:18-19*

Oh how near He is to those with shattered hearts—believer and non-believer—He is near! How His own heart breaks with you, only so much more—because He is also the most tenderhearted of all! Jesus, precious Jesus! Man of sorrows. Crushed for you iniquities, pierced through. He Himself died of a broken heart over our wicked sins. He suffered more than anyone has or ever will—marred beyond recognition as a human being. And that was only the physical pain. What about the emotional and especially the spiritual agony? Dear one, are you hurting this day? Has something or someone devastated you? Lean on Jesus. He is nearer to you than your own breath. Let Him hold you in His arms. Pour your heart out to Him. Let Him fill you with His forgiveness and renew your love. He is the only One who can heal your heart and even turn sorrow to joy. Only Jesus! He will do it. And He will, if you let Him, turn it to good and make you more like Himself. Let His resurrection spirit rise up in you! Let Jesus love you!

———————————————◇———————————————

Through your tears sing a song to Jesus, as a sacrifice of worship. He will make it a rainbow for you! You will sense His deep, tender love!

# JULY 11

*"But he who trusts in the Lord, lovingkindness shall surround him." Psalm 32:10*

He who puts all of his confidence, faith and hope in the Lord—who leans on the Lord completely—lovingkindness shall surround him. The glorious lovingkindness and mercy of the Lord Himself shall surround him. Do you not only believe in the Lord with all your heart, but trust Him—as a child trusts his father or mother to carry him through danger? Do you lean on the Lord in this way and not on yourself or others? In Jesus is your life. In Him alone. He is your hope and confidence. Do not throw away your confidence for you have great need of endurance—for soon He will come. Do not shrink back. Strengthen your faith, then your hope and then your love. Rise up in the mighty strength of the Lord. And humble yourself under His mighty hand—for all that is good in your life and in you is by His grace. All is a gift—every second, every breath. Let His lovingkindness and mercy fall upon you today and fill your heart. Depend on Him totally and not yourself. Let Him be Lord in every detail. Let His lovingkindness surround you in a cloud of His glory! See Jesus! See Him face to face today. Walk with Him, filled with His love. Trust Him with all your heart, for He is good!

————————————————◇————————————————

Draw a little stick figure of yourself and a rainbow around you of His lovingkindness and mercy! Bless Him today. Step out in a specific area of faith and trust, as an offering to Him!

# JULY 12

*"We will rejoice in you and be glad; we
will extol your love more than wine."*
*Song of Solomon 1:4B*

Oh, just knowing You, Lord, causes pure joy and love and worship to well up in us! It's so natural to sing to You all the time deep in our hearts! There's always a song for You deep down, even in trials and stormy weather! In the stillness and peace You've put in our hearts, there rises up a song! A song of beauty! A song of peace! A song of holiness! A song of joy! Yes, we rejoice in You! We are so glad in You. In You! That's the key! When we dwell in You, we rejoice, we have continual peace—a feast of Your glorious presence! How we adore You, Lord! Your lovingkindness is better than life. Besides You, we desire nothing on earth. You are our only good! We only want to love You, You alone are our life and all that matters is You! Your love is better than wine, better than jewels and riches, better than anything or anyone. We exalt You today! We extol Your sweet love! We lift it up for the world to see! The very love of the Messiah! We love You with an everlasting love as You first loved us! We extol Your love, full of joy!

———————————◇———————————

Dance unto the Lord today! In your dance lift up and extol His love full of joy! Rejoice in Jesus!

# JULY 13

*"Holy, Holy, Holy, is the Lord of hosts, the whole earth is full of His glory." "Here am I, send me!"*
*Isaiah 6:3, 8*

Do you hear that holy whisper, that awesome stillness and quietness of His holy presence? Do you see the heavenly hosts and angels and all of heaven bowing down on their faces before Him saying, "Holy, Holy, Holy"? Will you fall on your face today in His awesome, holy presence and cry, "Holy, Holy, Holy"? Oh, worship the Lord in holy array, dressed in His righteousness—made pure by the blood of His cross. Bow down so low before the Lord of hosts, the King of Kings, the great I AM. He is worthy of praise! He is Lord of all! The whole earth is *full* of His glory! *Full* of His glory! Honor and glory and praises and blessing and thanksgiving to You, Sweet Lord! We adore You! We are speechless before You! Oh, saint of God, worship Him in spirit and truth! Are you completely His? Is your life—"Not my will but Thine, Lord"? Can He have His way with you? Will you go anywhere and do anything for Him? Will you go through anything for Him because of what He's done for you? Will you say, "Here am I, send me, Lord!"?

———————————◇———————————

Worship the Lord in all of His holiness today. Be still and hear Him. Be willing to be sent by Him. Tell Him with all your heart, "Here am I, send me!"

# JULY 14

*"Go therefore, and make disciples of all the nations, baptizing (immersing) them in the name of the Father, and the Son, and the Holy Spirit, teaching them to observe all that I have commanded you; and lo, I am with you always, even to the end of the age." Matthew 28:19-20*

Go—make—baptize (immerse)—teach! Yes, that is our holy calling! These are Jesus' last words to us—the very purpose of our lives. He did not fill us with His salvation and resurrected life for us to simply hold it in selfishly for ourselves. No! The very Spirit of the Lord is to give. Yes, our lives are not our own now—they are His and He is the Giver. His nature is to give. The one who loves the most is the one who gives up the most. Give your life, dearly beloved of God. Give! Go into the part of the world He has called you to and preach the gospel. Then make disciples out of those new baby believers. See that they get filled with the Holy Spirit. Teach them all that Jesus has taught you—with the fear of God upon you. Give your life. Pour it out—this is your purpose in life. And know this—that He is well-pleased with you. Jesus is with you always. Always. Even until the end of time. How faithful is our God to those who love Him and serve Him with their whole hearts.

———————————◇———————————

Pray for someone to get saved this week (or many) and begin to disciple them. Teach them to do the same!

# JULY 15

*"Who is this that grows like the dawn, as beautiful as the full moon, as pure as the sun, as awesome as an army with banners?"*
*Song of Solomon 6:10*

Who is like the light of dawn? Isn't it our BRIGHT MORNING STAR, Jesus? He is the light of the world that lights our hearts and gives us a glow of His beautiful radiance! The path of those who love Him, who belong to Him and do His will, is like the light of dawn. When it's the very darkest, the MORNING STAR breaks through and grows until the sky is full of sunlight. Jesus is the sunrise in our eyes! He shines upon us brighter and brighter until the full day when we shall see Him face to face! As the lightning flashes from east to west, He will come, with His holy angels. He is purer than the bright sun in its full strength! He is more beautiful than the full moon on a starry night! He is regal, as awesome as an army with banners. His banner over us is love. He prepares a banquet for us in the presence of our enemies. Our cup runs over with the fullness of His precious love. He is more faithful than each sunrise and sunset. He gives us His own dear presence as often as we will let Him. He is costly above jewels and more beautiful than anything or anyone! He will never let you down for even a fraction of a second. He longs to pour His Spirit and love upon you as a sweet perfume! He is beautiful!

---◇---

Plan a morning to get up and see the BRIGHT MORNING STAR and the sunrise. Worship the Lord in that spot and bless Him in every way.

# JULY 16

*"For those who honor Me, I will honor, and those who despise Me will be lightly esteemed."*
*1 Samuel 2:30 D*

How good God is! Love believes the best! The Lord is our greatest encourager at every turn of the road. He's the lifter of our heads. **He** makes His face shine upon us. How gracious He is—those who honor Him, He honors! And those who are so hard-hearted that they despise Him? Does He also despise them? No, He lightly esteems them. He does not give us what we deserve. He saves us. He gives us His grace and mercy. He gives us time to repent, a multitude of second chances. But let us take His hand of mercy and not invoke His hand of wrath. Let us not break the heart of the One who was tortured and died for us. Our sins fall onto the fourth generation. And our blessings? To the 1,000th generation! How full of lovingkindness is our sweet God! His patient endurance is with us. Do you honor Him so that He can honor you? He will! He is looking for those whose hearts are completely His so He can **fully** support them! When you work for Him, He works for you! He is our miracle giving God! Do you believe the best of Him as He does of you?

❖

Find a special way to honor the Lord today—something just between you and Him! Determine to believe the best of Him and of others.

# JULY 17

*"And He said to them, 'Go into all the world and preach the gospel to all creation.'" Mark 16:15*

What is a command for? It is for absolute and immediate obedience. Obedience is better than sacrifice. Jesus said, "Go!" It's direct and easy to understand. Go! That means now, not tomorrow—for every second thousands of people die without Jesus. So, go! Where? Into all the world! First start with where you are, then ask later, after you've obeyed all—if there's another place. Keep going until the end. And do not limit yourself to time and space. Go also with your prayers—go into all the world—to every continent, every nation, every city—claim them for God's Kingdom. Speak His word over them. Preach the gospel. Preach the cross! Preach Jesus! To whom? To *all!* Yes, to all! To everyone you meet. Be brave and bold! Stand up for Jesus! Be a good soldier of the Lord. Carry tracts and give out hundreds and thousands every day. Give His message with a heart full of His love—to every creature! God is not wishing for any to perish but for *all* to come to repentance. Write it. Call it on the phone. Speak it. Pray for the salvation of the world. Consider every person a divine appointment from God. Work while it is day!

———————————◇———————————

Pray and ask the Lord for desire and anointing to be a fiery witness of His love and salvation. Bring people to Jesus!

# JULY 18

*"The Messiah in you, the hope of glory."*
**Colossians 1:27**

Oh, what a divine mystery full of glory and grace! To think that the Messiah not only gave His life and suffered for us, not only rose from the dead, not only reconciled us to God and gave us a relationship with Himself—but that He Himself lives in us! Halleluia! He desires to live in the deepest place of our hearts, making us holy unto Himself! Can we ever be without hope? No! Hopelessness is a lie from satan. We have the hope of glory living in our hearts. The Son of God dwelling in us by His Holy Spirit! Our lives are radically changed because He made us His home! Even the closest relationships on earth, even marriage is not that close. The Messiah *in* us! His kingdom *in* us! His presence *in* us! His heart and mind *in* us! His ways, His nature *in* us! *He* is our closet relative. *He* is our life! *He* is first. *He* is our love. The Messiah *in* us! Do you really understand that the Holy One lives *in* you? Then say, "Your will, not mine, Lord" all the days of your life—with every breath. Let your heart and soul continually praise and adore Him. Let His character be formed in you. Surrender all to Him, moment by moment. Abandon yourself to Jesus. Glorify Him! You were created to give Him glory forever! The Messiah *in* you, the hope of glory!

———————————⋄———————————

Commit to the Lord today your desire to love Him more and more, to honor and glorify Him in all of your days. Let Him speak to your heart. Thank Him for living in you—your hope and glory!

# JULY 19

*"I am my beloved's and His desire is for me.*
*Come, my beloved; let us go out into the country."*
*Song of Solomon 7:10-11*

Blessed, blessed words aglow in my heart. The great I AM, God Almighty, tender loving Jesus, Son of God is my own Beloved! He is your Beloved! There is no one like Him! No other name, no other love is as His to your heart—precious beyond words. Oh, come sweet Holy Spirit. Fill us with Yourself. We want to be like Jesus. How beautiful is this ownership. As a bride says to her groom—"I am my beloved's and he is mine. His desire is for me. We are drawn to each other." Is it that way with you? Is Jesus as a Bridegroom to you—that deep, sweet love between you? Do you absolutely belong to Him and know that He is yours? He looks at you and is totally in love with you. He says, "Come, my precious beloved! Come away with Me! Let us go out into the country!" Will you drop everything for your Beloved Jesus, the Love of your life? Will you let go of your cares and busyness? Will you let Him hold you in His loving arms and bless you in the way He wants to? Will you sing to Him? Will you minister to Him? Will you take His yoke and learn from Him? Run to your Beloved today! Rest in His arms. Enjoy Him for who He is. Let His sweet fragrance anoint you!

---

Plan a special time of a few days alone with the Lord somewhere away. Enjoy the beauty of His love and intimate fellowship! Love Him! Bless Him!

# JULY 20

*"And behold, I am sending forth the promise of My Father upon you; but you are to stay in the city until you are clothed with power from on high." Luke 24:49*

And who is the promise of our loving Heavenly Father but the sweet Holy Spirit. Jesus said He would send the Holy Spirit to us. He Himself was conceived into this earth by the Holy Spirit. The Holy Spirit came to Him at baptism (immersion) in the form of a dove. Jesus was *full* of the Holy Spirit and shortly afterwards He was attacked by satan with every temptation. He (the Father) freely gives the Holy Spirit to those who ask. The Holy Spirit is beautiful! He teaches us, helps us, gives us power to *be* witnesses. He comforts us. He convicts the world of sin and righteousness. He leads us. He heals and performs miracles. He is tender and can be grieved easily. He waits for us. Without the Holy Spirit we are dry. He comes to us at salvation, drawing us to Jesus, but what? Wait until you are clothed with His power from on high. Do not go out to do the works of God without the Holy Spirit. We need Him. Open your heart and let Him fill you. Let the Spirit of God and the word of God richly dwell in you. Let Him reveal Himself through you. Let Him speak through you in your mother tongue and in His heavenly language. Let Him use you for healings and miracles.

---

Trust in the Lord at His word today. Ask Him to fill you with His Holy Spirit. Receive His Spirit and power from on high. Wait and He will do it. It is His promise to you and He will keep it. Believe and receive.

# JULY 21

*"Then the Spirit of the Lord will come upon you mightily, and you shall prophesy with them and be changed into another man." 1 Samuel 10:6*

Be kind to the sweet Spirit of God. Do not blaspheme Him in any way. Surrender your will and your love to Him daily. Learn to be led by Him. Do not hold back. The Lord has good plans for you and wants to use your life as a great blessing to others—to lead them to Himself, to feed them the heavenly Bread of Life, to be poured out like wine on the altar for them, and to glorify Him. Let the gift of faith come upon you. Be filled with the Holy Spirit and step out in faith. Desire to prophesy, for it is God's will. Don't say a single word if it *is not* from God. Don't hold back if it is from God. It will be according to His word and it will come about. Pray much in the Spirit. Worship the Lord continually. Then the Spirit of the Lord will come upon you how? Mightily. God wants to use you mightily. And you shall prophesy. As you speak, whether in the Spirit or in your language—more words will come, even scriptures. It will be from the Lord. It will exhort and encourage and sometimes rebuke. You will be changed because you will be God's instrument—*if* . . . you walk humbly before Him continually. Keep a repentant heart.

---◆---

Bow before the Lord and ask Him to begin to give you prophetic words to speak at His will, in His timing. He will do it. Step out in faith and speak for Him!

# JULY 22

*"And His name will be called Wonderful Counselor, Mighty God, Eternal Father, Prince of Peace." Isaiah 9:6*

His name! That precious name! He is Savior, He is the Anointed One, the Messiah! He is Emmanuel—God with us, and on and on . . . and He is our Wonderful Counselor! Who else but the Lord Himself can really counsel us heart to heart? He knows us through and through, better than we know ourselves. He is the Comforter, the Everlasting arms. He is our wisdom and knowledge and understanding and righteousness and strength. He is wonderful and He is our good counselor. Let us always seek His will and counsel first and all else be only a confirmation of what He has told us. He is Almighty God, El Shaddai. Our sufficient Comforter. He is your strength and song and salvation. He is your shield, like the sunlight in its strength! He is your Eternal, loving Father. He is full of loving compassion for you, tender hearted and merciful. He knows your frame. He is *for* you. He will never let you down. He is trustworthy. He is the Prince of Peace! Who is peaceful like the Lord? His peace surpasses understanding! Peace on earth. God has called us to peace (shalom). He Himself is our peace!

---◇---

As you worship the Lord today, give to Him any areas that are difficult to trust in and receive Him as your Wonderful Counselor, Mighty God and Prince of Peace. Put all into His care and let the peace of the Messiah dwell in you!

# JULY 23

*"Who is this coming up from the wilderness,
leaning on her beloved?" Song of Solomon 8:5*

Have you been in the wilderness where it is dry and empty? Have you felt the scorching heat and been thirsty, longing for the rivers of life? Fear not, for your God will come to you as a torrent of waterfall, full of life! Seek Him earnestly during this time of testing. Let your faith be tested and be found faithful, shining as precious gold. Do you long to see Him as you did? To behold His glory? You will! Stand fast, soldier of God—He is there with you in this dry land. Will you prove your faithfulness to Him when there are no feelings of His sweet presence? He is there. Trust Him. He will never forsake you. His lovingkindness is better than life itself. He has brought you into the wilderness to speak kindly to you. In the valley there is a door of hope and you will yet sing on the mountaintops. Your lips will be filled with joy and laughter! You will come up from the wilderness leaning on your Beloved! Yes, you will lean on Him. You will trust Him in new ways, know Him in new depths. He is your Beloved, your Bridegroom! He has betrothed you to Himself forever. Lean completely on Him. Trust Him with all your heart!

---◇---

Find a twig to remind you of the wildernesses that the Lord takes you through. Find a ring and set it on top, representing His marital faithfulness to you. Bless Him today. Lean on Him.

# JULY 24

*"Lord, You know all of these things; You know that I love You." Jesus said, "Tend My sheep." John 21:17*

If we love Jesus, we truly love His people, for if we do not love our brothers and sisters, how can we say we love God? A new commandment He gives us—"love one another." And just how do we tend His sheep? We feed them. Some are newborns and need the pure milk of the word. Some are grown and need strong meat to digest. Jesus is the Bread of Life, the Living Water of life eternal! We feed them Jesus! Let them come to the Rock of their salvation and drink in the rivers of delight! It is the impartation of life that brings life! Jesus gave His life and so we live! We must be willing to pour out our lives. He blesses us so we can bless others. Our blessings are never to be coveted and held onto—they are to be given out as a mother or father gives all for their children. Dwell in Him until there is an overflow of His presence and life in you, changing and growing strong, then pour out to all around you, the goodness of His love in you. Where two or three are gathered, He is in your midst. May you have many, many spiritual children and feed them Jesus. Love Him, feed them!

--------------------◇--------------------

Pray this morning for five or more people that you can disciple and feed and pour your life into. Begin to do it weekly by His word and Spirit and anointing.

# JULY 25

*"For they are as the stones of a crown, sparkling in His hand." Zechariah 9:16*

Oh, bless You, Lord, for You alone make us beautiful! You take our lives in an ash heap and turn us to beauty as You fill us with Your lovely Holy Spirit! You heal our broken hearts. You bring deliverance from the evil one. You set us free from sin and sickness and sorrow, giving us a garland of joy and praise! You are our beauty! Out of Zion comes the perfection of beauty— Jesus, our Savior, our Lord, our Messiah! You are the King of Kings and Lord of Lords! In You are all the wonders of the glory of heaven and endless joy and peace! You are our Bridegroom in heaven, waiting to be joined to us! You rejoice over us, Your bride. You give us garments of salvation and wrap us in robes of righteousness. You alone make us pure and holy in Your sight. Let us shine for You this day! Let us sparkle with Your sweet love and glory as jewels in Your hand. Let us be a crown of glory to You, Lord! Give us pure hearts so the light of Your countenance may shine brightly. Give us Your desires and Your ways! Bless Your holy name forever!

---

Take a branch and make it into a crown. Wrap it in something shiny to remind you of Zechariah 9:16. Remember the crown of thorns Jesus wore to make you a jewel in His crown of glory now.

# JULY 26

*"Finally, brethren, whatever is true, whatever is honorable, whatever is right, whatever is pure, whatever is lovely, whatever is of good repute, if there be any excellence, and if anything worthy of praise, let your mind dwell on these things."*
*Philippians 4:8*

Oh, that we would take captive every thought unto the Messiah. That we would put on the mind of the Messiah. Is not the mind the battleground of the devil against us? Let us cover our heads with the helmet of salvation today and resist the devil's accusations. Our Lord Jesus is continually interceding for us before the throne of the Father. His scars count as our righteousness to enter into His holy presence. He has done all for us. Our part is to keep our mind as well as our heart for Him. Our heart or spirit is where He dwells. It is holy and sacred. Our mind is where the enemy attacks us. It is also where we can become weak and fall into sin. Therefore we must guard by disciplining our mind to be fixed on what is true, honorable, right, pure, lovely, of good report, excellent and worthy of praise. Dwell on these things. Dwell on what the Lord has done and is doing in your life. Is not Jesus excellent, lovely, and praiseworthy? Dwell on Jesus and He will keep you in perfect peace. Concentrate on Him.

---

Write out in a letter to the Lord how He is each of these things to you! Exalt Him today! Bless Him!

# JULY 27

*"Many waters cannot quench love, nor rivers overflow it." Song of Solomon 8:7*

Real love, His love can never be quenched. No matter what or who comes against it, it will not stop—the light will not go out. Severe persecution only strengthens and multiplies it for His Kingdom. Nothing will overflow it or drown it out, for love covers a multitude of sins. And isn't His love our very breath of life? All of our gifts and ministry become as a clanging cymbal without love. Oh, let us beware of loving Him as a form or routine and not as a personal, loving God. It is the relationship that is important, not the duty. Let us not become so dry and dead that we feel obligated to have time with our precious Lord. Let us rise up with excitement to meet Him in the morning and stay in communion with Him throughout the day—hearing Him, obeying Him, worshipping Him. He is worthy of all praise and honor—of **all** of our love and life. Greater love has no man than the one who lays down his life for his friend. Will you lay down your life today for your precious Friend, Jesus? Love Him today with every breath and cell of your body, with all of your heart and soul.

---◇---

Renew you love for Jesus today. Tell Him all day that you love Him and how dear He is to you. Take His own love to fill your heart. Love Him!

# JULY 28

*"But you shall receive power when the Holy Spirit has come upon you; and you shall be My witness both in Jerusalem, and in all Judea and Samaria, and even to the remotest part of the earth." Acts 1:8*

Oh, dear saint of God, let the sweetness of the Holy Spirit fall upon you this day. Ask and you shall receive. For your loving Father in heaven will not give you a stone if you ask for bread or a scorpion if you ask for an egg. Yes, there is a holy waiting in the upper room. Wait and then He will come. The Holy Spirit will fill you and you will go out with the fullness of God, dressed in His power to *be* His witness. He will teach you all things. He will be your anointing, your overflow, your absolute peace and joy, your overcoming spirit, your all in all, your very love. He will help you and comfort you. His gifts will flow from you and He will put His divine fruits and character in you. He is your gift—the Holy Spirit Himself! He is awesome, yet gentle. He is your promise and hope. Do not quench Him or resist Him or hurt Him with your words or thoughts or motives. Let Him fill you over and over. Deny yourself and live for Him. You must become less and He must become more . . . and more. Be with Him much. Be filled over and over. Humble yourself and He will lift you up. Pray in your heavenly language. Lay hands on the sick and heal them. Be His. Bring many people to Jesus.

---

Wait on the Lord today and receive the gift of the Holy Spirit. Live in His overflow!

# JULY 29

*"But as for me, I will watch expectantly for the Lord; I will wait for the God of my salvation, My God will hear me. Do not rejoice over me, O my enemy. Though I fall, I will rise; though I dwell in darkness, the Lord is a light for me. He will bring me out to the light, and I will see His righteousness. Then my enemy will see."*
Micah 7:7-8, 10

Are you in a low time? Has the darkness covered you? Is it hard to see the face of the Lord, to hear His voice? Do you feel dry and hopeless? Do you wish for His presence tangibly, yet not find it? Is your heart breaking in some situation? Do you feel forsaken and lonely? Fear not! The Lord is there in the darkest night. He has not left you and never will if your heart is for Him. He is allowing a crucifixion time but the resurrection light will come and it will be glorious! The enemy, satan, thinks that he has you down. He tries to torment you as he did Jesus in the garden and on the cross. But he is a defeated foe. The blood of Jesus is against him and he has already lost. He tries to rejoice over your pain. He doesn't know that when you rise again you will be **doubly strong** and full of more light and the power of God. He is deceived. You are victorious! **You will rise in Jesus** victoriously and full of Him!

---◇---

In spite of any depressing emotions offer a sacrifice of praise to the Lord for the victory He is bringing you. Rejoice for He has given you an overcoming spirit!

# JULY 30

*"Because He delights in unchanging love."*
*Micah 7:18*

Oh yes, Lord! What do You delight in? What pleases You? How can we bless You and show our deepest gratitude and love for you? Unchanging love is the answer! Faithful unto death! Trustworthiness and steadfast love like Yours!

But what are our poor hearts like? So often we are not completely faithful. We love when we are loved. So often we turn against those who differ from us. We often love ourselves too much. Or our love changes, up and down, according to our circumstances.

What is the answer? More of Jesus. Dwell in Him. Be full of the Lord. Let His Spirit and His ways fill your heart and mind. Dwell in His word. Pray continually. Look for ways to love people. Forget yourself. Set your affections on things above. **Set your heart on Jesus**. Recommit yourself to Him today—to be faithful to Him day by day, moment by moment—unchanging in your love for Him.

———————————◇———————————

Find at least one way today that you can tangibly begin to be more faithful to Jesus.

# JULY 31

*"I count all things to be loss in view of the surpassing value of knowing the Messiah, Jesus my Lord. That I may know Him and the power of His resurrection and the fellowship of His sufferings, being conformed to His death; in order that I may attain to the resurrection from the dead." Philippians 3:8, 10*

How many things? **All** things. My family, my job, my home and possessions? All things. My citizenship, my reputation, my interests? All things. They are as nothing compared to knowing the Messiah, as my Lord. If I were to lose all, and suffer great pain, it is still nothing compared to what Jesus went through for me on the cross—compared to my intimate relationship with Him! Knowing Him—that is my goal! God Himself is my goal! To know Him more and more and to make Him known! That I may know His sufferings, and die to my own ways and selfishness. That I may abandon all unto Him and say in everything—"***Not my will but Thine be done***." That I may know the power of His resurrection! That I may rise up to new life with Him and really live His very life here on earth— bringing His eternal fruit and glory! That I may rise up and see Jesus face to face!

---◇---

Imagine all was taken from you—now worship the Lord in spirit and truth—thanking Him that you have **Him**—and He is better than life!

# AUGUST 1

*"And he who does not take his cross and follow after Me is not worthy of Me. He who has found his life shall lose it, and he who has lost his life for My sake shall find it." Matthew 10:38-39*

If we love Jesus, then we must go His way and not our own. We must go the way of the crucifixion, and then resurrection will come. We must trust Him without leaning on our own understanding. We must acknowledge Him in all our ways and He will direct our path. We must take up our cross daily and follow hard after Him. He set His face like flint to Jerusalem, to die. We must endure insults for His sake, and inhospitable behavior. We must turn the other cheek and often be made to look foolish for His sake. We must be willing to be treated shamefully, even spit on, just as He was. For if we hold on to our own life, our own way, we will lose Him because He will not be Lord over us. If we lose our lives, totally surrendered—day by day—giving all to Him—then we will gain our lives—for He is our very life! Let us be found in Him this day, ready to do all that is in *His* heart whether it be difficult or easy. Will you go anywhere and do anything for Jesus?

———————◇———————

Carry Matthew 10:38-39 on a little paper in your pocket today to remind you to go His way in every situation. Let the peace of the Messiah dwell in you.

# AUGUST 2

*"Therefore, the soldiers did these things. But they were standing by the cross of Jesus, His mother, and His mother's sister, Mary the wife of Clopas, and Mary Magdalene." John 19:25*

And so we see the two things before the crucifixion—the criminals and the devoted faithful. Jesus was the Holy One between two criminals. The light and the dark. And isn't it so, as time draws near to the end—the light gets brighter and the dark gets darker, the contrast more and more striking? The evil one begins to pull down in all ways of immorality, raising up the occult and deceptive religions that tickle the ears and exalt self. The Almighty One, our God, begins to pour out His Holy Spirit revealing His Son Jesus in whom there is salvation, preparing for a ripe harvest and revival that will cause cities and nations to see Him as He really is. One day every knee will bow and every tongue confess that Jesus, the Messiah is Lord, to the glory of the Father! Let us pray today for revival, for the gift of repentance, for the gift of intercession and unity in the body of the Messiah, His congregation. Nothing is too difficult for Him. Jesus is Lord!

———————————◇———————————

Ask the Lord to use you in intercession and bringing unity and repentance (self first) to your part of the body of the Messiah. Humble yourself under His hand today.

# AUGUST 3

*"Go forth from your country, and from your relatives, and from your father's house, to the land which I will show you." Genesis 12:1*

Go forth! Go forth! This is the word of the Lord. He does not ask, He commands, for He knows His purposes. He knows what we are created for. He knows! It is **His** call that you hear. It is your Lord that is trusting you to do His will. He sets you aside to anoint you for His holy purposes. You are His choice! Will you be a willing vessel of honor for Him? Will you choose to glorify Jesus with your life?

Count the cost and go forth! If you must leave your country or city then go. If you must leave your dear relatives, then put them in His care and go!

Go to the land that He shows you. He has a good plan for you, with a future and a hope, not for calamity. Fear not, for God is with you!

Precious soldier of God, go forth. Follow your Lord with all your heart. You will never regret it but only grow stronger. Let Him use your life as a sweet fragrance of Himself. Be strong and take courage! Go forth for God! Go forth!

---◇---

Pray today and say to the Lord that you will go anywhere and do anything that He asks. Wait on Him for instructions and then go forth!

# AUGUST 4

*"And I will make you a great nation, and I will bless you, and make your name great; and so you shall be a blessing." Genesis 12:2*

The Lord your God is in the midst of you. He, the Almighty One inhabits your praises. He, the One who humbled Himself to the point of death, knows every hair on your head. He knows your frame. He knows your strengths and weaknesses. He has chosen the foolish things to confound the wise. His ways are higher than yours. He knows the way you take. He promises to give you a hope and a future. His ways are excellent. He is completely trustworthy. He gives you His Kingdom. He gave His Son. He gave all. He will not withhold any good thing from you if you walk with Him in integrity. He is able to do exceedingly, abundantly more than you ask or think. Do not limit Him. Open your heart. Strengthen your faith. He made the Jewish nation great and full of blessings. There is still more with them of His blessings to come. Will you give Him little seeds of faith in different areas of your life? Really give them to Him? Let Him turn these seeds into great nations of His will. Let Him make you a great blessing.

―――――――――――――◇―――――――――――――

Trust the Lord to give growth to all you give Him. Let Him make a great nation from your faith!

# AUGUST 5

*"And I will bless those who bless you, and the ones who curse you I will curse. And in you all the families of the earth shall be blessed."*
**Genesis 12:3**

Oh, Lord, You are the great Blesser! There is no one like You. You set up conditions for us to be blessed, and how You love to do it, as a Father loves to give to his little child—it is a chief delight of Yours to bless us abundantly! You send showers of blessing, overflowing until we cannot contain it.

You said to Abraham and to all Jewish people—"I will bless even those who bless you and I will curse those who curse you." With Jesus, the Messiah in our hearts it is the same promise! All who have You, Yeshua (Jesus), will be blessed. How strongly You are *for* us, upholding us, supporting us, defending us! Thank You, that we are the very apple of Your kind eye! It is the same today—those who bless the Jews (or all who have given their hearts totally to Jesus) will be blessed. Those who curse the Jews (or Messianic Jews or true believers) will be cursed.

And in you, oh Jews, all the families of the earth shall be blessed. For you, Messianic Jews, in these end times shall carry the gospel to all nations where you have been scattered, in great power and love, to the glory of the Father!

---

Today, pray for all Jewish family or friends to come to Yeshua (Jesus), the Messiah, the Lord of glory. Then go and share the word, the gospel with them in the power of His love!

# AUGUST 6

*"Behold the days are coming," declares the Lord, "when I will make a new covenant (new testament) with the house of Israel."*
*Jeremiah 31:31*

Awake O Israel! Put away your sleepiness. Rise! Shine! For your light has come! The glory of the Lord has risen upon you! The veil is lifting. You are beginning to see the face of your Messiah and King. Your eyes will see the One whom you pierced with your sins and you will mourn. But your mourning will be turned to joy. Your eyes will behold the King and you will come rejoicing, with everlasting joy upon your heads. The One who was crowned with thorns for your sins and sorrows will crown you with His own glory. You shall go out with joy and be led forth with peace. The mountains and the hills shall break forth before you. There will be shouts of joy and all the trees of the field will clap their hands. Your ashes will be turned to beauty forever. For this new covenant will be made in your hearts. The King of glory, the Holy One of Israel will dwell in your hearts! And you shall go forth in great shouts of joy, skipping as calves. The nations shall see it and rejoice. They will bow down to your God, Yeshua Ha Mashiach (Jesus the Messiah)!

---◇---

Find a map of Israel and pray for Israel today—for her leaders, her people, for the peace (shalom) of Jerusalem.

# AUGUST 7

*"For I do not want you, brethren, to be uninformed of this mystery, lest you be wise in your own estimation, that a partial hardening has happened to Israel until the fullness of the Gentiles has come in." Romans 11:25*

The Lord causes all things to work together for good to those who love Him and are called according to His purpose. The message of salvation in Yeshua (Jesus) was to go first to the Jews. They were to take it all over the world. The first congregation was all Jews, and they did that, but with much persecution from the hypocritical, hardened Jews. Continually, the Holy Spirit through Jesus, through Peter, through Paul and many others, brought the message to those hardened Jews. Finally, the Holy Spirit began to draw the rest of the world, the Gentiles and they were given the message to spread everywhere. Today, Jews are coming to Jesus. The fullness of the Gentiles is coming to an end. Salvation has come through the Jews and is now going back to them. Glory to God for His unfathomable ways, for His divine mysteries revealed, for His kindness in turning all to good for us. Bless you, O Jew, bless you, O Gentile. Bless the Lord! Hallelujah! The wall between us is coming down and Jesus is our peace (shalom)! Let us glorify Him together and exalt His name! Glory, glory, glory to You, Lord! Glory to Yeshua HaMashiach forever!

---

Rejoice in the Lord today for His excellent ways. Reach out to Jews and Gentiles in your neighborhood. Pray for the Jews to turn to their Messiah!

# AUGUST 8

*"And thus all Israel will be saved."*
*Romans 11:26*

How can it be? Don't the Scriptures speak so often about a remnant of Jews being saved, becoming Messianic Jews? Which is it? Part of them or all of them? Could it be that both things are right? God's ways are so much higher than ours.

Through the centuries for the last 2,000 years there have been Jews saved, loving their Messiah, Yeshua, with all their hearts. Even in the holocaust many were saved and the gospel went through those torture camps. There has always been a remnant after the first revival in Acts, that turned the world upside down with the good news.

If the Jews rejecting Yeshua (Jesus) brought salvation to the rest of the world, what will happen when they accept Yeshua (Jesus)? Will it not mean life from the dead? Yes, the mighty resurrection power will sweep this earth. Jews will awaken and see their Messiah and give their hearts to Him! In a single day, the Scripture says, Israel will be changed forever, saved! All Jews there will know their Lord! And so it is that all Israel will experience a Holy Spirit led revival and know the Lord. They will be a light of glory and salvation to the nations. They were chosen for this purpose alone! To glorify their Messiah before the nations!

---◇---

By faith, thank the Lord for Israel's coming salvation! Rejoice and dance! Then pray for the Jews around you and for Messianic fellowships.

# AUGUST 9

*"For I could wish that I myself were accursed, separated from the Messiah, for the sake of my brethren, my kinsmen." Romans 9:3*

What are those words? Are they not impossible? No! Nothing is impossible for God. These words come from the very heart of God.

Paul, like Moses wished Himself accursed, blotted out, separated from the Messiah, for the sake of his fellow Jews, his people. Paul, who was called to the Gentiles always went to the Lost Sheep of Israel first. Jesus always went to the Lost Sheep of Israel first. The Jews have been chosen first by God to bring salvation to the world.  They are a key to world salvation.

Have you ever said to the Lord, "Do whatever You need to do to save this person, or this city or this nation?" Have you ever said, "Take my life if it will bring salvation to this person?" But to say, "Take my salvation to save this person"—that comes from the Holy Spirit. It is supernatural. Still, Paul said it and meant it. So did Moses. God heard them and answered, but spared them. God heard Jesus and answered but did not spare Him. And so, we are saved. Praise God! Praise God!

———————————◇———————————

Get on your knees and ask the Lord to give you His own heart when you pray for salvations. Let His tender love and urgency flow through you.

# AUGUST 10

*"I will call those who were not My people, 'My people,' and her who was not beloved, 'Beloved.'"*
*Romans 9:25*

Oh dear Gentile, what a glorious thing that the Lord of the universe has called you! Not that you loved Him but that He loved you first and while you were yet a sinner, not even looking His way—He came and died for you—laying His perfectly holy life in the dust for you. You were not seeking Him, but by His Holy Spirit, He began to draw you with everlasting lovingkindness. He began to call you and to give you ears to hear Him. Then as you came near, He began to take away your spiritual blindness and let you see a glimpse of Himself. And when you repented and gave Him your heart, you saw Him face to face! It was then that you fell in love with Jesus! You trusted Him and you were changed on the inside, never to be the same. Now you are His! You belong to the Lord! You are *His* "Beloved!" It was His plan long ago to come and pursue you, to seek you and to love you, to give you Himself, the Lord of Love!

---

Thank the Lord today for His sweet Holy Spirit pursuing you and drawing you to be His beloved. He pursues you this day also—to draw near and give Him your love!

# AUGUST 11

*"I was formed by those who sought Me not. I became manifest to whose who did not ask for Me. But as for Israel He says, 'All the day long I have stretched out My hands to a disobedient and obstinate people.'" Romans 10:20-21*

Oh, what a divine mystery—that the Jews rejecting their Messiah brought salvation to the world! The Jewish Messiah became manifest to those who were not even looking for Him. The kindness of God is better than life itself. His love is always flowing, always giving. It has no end. It's depth is incomprehensible. He lavishes it on us, even those who do not ask. It is the river of delight and joy! When the Lord of heaven begins to turn His face to look upon us, we are changed—never to be the same. The glory of His countenance fills us with His sweet love and nature.

But you, Oh Israel! To you, His firstborn, His chosen treasure—He has stretched out His nail-scarred hands all day long. He has called you with an everlasting love. Leave your disobedience and obstinance in the ashes. Run to your Savior, Your Messiah, the Holy One of Israel who loves you. Run to His open arms.

---◇---

If you are Jewish or Gentile, make a commitment before the Lord today to pray for one Jewish friend for a month—to be saved and walk with the Lord in closeness.

# AUGUST 12

*"For the gifts and calling of God are irrevocable."* Romans 11:29

How often this verse has refreshed my soul. Lord, Your goodness and faithfulness are constant and true. We as frail human beings are not able to keep our commitments as You do. We are not always faithful in our thoughts and emotions, as You are. Your promises are true. They come to pass in spite of us. And You uphold faithfulness even when we don't. You give Your precious gifts, Your gracious calling, and You do not relent. How often does the worker feel so unworthy, yet You bless and anoint his calling, his gifts with the power of Your Spirit. You use us for Your sweet glory, in spite of ourselves. A man's gift makes room for him. It is *You*, not us. We are only the instruments. We are only the messengers. We must decrease and You must increase. Let each one in this finely tuned orchestra play his melody. Let the music be sweet to the Master's ear. Let it drive out the enemy. Let it bring new life and love to all who have ears to hear. Glorify, Yourself, Lord in us!

---◇---

Fall on your knees and give back to the Lord every good gift He has given you so that all may glorify Him and magnify His name.

# AUGUST 13

*"But we have this treasure in earthen vessels, that the surpassing greatness of power may be of God and not from ourselves."* 2 Corinthians 4:7

What would you do if you looked in an old clay pot and saw dazzling, sparkling jewels shining out? You would treasure that pot. You would put it in a special place. You would use these jewels for special occasions. You would guard it and cherish it.

Imagine! The Lord calls us *His* treasure! We are not just *a* treasure. In fact, without Him, we are not a treasure at all. It is His priceless gaze upon us, His transforming touch that makes us a treasure. *He* is the One who lights up our lives and causes us to shine and sparkle as we were created to do. It is *His* very nature in us that causes us to shine. We live to give Him glory!

He has chosen for us to live in earthen vessels, weak human bodies that are destined to die and be raised later. This surpassing greatness of the treasure in us, the very power of His Spirit, is of Him and not us. We exalt Him, our glorious King! We are His treasure! Let our inner beauty grow strong unto Him!

————————————◇————————————

Find some clay pot or mug and put a shiny jewel (imitation) inside to remind you of 2 Corinthians 4:7. Thank Him for making you His jewel!

# AUGUST 14

*"You have made my heart beat faster, my sister,
my bride; you have made my heart beat faster
with a single glance of your eyes."*
*Song of Solomon 4:9*

Our God is love! The Lord of love! He is the creator of love, the creator of marriage, of friendship, of deep relationships. He created the bright morning sun, the majestic mountains, the glorious oceans and forests and romantic moonlight. One touch of His sweet love and our lives are changed! His love is strong and beautiful bringing new life, eternal life. One look in the eyes of Jesus and we only fall more in love with Him. Those kind, majestic, piercing, loving eyes! Is there anything like looking into the eyes of the Son of God? Doesn't it truly make our hearts beat faster? Just a single glance, as a bride with her groom!

But what does it say? His sister, His bride! We, the believers are His lovely bride! There is nothing like that "bridal love!" And *He* is saying that we, His bride have made *His* heart beat faster with a single glance! Do you know that Your Bridegroom Jesus is in love with you, that you affect His heart?

───────────────◇───────────────

Make a picture of what it will be like at the wedding supper of the Lamb, when we see Jesus face to face and embrace Him!

# AUGUST 15

And the glory—(the honor, splendor, radiance and fulness of His presence.) . . . the glory that You have given Me—I have truly given to them! The Father in His gracious and lavish giving of Himself, giving of His eternal love, has also given His precious glory. His is the kingdom and the power and the glory forever—His! It's *His* glory. No one can have it or even see it unless *He* gives it. Glory to God in the highest! In the highest is where He is given perfect glory! But He wants His kingdom to come on earth as it is in heaven. He wants the whole earth to be filled with His glory! Alleluia! The glory of the Lord shone around them. Arise, shine, for your light has come and the glory of the Lord has risen upon you! The glory that the Father gave Jesus, He has given *to you!* It is *yours!* Do not tarnish it or abuse it or ignore it. Walk in it so that you may be of *one heart* together in the overflow of His love and Spirit! When you are one, brothers, sisters, husbands, wives—He will command a blessing! Revival will come! His glory will cover the earth! He has crowned you with glory and honor! Give glory to God!

---

Take as much time as you need in worship today until you are dwelling in the holy of holies. Get on your face and receive His grace, anointing and glory so that you may be one.

# AUGUST 16

*"His mouth is full of sweetness, and he is wholly desirable. This is my beloved and this is my friend!" Song of Solomon 5:16*

His mouth, the mouth of Jesus, is full of love and kindness, sweetness. Even His judgments are kind, for no one cares for our hearts as He does. He is our Good Shepherd who lays down His life for us. His ways are so excellent and He is full of goodness and mercy. He knows the right word for every situation. He is ***beautiful*** for every situation. His wisdom and knowledge bring comfort and hope. He is the only One who can satisfy all of your needs. And He knows you better than anyone. He has understanding and patience and faithfulness. He is full of love and joy and peace. Jesus is wholly desirable. Do you desire Him more than anyone or anything? Do you desire to know Him better, to love Him more, to make Him known? He is wholly desirable. Drink from the wells of His deep love. There is life in one glance at Jesus. He is not only your Father, your Brother, your Friend, but He is your Beloved. You are also sweet to Him. You are desirable to Him. Spend time with Him, your Beloved and your Best Friend!

---◆---

Lay yourself before Him today. Say that you will be completely His, that He is totally desirable to you—your Beloved and Friend.

# AUGUST 17

*"But thanks be to God who always leads us in His triumph in the Messiah and manifests through us the sweet aroma of the knowledge of Him in every place." 2 Corinthians 2:14*

Who **always** . . . God always leads us in His triumph in the Messiah. **His** triumph. It is His triumph that we live in. He has already won the victory by his death and we just need to walk in it. Let us enter into His triumphant army with a shout of praise! Begin to march, precious soldier of God. Put on your armor and stand up for Jesus even at the cost of your life. No weapon formed against you will prosper. Walk by faith. Do not look at your stormy circumstances. Look at Jesus!

In the days of Queen Esther, those who wanted to be the queen would spend one year with oils and spices and perfumes in order to prepare for the king to choose them. But **you** have been chosen! You are a holy nation. The King of Kings, the Lord, has chosen you! The Messiah manifests His sweet and glorious presence through you! You are a fragrant perfume of His character! You bring the beautiful knowledge of the Messiah into every place, by your presence. He is in you!

───────────────◇───────────────

Get some perfume or oil and consecrate yourself to be a lovely fragrance to the Lord!

# AUGUST 18

*"For if you forgive men for their transgressions, your heavenly Father will also forgive you. But if you do not forgive men, then your Father will not forgive your transgressions."*
*Matthew 6:14-15*

Why is it so? Why does God require this forgiveness of us? Isn't His love unconditional? Yes, indeed it is! Why does He (Jesus) single this thing out of the prayer (the Lord's prayer) and make this condition?

It is because our wounds are so microscopic compared to what Jesus went through in His death for us—that there is no comparison at all. It may not feel like that. You may have been dealt with unjustly—but what about the Son of God? The Holy Son of God who was marred beyond recognition? We have not yet resisted sin to the point of blood. And *He* is the only One who truly understands suffering. He wants you to go on to the resurrection stage. No healing of heartbreaks will come without forgiveness. Only a root of bitterness will grow and branch out and torment you and others. The message of salvation is forgiveness and love. Make it your life to continually forgive and love as Jesus does.

---

Write down all people you need to forgive or ask forgiveness. Pray and go to that person if possible. Be healed. Be free. Love with Jesus' love.

# AUGUST 19

*"Do not speak against one another, brethren. He who speaks against a brother or judges a brother, speaks against the law; but if you judge the law, you are not a doer of the law. There is only one Lawgiver and Judge, the One who is able to save and destroy, but who are you who judge your neighbor?" James 4:11-12*

Oh, Lord, give us repentant hearts. Put the fear of You upon us. Let us be careful, Lord, not to touch Your anointed with our tongues. For we touch the apple of Your eye. When we have done it to one of these (our brethren) we have done it unto You. Have mercy upon us, Lord. Put in us a desire for unity without compromise. You said that the world will know us by our love for one another. Oh, that we might break down the walls, for You are our peace—and where unity is, You command a blessing of life forever. Let not the enemy continue to divide Your house—for he knows that our humble hearts and unity will usher in a revival and You, Lord Jesus, will rule the land! Rise up, precious soldier of God! Be valiant! Go to your brother (or sister), get things right, then take your gift to the altar. Lord, put a seal over our lips, that we may bless and bless.

---

Pray and ask the Lord if there's any relationship that you need to make right. If so, do it. Ask Him to help you see people with His eyes and to love with His heart and to bless with His words.

# AUGUST 20

*"Let the word of the Messiah richly dwell within you, with all wisdom and teaching and admonishing one another with psalms, hymns and spiritual songs, singing with thankfulness in your heart to God." Colossians 3:16*

Dear precious saint of God—let's be filled with His Spirit at all times. Let's keep our relationship with the Lord new and alive. Let the fire of His love fall upon you that you may rise up with new healing love, that you may shine and sparkle with His dazzling life and love. Yes, it's a precious, costly relationship—the very life of Jesus that is in you. Let it not become a religious routine. How we tend to fall into unhealthy patterns. "This is the time we worship, then we pray and read the word. Now we have fellowship." No! His life is in you *all* the time—prayer and worship and the word must be part of your life at all times, not only set times. Yes, the special time with Jesus daily is the *most important* thing in your life! But let Him be alive in you. The Lord will do things at unexpected times—to your joy—if you will be so tuned in to Him, dwelling in Him, in love with Him. Let His word, His prayers, His worship *richly dwell* in you! Live in Him continually. Keep a thankful heart. Keep a song. Keep a prayer in your heart at all times. Do not stagnate. Love Him.

---

Bow your head and let the fresh waters of His holy Spirit fall upon you as a waterfall, refreshing you and filling you up to the overflow. Walk in Him and with Him. Concentrate on Jesus.

# AUGUST 21

*". . . work out your salvation with fear and trembling."* Philippians 2:12

Yes, there is the taking on of salvation when we repent from our sins, as we turn to Jesus with all of our hearts. He then becomes our Savior our Lord as we surrender ourselves totally unto Him, to follow and obey. He becomes our life, our all in all, our love. But the working out of our salvation is day by day. Yesterday's manna will not be for today. We must take up our cross *daily* and follow Him. We must be yoked with Jesus, for He is humble of heart and His burden is light.

Do we have the right perspective or are we too extreme? Do we blatantly say, "I'm saved and nothing can stop that" or do we know that we ourselves can walk away or fall away by just standing still and not running the race—or by sin? Many of God's saints did. Do we say, "I must work to be good enough. I must serve God a certain way or He won't keep me?" It is by grace you are saved and He will sustain you to do good works by His Spirit. The bottom line is that we must stand at the feet of Jesus *daily* and say, "I'm Yours, Lord. Fill me. Let me do Your will today. Lead me. Speak to me." Salvation belongs to the Lord. It is a fearful thing to fall into the hands of the Living God.

---

Today fall on your face and commit yourself in a new way to working out your salvation (or walk) with the Lord. Give Him time to speak to your heart and minister to you.

# AUGUST 22

*"Humble yourselves in the presence of the Lord, and He will exalt you." James 4:10*

Oh, beloved seeker of God, let us draw near to the throne of grace and receive the kind gift of repentance. Let us be open and broken before Almighty God, so that He might pour the balm of Gilead on us and heal us. Oh, Lord, create in me a clean heart. Renew a right spirit within me. Cast me, not away from your presence, Oh Lord. Take not Your Holy Spirit from me. Restore unto me, the joy of Thy salvation and sustain me with a willing spirit. Then I will teach transgressors Thy ways, and sinners will be converted to Thee. For a broken and contrite heart You will not despise. Wash away my sins with Your holy blood. Give me a pure heart that I might see Your face in all it's beauty. Lord, grant us humble hearts before You all our days, that we might cast ourselves at Your feet and cry, "Holy, holy, holy." How desperately we need You. You give us every breath. Let us exalt You dear Jesus, with a humble heart! You can lift us up, at Your will. Glory and honor to You forever!

---

Pray and ask the Lord to show you often your heart so that you may have continual repentance and restoration and live a sanctified life in His presence.

# AUGUST 23

*"By this all men will know that you are My disciples, if you have love for one another."*
*John 13:35*

And what is the enemy's tactic but to divide. Satan, the deceiver and liar of our souls, who's job is to falsely accuse us is busy throughout the earth, trying to divide and separate believers—to bring hurt and strife and disunity and bitterness. If he can keep believers away from being bonded in the unity of the Messiah's love, then the gospel will not spread and multiply as it should.

But God's love is stronger than death. ***Nothing, absolutely*** nothing shall separate us from the love of the Messiah. And where unity and love of the brethren is strong, He ***commands*** a blessing. The sweet oil of anointing covers us from head to foot. For love covers a multitude of sins. ***His love never fails***. What a great weapon we have against the enemy for winning nations— love one another. Jesus makes it so simple—just love God with all your heart and love one another. If we do these two things ***all*** men—***all*** men, will know that we are His! Dear brother, sweet sister, make sure your relationships are right and good—first with God and then with others. Love and forgive as Jesus does. Bear ***His*** image today!

———————————◇———————————

Make a list of people hard to love and pray over it. Commit to love them with Jesus' love and take action!

# AUGUST 24

*"For His lovingkindness is great towards us."*
*Psalm 117:2*

The love of God is stronger than anything in the universe. It is far beyond our comprehension. Who can grasp the depth of it? It remains forever. It was there before the worlds or heavens were created. It is unconditional and unchanging. It is for *all*, even the most wicked. It is glorious! It turns the ashes to beauty in our lives and puts a garland of praise and joy in our hearts. Oh the depth and the width and the height of the fullness of God—for God Himself *is* love! And His love grows because it is alive. It grows deeper and greater for our family and children and friends. Truly our love for Him grows the strongest of all and without it we would fall. It is His kind grace that carries us.

So also, sin on this earth hurts Him more and more. His heart breaks more and more—still He withholds judgment so that all may turn and repent and taste of His love forever more. There will come a day when it will end—Judgment Day. His love will then overtake all. He even judges in lovingkindness. Taste His love fresh today!

––––––––––––––––––––– ✧ –––––––––––––––––––––

Kneel down and ask the Lord to immerse you in His love. So that you may be filled up with the fullness of God!

# AUGUST 25

*"Be hospitable to one another without complaint." 1 Peter 4:9*

Let us be full of grace as Jesus is! Let us open our homes and hearts to those we know and love and to those we don't know so well. Let us not complain but see it as an opportunity to show His love! Maybe it will be inconvenient. Maybe it will interrupt your plans. Maybe God has sent this person to you for a reason. Will you minister to that person? Will you do it as unto Jesus? Maybe, instead, that person will minister unto you.

We are to show kindness and hospitality, especially to orphans and widows—to the poor and the sick, to those in prison and in trouble—for they are on God's heart The Lord even makes it possible that at times we may be ministering to angels that He has sent.

There is always a great blessing to receive as you give out your love and hospitality—great because you are doing it unto Jesus! You will see His mighty work in your midst. Praise to Almighty God, Maker of the universe, who stooped to wash the feet of His disciples.

———————————————⟡———————————————

Pray and ask the Lord who you can show hospitality to and what you should do. Go with His words and His love!

# AUGUST 26

*"And after you have suffered for a little while, the God of all grace who called you into His eternal glory in the Messiah, will Himself perfect, confirm, strengthen and establish you."*
*1 Peter 5:10*

That universal question—"why is there suffering?" The answer is that it came with sin into the world and spread like a disease. No one is free from it completely. The sinless Son of God suffered the most—He, who sweat great drops of blood, whose heart was broken over our sins, who suffered beyond recognition on the cross. He knows pain and suffering more than anyone. And He can comfort more than anyone. His Spirit is the "Comforter."

But suffering is always temporary. In His kindness it comes to an end. One day when judgment comes—all suffering will stop forever—but those without the Messiah will go to everlasting separation from God. There will not be even the influence of His mercy or grace in that place—a place called hell which was created for satan, not for man.

God works *all* things for good to those who love Him. He uses the suffering to purify us and make us shine His reflection—pure as gold. He confirms us, strengthens us, establishes us and prepares us for living in His eternal glory. Suffering is short, His glory is forever!

---

⬦

---

Thank the Lord for any suffering that has come your way. Ask Him to make you like Jesus in it. Thank Him that it is temporary and that He will establish you.

# AUGUST 27

*"But to the degree that you share the sufferings of the Messiah keep on rejoicing; so that also at the revelation of His glory you may rejoice with exultation." 1 Peter 4:13*

To the degree. Do you suffer for the Messiah? The Bible says that all who live godly will be persecuted. *All* who live godly. How do you suffer for Him? Some suffer by others' mockings or being rejected for the message of the Messiah, or treated unfairly. Some suffer by being falsely accused or slandered. Some are arrested or beaten just for loving Him or for sharing His message. Some of our brothers and sisters, even now, are tortured and killed because they stand for Jesus. They honor Him and so are degraded and scorned on earth. Whatever way you bear His reproach, He sees you, He upholds you, He is pleased with you. Your reward in heaven will be forever! If you have not always stood for Jesus, remember Peter and repent. Do not despair. Stand up again. Let Him wash away your tears and run the race! You will win by your perseverance. Rejoice, precious soldier of God! Keep His song in your heart at all times! You are a trumpet of His glory! At the revelation of His glory you will rejoice with great exultation! Do not be weary. The Son of God is with you! Rejoice for you are His!

---

Cast upon Him the area of suffering you have. Let His supernatural peace and grace fill your heart full! Be strong in the Lord! Rejoice!

# AUGUST 28

*"For you have been called for this purpose, since the Messiah also suffered for you, leaving you an example for you to follow in His steps, who committed no sin nor was any deceit found in His mouth; and while being reviled, He did not revile in return; while suffering He uttered no threats, but kept entrusting Himself to Him who judges righteously." 1 Peter 2:21-23*

Have you ever thought of suffering as an opportunity to learn to respond as Jesus did? Maybe even in small sufferings and pains we can begin to imitate the Messiah, and follow in His steps. For He committed no sin. He had no resentment or anger or bitterness in His soul as He was nailed to the cross. Surely those who hammered the nails could have looked into His eyes and softened their hearts to be saved. Out of Jesus flowed a fathomless ocean of forgiveness and eternal, godly love! He embraced the world with divine love and commitment. The Son of God hanging there for our sins without a word or thought of hurt, was entrusting Himself to the Father of righteousness. God does not cause suffering and pain but He uses it to transform us into His image so that we may **see Him** and know **His weight of glory!** Let us learn to respond as Jesus to pain in our lives. Let us hold Him closer than our pain.

---

Give to the Lord any large or small suffering that you have. Ask Him to help you bear it as He would and begin to praise Him in the midst of it!

# AUGUST 29

*"Above all, keep fervent in your love for one another, because love covers a multitude of sins."*
*1 Peter 4:8*

People all over the world are looking for love—the orphan, the widow, the poor, the rich, the drug addict, the righteous, the unrighteous. They look for friendship love, romantic love, parental love. It is a constant longing of the human heart, as needful as the air we breathe. Yet even when we find it, it does not satisfy us fully unless we have first found the One who bore our sins, the One who said, "It is finished" and committed Himself into the Father's hands, the only One in all of eternity whose bloodshed makes us clean, the One who first loved us. We must be full of His everlasting "agape" love before we can really love one another. For God Himself *is* love! His love brings eternal life and is infinite.

Above all, brothers and sisters—(so loved by God)—*above all*, keep fervent in your love for one another. You may fall short, you may do the very thing you don't want to do. You may say the wrong thing, you may hurt the very one you love the most—but loves covers a multitude of sins. Jesus' love covers you. Let your love for each other cover. *Love covers*. It forgives, it loves again, it believes the best, it protects, it does not speak against, it bears all things, it is truthful, it is patient, it endures, it never fails. Fervently love, for love covers!

---

Bring to the throne of God anyone you find difficult to love or have conflict with. Cover them with your love and prayers. Now act on this love, with or without feelings. Find a way to show your (His) love.

# AUGUST 30

*"There I will give you my love."*
*Song of Solomon 7:12*

Come away with Me! Come, My beloved, let us go away together. Come away with Me and rest. You have said that your heart longs after Me as a deer panting for water. You have hungered and thirsted after Me. You desire deep in your heart a greater intimacy with Me. It is there for you any time you want—just come. I will give you rest for your soul. I will give fresh oil of anointing. You shall be as a well watered garden blooming with beauty and joy and fragrance! Come into My loving arms. I am here, waiting for you. Do not ask for anything. Do not lay anything on My altar—your presence is enough. Just be with Me. Let us enjoy one another. Let Me give you a new song of peace! You are a rare, exquisite jewel in My crown, My beloved. I am in love with you. As you love to be with Me and please Me, so I love to be with you. For these precious times I gave My life. My suffering and blood poured out for you was to make you clean and pure, holy in My sight—so I could **dwell with you** in deep, unspeakable union and love. You are My glory. Receive My heart overflowing with love for you!

---

Be so still in His presence. Forget time and cares. Dwell in Him as long as possible. Let Him pour His love out. Just receive. Enjoy your Lord in intimacy, filled with His presence.

# AUGUST 31

*"For Thou didst form my inward parts; Thou didst weave me in my mother's womb. I will give thanks to Thee, for I am fearfully and wonderfully made." Psalm 139:13-14*

Can anything be more clear? We are formed in the womb by the Lord Himself—with awe and wonder—a holy work . . . yet people throw away their babies in abortion. What madness, to throw away a life at it's beginning. The enemy himself is the one guiding these thoughts and actions. Have you seen the photos of babies in the womb burned to death or suffocated or suctioned into pieces? It ought to sober us to prayer and action against this holocaust. It is not the baby's fault. The baby is not immoral. Why should this precious, innocent one suffer? Should a mother's womb be such a dangerous place? Certainly not, it was created for the opposite—comfort, nourishment and love—a place of blessing.

What a true wonder it is that the very love of a man and woman together in unity can bring about a new little life! What an honor and privilege that our Creator and Heavenly Father has given us free will and the ability to conceive. It is His doings, not ours. Each child is His gift to us and to the world. Each little personality is created uniquely to glorify Him and love the world with His love. Each one is an eternal being. Let us worship and honor and bless the Lord for the gift of life! Glory to the Lord!

---◆---

Hold out your hand. A three-month-old baby in the womb is that size—has a heartbeat, fingers, toes, eyelashes, etc. Thank the Lord for life and for babies. Pray for the pro-life workers in your area and find a way to help

# SEPTEMBER 1

*"And exchanged the glory of God for an image in the form of corruptible man . . . they exchanged the truth of God for a lie . . . . For this reason God gave them over to degrading passions, to a depraved mind." Romans 1:23-28*

Dear brother, dear sister, dear elderly, dear little one—take warning from the Lord. See the signs of the times. In the last days men will be lovers of self, of money, boastful, arrogant, revilers, disobedient to parents, ungrateful, unholy, gossips, unloving, brutal, haters of good, treacherous, lovers of pleasure rather than God. You, avoid these things. You stand firm in the Lord. Fear God, honor Him and not men. Beloved brother or sister, do you see that many are exchanging the glory of God for corruption and the truth of God for a lie? Women and men are turning to degrading passions, exchanging natural function for that which is unnatural. They are burning in homosexual desire, depraved, committing indecent acts. So, lawlessness comes. The door is opened to all kinds of evil. But O, how the heart of God aches. His pain grows as the depravity continues—for He loves the sinner but hates the sin. He longs to free the person unto His own glorious love, unto peace and holiness and purity. Beloved, we must reach out with the love of the Messiah to a sick and dying world. We can bring comfort and honor to our Lord!

---

Today, pray for homosexuals in your city and if you know some, share the love of the Messiah with them in word and deed, without compromise.

# SEPTEMBER 2

*"But as many as received Him, to them He gave the right to become children of God even to those who believe in His name, who were born not of blood, nor of the will of the flesh, but the will of God." John 1:12-13*

As many as received Him—for God is not willing for any to perish, but for **all** to come to repentance. Therefore He said, "Go into the world and preach to **all** creatures, the gospel." Yet, we have our precious free will, with which we can bless or damn ourselves eternally. Jesus held out His arms on the cross, opened wide to you. He gave all. He gave His life—His holy life. In exchange He took your sins which caused Him untold agony. But to those who received Him He gave the right to become children of God. We speak of rights. Have you received Him? Has He given you that right? Are your sins forgiven? Do you dwell in Him? Is He your life and your love? This is the new birth. Spiritual, not physical. How does it happen? Not by the will of man, not by physical blood, but only by the will of God. Only by His will. When is the moment of salvation in a person? It is a divine secret. It belongs to Him! But we see the fruit! We see the totally new life that is born unto God. Bless His holy name and all His ways!

---◇---

Pray and make sure you are saved. Ask Jesus to forgive your sins and be the Lord of your life. Then tell someone of His glorious salvation today!

# SEPTEMBER 3

*"For if these qualities are yours and are increasing, they render you neither useless or unfruitful in the true knowledge of our Lord Jesus, the Messiah. For he who lacks these qualities is blind or short-sighted, having forgotten his purification from his former sins. Therefore, brethren, be all the more diligent to make certain about His calling and choosing you; for as long as you practice these things you will never stumble." 2 Peter 1:8-10*

If **these qualities** are yours and **increasing**, you will be fruitful. What qualities? These of life: applying diligence in your faith, supplying moral excellence, and knowledge (revelation knowledge), and self-control, and perseverance, and godliness, brotherly kindness, and godly love. Are you increasing in each one of these? Then you are fruitful and useful to the Lord in His kingdom. If you lack these qualities, you friend, have backslidden. Check yourself to see, because sliding back comes subtlety. It can even come from being too busy serving the Lord, in activities and not in the heart. Therefore, be all the more diligent to be sure of your calling and His choice of you. For as long as you **practice these things** you will **never** stumble. Never! How clear the Lord makes it for us. You will **never** stumble. How important this word is to keep us from falling. Test yourself. Are you increasing in these qualities? Are you strong in some and weak in others? Take it to the Lord.

---

Pray and search your heart. For the qualities you are increasing in, let the Lord affirm you. If you are lacking in any—repent and do your first works. Strengthen yourself in the might of the Lord. Go forward.

# SEPTEMBER 4

*"And I saw a new heaven and a new earth; for the first heaven and the first earth passed away, and there was no longer any sea." Revelation 21:1*

Dear beloved one, let us praise the Lord together that He is bringing a new heaven and earth for us. He gives us new hearts, not just repaired hearts. So, He gives a new heaven and new earth. There, we will sit at the heavenly wedding banquet, totally in love with our Bridegroom Jesus—finally one with Him completely, finally pure and holy without blemish. Those sins that followed us around and pulled on us will be gone forever. Those illnesses that dragged us down and those sorrows that oppressed us will be gone. The brightness of His countenance will forever light our hearts with the sacred oil of joy! We will be holy as He is holy. We will be able to worship Him in pure Spirit and truth in the way He is worthy to be worshipped. And we will be one bride without divisions. The sea divides the land of peoples but in the new heaven we will have *no divisions* but will adore Him together with one heart! Bless His holy name forever and ever!

---

Make a picture of the new heaven—with jewels on the throne and gates of pearls, streets of gold—now write on it all the glorious qualities we will have as the bride of the Messiah. Bless Him. Bow down and bless Him! Adore Him!

# SEPTEMBER 5

*"If I, then, the Lord and the Teacher, washed your feet, you ought also to wash one another's feet." John 13:14*

Can you imagine Jesus washing your feet, serving you, getting on His blessed knees before you and washing your feet? The King of Kings, the One who created all, stooping to wash your dirty feet? Yet He does it in many ways all the time. He, the Most High, humbles Himself to be with you, to care for you, to do every little thing to show His love for you. Have you ever noticed how He answers the details of your life, even some things before you ask? He is a kind and loving Father. He loves to care for your needs. The truth is that we are to wash His beautiful, nail-scarred feet, with our adoration and devotion and serving Him. Oh my brother! My sister! Have you ever cried out to God to be submerged in His love? Do you want to be filled up with His love? Then, here is the starting point—we must wash each other's feet. We must love each other in truth, in sacrifice. Jesus said over and over—a new commandment I give to you—"Love one another as I have loved you." By *this* all men . . . how many? *All* men (or people) will know that you are My disciples, if you have love for one another. Do you want to obey His every commandment? Then, love the Lord your God with all your heart, mind and strength and soul. And love your neighbor as yourself.

---------------◇---------------

Get on your knees and pray for the love of the Messiah to fill your heart for your brothers and sisters, especially any who irritate you. By faith, show them an act of love and grow in that love. Wash their feet.

# SEPTEMBER 6

### *"Love is patient."* 1 Corinthians 13:4

Why is it, my brother, my sister, that in this glorious chapter on God's "agape" love—that "patience" is the first attribute mentioned? Isn't it of utmost importance? God is love, we know. Think of His patience with us. If He weren't patient there would have been no Savior coming to earth for us and for most of us, no physical birth either. The world and all of mankind would have been blotted out a long, long time ago—and rightly so, for breaking His heart with such grief over our sins. If He were not patient, He would not be withholding Judgment Day right now. If He were not patient we would never have known of His infinite love, mercy, grace, goodness, faithfulness, holiness and all of His glorious attributes. But He *is* patient. He is not willing for any to perish. Yes, we have suffering on earth, but what about Jesus' suffering? He was beyond recognition and that was only the outer suffering. If God were to wipe out all evil, we too would perish for we have some—we are not yet made perfect. So, He waits, to His own suffering, for all to turn and be saved. And are we patient with each other? Are we loving and kind when wronged? How deep is our love? Is it words? Do we love those who hate us and mistreat us, as Jesus did? Love is patient.

———————————◇———————————

Thank the Lord for the patience He's given you, especially in certain areas. Ask Him to give you more in other areas. Go to a person with whom you are not patient. Love that person with the very love of the Messiah.

# SEPTEMBER 7

*"Consider it all joy, my brethren, when you*
*encounter various trials, knowing that the testing*
*of your faith produces endurance and let*
*endurance have its perfect result, that you may*
*be perfect and complete, lacking in nothing."*
*James 1:2-4*

Tribulation brings about perseverance. Exult in your tribulations. Perseverance brings forth proven character (as gold—to the glory of Jesus) and proven character brings hope and hope does not disappoint for the love of God has been poured out within our hearts through the Holy Spirit who was given to us. "You have kept the word of My perseverance, therefore I will keep you from the hour of testing which is about to come upon the whole earth." Oh Lord, how vital it is that we let You prove our characters and purify our hearts. It is difficult for Your lovely Holy Spirit to dwell in our flesh at times. How often we grieve Him with our unwholesome words and attitudes toward one another. How will we overcome unless the Son of God is truly Lord, and truly reigning in us—that our will is dead and His will is alive in us? Consider it joy that the Holy Spirit is at work in you, even more so in trials, to give you endurance which will make you perfect and complete, lacking in nothing! Rejoice, He will never fail you. He who began a good work in you will be faithful to complete it—to perfect it. We need not only to endure but to persevere, actively with a song of joy in spite of all. Can you sing to the Lord during the darkest trial? This a beautiful and real worship unto Him.

⎯⎯⎯⎯⎯⎯⎯⎯⎯⎯⎯◇⎯⎯⎯⎯⎯⎯⎯⎯⎯⎯⎯

Sing and dance to the Lord today! Thank Him for making you perfect and complete, lacking nothing through your trials!

# SEPTEMBER 8

### *"When the Son of Man comes, will He find faith on earth?" Luke 18:8*

How difficult it is for the Holy Spirit to live with our flesh. We so often limit Him by our little faith or our lack of love for each other or our lack of unity in the body of the Messiah. The Spirit in us groans and longs of the day of redemption. So our own will does the same as we long to be with the Lord physically as well as spiritually—to finally see Him face to face and dwell with Him forever more!

Yet, there is hope, for if we have faith, trusting faith as a child, we shall enter the kingdom of heaven. If we have faith as a mustard seed, the Lord will cause it to grow. He meets us where we are. We are made righteous, to live by faith in the Son of God. Our faith along with the divine revelation of Jesus and what He has done for us, saves us. Our faith, with His divine touch heals us. Faith comes by hearing (revelation) the word of God. Take up the shield of faith. Stand firm. Lengthen your tent pegs. Trust God with all your heart and do His will.

———————————————◇———————————————

Make a big shield of faith. Write on it all the things you have great faith about. Then write in small letters the ones you have less faith—as mustard seeds. Pray for your faith to grow. Memorize verses you have revelation on.

# SEPTEMBER 9

## "My God, My God, why hast Thou forsaken Me?" Matthew 27:46

The most grievous shriek in all of eternity, in all of the universe! The Holy Son of God, sinless and innocent and pure, with our vicious sins upon Him, crying out in despair to His Father—but at that point broken off from the Father into utter darkness and hell, because of our hideous sins. The isolation and sorrow deep down as He called, and no answer came. Even unable to say "Father" but having to say "God." Now, Jesus the Son of **Man**, so identified with us, carrying our wickedness, asks why. Surely He knew why but He had to go through the weight of our sorrows and experience rejection. We **do** ask why when we are grieving, even if we know why. It's the pain of it that causes us to ask it. For Jesus had already said, with great agony of heart. "Thy will be done." He drank the bitter cup.

And what about the Father? It's a divine mystery that He allowed His Son to be crushed for our iniquities. We know nothing about this type of sacrificial giving—to the point of voluntary grief and suffering. Would you give up your child to suffering and death to save an evil person? Oh, the heart of God! The greater the sacrifice, the deeper the love. The Father had to turn away from His Beloved Son, the joy of His heart, in His greatest moment of agony. He could not look upon the sin. But through that **precious** blood of Jesus, He heard His cry for us—"Father forgive them!", and He answered—for us! The Father's pain was so great that it's not even written. It's His secret. The love of God—so unspeakable!

---◇---

Today, minister to the heart of the Lord in thanksgiving for your salvation—deeply. Bless His heart with your love to Him in a special way.

# SEPTEMBER 10

*"Truly, I say unto you, to the extent that you did it to one of these brothers (sisters) of Mine, even the least of them, you did to Me."*
*Matthew 25:40*

What blessed words to hear from Jesus: "Come you who are blessed of My Father, inherit the kingdom . . . for I was hungry and you gave Me something to eat, I was thirsty and you gave Me drink; I was a stranger and you invited Me in; naked and you clothed Me; I was sick and you visited Me; I was in prison and you came to Me." The point is that any kindness or love we show to a brother or sister is as if we did it to Jesus! How often we feel His presence when we do these things. His love wells up in our hearts and He strongly uses our words and actions and even the look in our eyes to bless that person. He faithfully meets us and fills us. But the best is that He identifies so much with the hurting person that He says—"you did it to Me." When you love someone very deeply and someone else ministers to them, it's as unto you. The opposite is true too—when we don't do it, then we bypass Jesus, not caring for Him, hard-hearted. And if we hurt a brother or sister, we hurt Jesus. How often we hurt the ones we love—and it hurts Him too! Let us treat each other as we would Jesus!

---

◇

Make a commitment to see each other as Jesus sees us. To really love one another. Pray and ask the Lord to send you to a hospital or prison, orphanage, etc., to minister His precious love.

# SEPTEMBER 11

*"On the secret place of His tent He
will hide me." Psalm 27:5*

Thou, O Lord, art my hiding place. I hide under the shadow of Your wings. In that secret place, You hide me.

Dear saint of God, is your life hidden with the Messiah? Do you dwell in that precious, secret place with Him? He is your Almighty Protector. He surrounds you with songs of deliverance. In times of trouble, He takes you in and hides you. In the secret place of His tent He will hide you. Some in hostile lands are hidden away in prisons—although they are beaten and persecuted for the Messiah, they are hidden in the secret, holy dwelling place with Him. Their faces shine like angels to their persecutors. They praise Him as they endure pain and slander for His name's sake.

But you, precious one! Are you too hidden away in that secret place? Let Him hide you in His holiness today. Dwell there with Him, where no one else can see—in that sacred sanctuary with Him. Adore Him! Give glory to Him! Return there many times during the day to worship Him! Glory to His holy name! Worship the Lord in the sweet secret place!

---◇---

Let all of your cares and plans go and worship the Lord in holiness today. Be much with the One who bore the crown of thorns for you. Adore Him in the secret place. Bless Him!

# SEPTEMBER 12

*"Seek ye first the kingdom of God and His righteousness, and all these things shall be added unto you." Matthew 6:33*

Do you seek Him first? Is He the first in your day, in your priorities, in everything you do and say, in your life? If not, then get rid of any idols right away.

Seek *His* kingdom, not your own and not the world's. Seek *His* righteousness, not your own good ideas, although they may seem right or holy. Seek His way of doing things, not your own, or your group's way—but *His way*.

In our fast-paced world, it's not only hard to keep priorities right and to keep from busyness or running from one thing to another—but it is hard to keep a clean slate of your time. Of course practical things and work must be done—but in your free time, is He first? Are His ways and His will being done?

Many saints of the past who ushered in revival did not plan full days and then ask the Lord to bless it. They put Him first. They spent hours with Jesus in the morning, then they did what He asked—exactly what He asked—hitting the target in obedience. How blessed their eyes and ears to see and hear the Lord so keenly. Will you sacrifice certain things to put Him first and to do His will? He will truly add all things unto you!

––––––––––––––––––––◇––––––––––––––––––––

Begin to take one day a week and keep it for the Lord—free to be with Him and do His will.

# SEPTEMBER 13

*"My children, with whom I am again in labor*
*until the Messiah is formed in you."*
*Galatians 4:19*

Are you laboring for the Lord and for those He has given you? Have you prayed earnestly for those you are with daily? Have you shared the gospel with them and seen them come to Jesus? Be in labor and give new birth to those who are open to the Lord. Then begin to build them up in the Lord. Teach them the word by the power of the Holy Spirit. Teach them to pray. Teach them to worship and to know His presence intimately. Teach them to evangelize when they are yet babies in the Lord with no fears. Teach them to spend time alone with the Lord—the most important thing in life—to know Him, to love Him, to make Him known. Teach them to serve Jesus, but more than that, to know His character. Teach them to walk in integrity and holiness with a humble heart, not in pride, not in self-righteousness and judging—but to serve and wash feet. Teach them sweet communion with Jesus. Be an example, be an imitator of the Messiah. Teach them to repent quickly and keep a clean heart continually. Spend much time with them. Love them with the very heart of the Lord until the Messiah is formed in them.

---◇---

Pray for one person in whom you can pour your life and raise up as an evangelist and discipler of others—who will multiply the kingdom of God! Let the Messiah be formed in us all. Praise God!

# SEPTEMBER 14

*"My brethren, do not hold your faith in our glorious Lord Jesus, the Messiah with an attitude of personal favoritism." James 2:1*

Lord, have mercy on us, for in our hearts we often show favoritism. But You have chosen the foolish to confound the wise. You have chosen the poor to be rich in faith. For money can be a thief of God. It is hard for a rich man to enter the kingdom of heaven, but the poorer nations and minority groups are bowing their knees to the Lordship of Jesus. Often those most poor (as the widow that Jesus pointed out) are the most giving. Is not giving a sign of love? God gave us Jesus!

Jesus is our glorious Lord, and how richly He loves us! How He lavishes His beautiful love upon us all—all! All are touched in the harvest—all are reached in a revival—all. He does not pick and choose and show personal favoritism. He gives Himself to any and *all* who have a repentant and willing heart. How dare we show favoritism in the body of the Messiah, causing divisions, strife, jealousy and competition—grieving the Holy Spirit! We try to conform people to our image of what a believer should be instead of seeing the Messiah formed in them, instead of loving the unlovely. How hypocritical we are. Let us repent and love *all* with His love!

---

Think of someone who irritates you or is unlovely to be with or someone you have looked down on. Repent and love that person with Jesus' love. Point them to Jesus, not yourself or your own ideas.

# SEPTEMBER 15

*"Now I rejoice in my sufferings for your sake,
and in my flesh I do my share on behalf of His
body (which is the congregation) in filling up that
which is lacking in the Messiah's afflictions."*
**Colossians 1:24**

Oh divine mystery—to rejoice in sufferings! For the Messiah's sake?—yes, that is our heart's desire. For others' sake?—that is more difficult. For our enemies' sake?—a divine mystery. God will use any willing heart. Rejoice in your sufferings. Offer your life to the Lord, daily, as a sacrifice of love, to do as He wishes. You can do all things through the Messiah who strengthens you—all things—even suffering and rejoicing in it. Your life is His.

But what does it mean—filling up that which is lacking in the Messiah's afflictions? Wasn't His death enough? Oh, yes, it was exceedingly, abundantly more than enough. The blood of Jesus saves us. But His beloved people still suffer. They still have persecution and will even more so as the days grow darker until the end of time. Yet His light shines brighter in the darkness. A match in total darkness can be seen 11 miles away—how much more the brilliant light of the glorious Son of God! Still, He suffers with us as we suffer for Him, as we fill up this pain that He sees us (His beloved) go through for Him—until that final day, when no man can work for Him, when time stands still and we embrace our Bridegroom, Jesus.

❖

Today, if you are persecuted for Jesus. Rejoice—for His kingdom is at hand! Pray for those under severe persecution for the gospel (beatings, torture, killings) that they will remain faithful to Him. Pray for any who have denied Him, to take His grace and mercies and come back to Him.

# SEPTEMBER 16

*"And we proclaim Him admonishing every man
and teaching every man with all wisdom,
that we may present every man complete
in the Messiah." Colossians 1:28*

Are you proclaiming Him in word, deed and character? Have you taken His divine nature and promises and proclaimed them boldly? If not, ask the Lord to help you do it, and do it by faith. Admonish or warn every man of the life and death decision of repenting and coming to Jesus, or perishing for lack of knowledge or a hardened heart. **Every** man. Go into **all** the world and preach the gospel to all of creation. Have you gone into your world? Have you heard His call to go to another land or another people? Go! Proclaim! But also teach. Did not Jesus say to teach all that He's taught us? To make disciples of **all** nations? Teach, with the fear of God upon you. Teach His word, by His Spirit, giving life to those who hear. Teach with **all** wisdom. Acquire wisdom, and prudence, knowledge and understanding. Have discretion and counsel and instruction. Let wisdom be as a garland of grace and crown of beauty upon you. Seek her as a jewel. And present **every** man, everyone you win and disciple for Jesus, **complete** in Him!

———————————◇———————————

Pray for the fear of the Lord and wisdom to disciple new believers around you. See it through until they are complete in Him and serving Him, loving Him with all their hearts.

# SEPTEMBER 17

*"For this cause a man shall leave his father and mother, and shall cleave to his wife; and the two shall become one flesh." Ephesians 5:31*

The beautiful mystery of marriage—the love of the Messiah making us one! The relationship with the parents changes (although as dear as ever) and the spouse becomes the closest relative. The oneness grows and grows and it glorifies the Lord and shows the world Jesus' love—then one lays the other into God's loving arms at the time of death. The marriage is then given over to the love of the marriage Lamb in heaven. There is only one marriage in heaven—Jesus and His bride, His people (made up of Jew, Gentile, every tribe and tongue on earth).

What about Jesus Himself—our heavenly Bridegroom? He gave Himself for His bride and He provides for her on earth. But one day He will be joined to her forever at the marriage supper of the Lamb. He left His Father to redeem her, and now, He waits in heaven for her to finally come to Him. She will be pure and holy bearing His image in the fullness of God. He will be wed to His bride and they will be *one!* Jesus is our closest relative throughout eternity. This marriage will never end!

———————◇———————

Imagine being holy unto the Lord without a spot or wrinkle! Imagine Him waiting for you, rejoicing over you—one with you forever!

# SEPTEMBER 18

*"But the things which proceed out of the man are what defile the man." Mark 7:15*

From the heart to the mind to the tongue comes that which defiles a person. The heart is desperately wicked and deceitful until the Son of God comes to cleanse it. We are people of unclean lips. Let the cherub bring charcoal from the altar to cleanse us and prepare us to say, "Here I am, Lord, send me."

What do you talk about the most? That is your god. What is it? If it is not Jesus, then you have fallen, my brother, my sister, and you need to return to your First Love and do the deeds you did at first. You need to be restored so that your lamp will not go out. Come to Him if you are weary and heavy laden. He will give you rest for your soul.

Turn from idols in your life at once, this very day. Do not tolerate them even if they are good things like a son or daughter, a parent, a spouse, a ministry, a congregation, a gift from the Lord. For the enemy tempts subtly with good things. He is deceptive. Come back to Jesus with all your heart.

---

Let the Lord search your heart for any idols. Test your thoughts and speech. Repent. Do your first works. Love Jesus with all your heart!

# SEPTEMBER 19

*"All the ends of the earth will remember and turn to the Lord. And all the families of the nations will worship before Thee. For the kingdom is the Lord's and He rules over the nations."*
*Psalm 22:27-28*

All the earth! Can you imagine? All the ends of the earth! Every hidden tribe! Isn't this what we long for? But do we pray it? Or is it too big of a prayer? The Lord will not forget a single person. He has us inscribed on the palms of His hands. He has the precious scars to prove His love. Not all will be saved because not all will come to Him, but every nation and every people group no matter how large or small will experience revival in the end. The Lord will pour out His Spirit upon *all* flesh. There will also be great tribulation. He will give every chance up until the end. Even those who will shake their fist at God and worship demons will have an angel to preach the gospel to them. In the end, families of every nation will worship Him. All the nations will finally come and give Jesus (Yeshua) honor as King of Kings and Lord of Lords! He is the Sovereign Lord who rules over all of the universe! Bless His holy name!

---

Today, do a short Bible study on the sovereignty of God! Then worship Him!

# SEPTEMBER 20

*"The secret of the Lord is for those
who fear Him." Psalm 25:14*

To whom does the Lord reveal His secrets? To those who fear Him. To those who reverence Him in awe! Who is it that really hears Him, that really has His word for the moment? Those who fear and honor Him. Those who are completely His, unwavering in faith, trustworthy—it is these ones in whom He will trust with His own secrets of wisdom and knowledge and prophesy. What honor He bestows on them because He loves to tell them His innermost thoughts and plans. They are acquainted with His ways. They have a certain intimacy that most miss. In fact, they often walk a lonely road without much earthy fellowship because they are ahead of most people. Their time is with God. He directs their every motion. They only speak what He tells them because the fear of the Lord is on their tongues. They must be careful how they walk, keeping a humble heart, for if they allow the slightest bit of pride, their fall will be so great, often taking many with them. Will you too be trustworthy to the Lord, in that higher place where He can reveal His secrets to you?

---◇---

Fall on your face and ask for the fear of God and a humble, faithful heart—to be worthy to know His secrets.

# SEPTEMBER 21

*"How beautiful you are, my darling, how beautiful you are. Your eyes are like doves behind your veil." Song of Solomon 4:1*

That glowing bridal love—first love! There is nothing like it, in our love for Jesus, also in love for our spouses or dearest ones. We see only His beauty. We are captivated as we behold Him. We cannot turn our eyes away from Him and His overwhelming love! We say again and again—"How beautiful You are!" We are totally in love. All we can think of is Jesus. He in turn, radically changes our lives as He comes to dwell in out hearts and we are made into a new image—His very image as we go to the mountain tops and through the fiery trials of the valleys. How beautiful You are, Lord!

And He is totally in love with us too! Beholding us! He looks into our eyes behind the holy veil. One glance and we are changed, going from glory to glory. The sunshine of His gaze purifies us and makes us holy and full of adoring love. Our eyes are as innocent as doves, full of His peace. Let us be as homing pigeons, too—always returning to our first love, our bridal love. How beautiful! How beautiful! How beautiful!

---◇---

Take time this day to gaze into the piercing eyes of Jesus. Let Him fill you with bridal love for Himself and also the one who is dearest to you! Be His!

# SEPTEMBER 22

*"But if we walk in the light as He Himself is in the light, we have fellowship with one another, and the blood of Jesus cleanses us from all sin."*
*1 John 1:7*

How the Holy Spirit keeps us in the light! If we obey His promptings, our hearts will be laid open in His piercing light. Things will come up that we didn't even know were there and He will correct us. He patiently disciples us and loves us. Jesus is light—so brilliant and bright that the human eye cannot look on His holiness. But we walk *in* His light and we too are lights in the world. Therefore we must walk in the light together loving one another, open and honest with each other. Let us keep short accounts and live lives of forgiveness, letting nothing build up—no bitterness or resentment, no unforgiveness. Let us walk as He walked, who said, "Father, forgive them. They don't know what they're doing."

These are blessed words "the blood of Jesus (Yeshua) cleanses you." It is not "cleansed" or "will cleanse," but "cleanses." Right now, His blood cleanses you. The eternal fountain of His love is in the holy blood that cleanses you. Right now, let Him make your heart whiter than snow. He is able to make you stand before the Father blameless and full of joy!

◇

Ask the Lord to cleanse you freshly today. Bring all to the light. Let Him search you. Forgive anyone and everyone that He brings to your mind.

# SEPTEMBER 23

*"Faith, hope and love, but the greatest of these is love."* **1 Corinthians 13:13**

Faith comes by hearing the word of God. It is the substance of things hoped for. Hope does not disappoint for the love of God is shed upon our hearts. Love is from God. In fact God Himself *is* love. Keep yourself in the love of God. His love never fails.

When you've lost faith, hold onto hope. When you've lost hope, hold onto love. God is love. Draw up from the wells of His eternal love and build your hope up. He is the God of hope who will fill you again and again. Nothing is ever hopeless for He causes *all* things to work for good if we love Him and serve Him. Be faithful to Him who gave the greatest love to you by laying down His life for you. If you have faith as a mustard seed, He will cause it to grow into a huge tree. Nothing is too difficult. Nothing is impossible for God. You are justified by faith. Jesus gave His life to make you righteous. Soldier of the Lord, take up your shield of faith. The Messiah is in you, the hope of glory. Pursue love. Love the Lord your God will all your heart, soul, mind and strength.

———————————◇———————————

Pray for fresh faith, hope and love in an area in your life. Now act on each one in a tangible way. Let God be God. Fill up on His love.

# SEPTEMBER 24

*"All my desire is before Thee." Psalm 38:9*

Oh Lord, all my desire is before Thee. My heart is laid open to You that You may have Your way with me. Do what pleases Your heart, precious Lord. Fill me with Your desires. For only in sweet surrender to You am I truly free. You, the Son of God have set me free indeed. Oh Lord, let me grow in abandonment to You, to the love of the Messiah. Let my trust and love for You bring lasting fruit, holiness and the power of Your presence. For You live *in* me. You do not desire to be only close to me on the outside but in me. You desire continual fellowship with me, and in Your presence alone is fullness of joy! Let me *be* a worship unto You, rejoicing, giving You glory. Let Your awesome peace fall upon me and direct my soul. Let my will die and my spirit live, unto You. Let me be conformed to Your image, Jesus—to see others as You do, to think as You do—to love as You do—to be like You, Lord—that is all my desire! Have Your way!

———————————◇———————————

Worship the Lord in total surrender this morning for Him, full of Him!

# SEPTEMBER 25

*"Now you write to the Jews as you see fit, in the king's name, and seal it with the king's signet ring." Esther 8:8*

Yeshua (Jesus) has given us His name—the name above all names. It is higher than any problem, higher than any pain, higher than any illness. It is above all. His name is higher than governments, even above the workings of the universe. In Him all was spoken into existence and has its sustenance. And He is at the end of all things. He goes with us, for He is the way. He is the life and the resurrection. He is alive forevermore. He trusts us with His name, His precious name. Do all in the name of your King—King Jesus, who is Lord of heaven and earth! Then seal it with His seal, His signet ring, making it irrevocable. Seal it with the Holy Spirit—the King's signet ring. He who establishes us with you in the Messiah and anointed us is God, who also sealed us and gave us the Spirit in our hearts as a pledge. You were sealed in Him with the Holy Spirit of promise. His calling on your life is irrevocable for it is decreed by the King Himself, the Holy One, the Lord of love. He will make you like a signet ring for He has chosen you.

---

Find a ring to wear on a different finger today to remind you all day to pray in His name and seal it with His beautiful Holy Spirit.

# SEPTEMBER 26

*"But the Lord of hosts revealed Himself to me."*
*Isaiah 22:14*

The Lord of hosts! Of all heavenly beings; angels, cherubim, seraphim, of those great saints who have gone before us, the King of all kings and Lord of heaven and earth, this great God, has revealed Himself to you. He has humbled Himself and made Himself vulnerable. He has stooped to earth to reveal Himself to us all. And isn't it His nature to do so? For His name is also "Elohim" which means "God who reveals Himself." Our Triune God is One who constantly loves and gives Himself. He created us for Himself. We were made to love Him, to enjoy Him, to worship Him. Blood and flesh do not reveal Him, but He Himself reveals Himself, a divine, heavenly mystery. The Son of God (Son of Man) is revealed. The manifestations of the Holy Spirit are revealed. The glory of the Lord is soon to be revealed. But we know not of the far surpassing glory of the Lord to be revealed in our hearts. Has He revealed Himself to you in a precious and tender and sacred way? Is He still revealing Himself to you? He will. For if you seek Him, you will find Him!

———————————◇———————————

Alone in a quiet place, ask the Lord of hosts to reveal Himself, something new about Himself to you today. Open your heart to receive!

# SEPTEMBER 27

*"Because this people draw near with their words and honor Me with their lip service, but they remove their hearts far from Me, and their reverence for Me consists of tradition learned by rote." Isaiah 29:13*

Do you draw near to Jesus in the way that you did at first when your heart was full of love for Him? Every verse jumped into your heart. You sang every song with a heart of adoration. You were in awe of Him. He was your every thought. He was the love of your life. Is it still like that or have you slipped some? Do you know that it is so possible to sing to Him, even to pray to Him with all the right words, yet your heart be far, your thoughts on something else (maybe on something good but not on Him). You, dear one, can do His works, serving Him, and still have your heart be far from Him. You can reverence Him with a daily quiet time and it can become routine or as a duty far from Him. If this roteness continues unchecked, it will become a mere tradition and your fiery love for Jesus will be only a memory. Let the Holy Spirit have His way. Awake, O sleeper! Arise, for the glory of the Lord is upon you! Rise and walk in the name of Jesus! Drink of the Living water! Eat fresh manna! Sing a new song to the Lord! He will make a roadway in the wilderness! Stir up your heart of love! Love Jesus! Forget all else! Concentrate on Him!

───────────◇───────────

Find new, creative ways to spend time with the Lord each day. Study a book of the Bible, memorize verses, listen to a tape, do a prayer walk, a dance, a song, a love note. Pray around your neighborhood, do a fast, take communion, have a foot washing. Stir up your love and show it to Him in new ways.

# SEPTEMBER 28

*"The everlasting God, the Lord, the Creator of*
*the ends of the earth does not become weary or*
*tired. His understanding is inscrutable."*
*Isaiah 40:28*

He is the living God enduring forever. His kingdom shall not be destroyed. His dominion will be forever. The King shall reign. Jesus shall reign forevermore. He is the Lord, the Creator. He does not become weary or tired. He is eternal youth. His zeal will accomplish His will. The nations will come to Him. He is the Resurrection and the Life! His understanding is infinite. He walked the dusty roads of Israel—He did become tired as a human—He understands. But He has risen! His glory only shines brighter and brighter—and so do you. Weary soldier of the front lines, rest your head in His arms. Let Him fill you with fresh new Living Water—His Holy Spirit! Be renewed in Him, refreshed by His presence. Let Him restore your soul. He is the God of hope and strength and peace. Forget all your circumstances. Cast them to Him. He cares for you. Let the Good Shepherd lead you to green pastures, to still waters, to His quietness, His lovely presence. Come away with Him and rest. Then rise up with new strength in your heart and mind! Sing to the Lord a new song!

———————————◇———————————

Offer to the Lord the first fruit of each day, of each week (Sabbath rest on Saturday or Sunday). Be filled. Let His peace be your strength.

# SEPTEMBER 29

*"He gives strength to the weary and to him who lacks might He increases power." Isaiah 40:29*

He who never slumbers, who does not become weary or tired, will give you new strength, His strength—by His Spirit. The supernatural strength of God will carry you through for God is the strength of your heart. You will accomplish amazingly all that He has for you, without weariness. Dear saint of God, are you lacking might? Let His power come to you this day, fresh and new. He promises to increase your power. *He* is your strength. Walk in *Him*. Do not lean on your own strength. Learn to say, "no"—do not use His time unwisely. Do all for the glory of God and unto Him! Store up precious time alone with the Lord! Renew yourself in Him! Deny yourself of the pleasures that please the flesh, even good fellowship if it is in excess. *He* is the Lord of your life, not schedules. Discipline yourself to spend a good amount of time with the Lord daily. Go to bed early and get up before the devil does. Take the strength that God gives you as the sunrises each day! Walk in *His* power!

---

Plan some extra time with the Lord besides your daily time. Steal away with Him even if it's only ten or fifteen minutes. Look for time to be with your Beloved Jesus!

# SEPTEMBER 30

*"Though youths grow weary and tired, and vigorous young men stumble badly, yet those who wait for the Lord will gain new strength."*
*Isaiah 40:30-31*

Youths grow weary? Tired? Yes, they can if their priorities are not God's priorities. Yes, they can if they are running the race without pastoral care. Yes, they can if they become slothful and without vision and purpose. Yes, they can without the right encouragement and prayer covering.

And vigorous young men can stumble badly. **Vigorous** young men. Stumble **badly**. It can happen for the zeal of the Lord must be accompanied with character development and sanctification of the Holy Spirit. After repentance must come the seeking of the Lord with a humble spirit, the learning to surrender all and do His will—the purging of the Holy Spirit to make one holy.

Those who wait—who unite themselves to God, trusting Him—will renew their strength or gain new strength from Him. His strength upholds and gives peace and divine confidence and boldness in the Holy Spirit. His strength is eternal, not earthly. It is without strife. It regenerates and makes things easier. It also gives God glory, not man. It makes the impossible to be possible. Soak in the rays of the Son.

———————◇———————

Let your spirit be tempered by God today. If you are weary take His strength. If you are full of zeal, take His peace. Wait on Him until you are filled then go out to do His will.

# OCTOBER 1

*"They will mount up with wings like eagles. They will run and not get tired. They will walk and not become weary." Isaiah 40:31*

Those who patiently wait on God for His will, His way, His timing, will experience a fresh outpouring of His Spirit, a newness of His presence, an undergirding by the Holy One. They will mount up over their circumstances, over their own weaknesses, up to the heavenly places with Him. As an eagle floats upward, soaring, letting the wind carry him, so the believer will rise up, carried by the Lord Himself in His resurrection spirit. They will taste of the high places. The fresh clean air of heaven. They will have strength to run and keep on running. They will not get tired for they will see their Masters' face! They will keep on walking and not fall by the wayside. They will not faint or be overwhelmed. They will see things as they really are, in spirit and truth—and they will worship God with all their hearts. His song will be in them, the song of heaven! And they will sing to all who will listen, to all who will join the race. They will run and they will win!

———————◇———————

Wait on the Lord this day. Renew your heart and mind in Jesus. Take new strength and run with Him! Run with new joy!

# OCTOBER 2

*"Rejoicing in hope, persevering in tribulation, devoted to prayer." Romans 12:12*

Dear precious one who loves God, isn't this verse music to your ears? Our God is a God of hope who does not disappoint for His love has been shed abroad in our hearts. He is the God of hope who fills you with all joy, *all* joy, . . . and peace, in believing, so that you may abound in hope. Yes, you may abound in hope by the power of the Holy Spirit. It is His will for you to have abundant faith and hope and love so that you may go on your way *rejoicing in hope!* Rejoice in it. Take hold of it and do not let it go for one minute. There is always hope in the Lord. When all seems hopeless and impossible, Jesus is the Resurrection and the Life! Our God is a God of new mercies and beginnings! Rejoice in hope, dear saint! Persevere in tribulation. And here's the key—be devoted to prayer! Cling to the Lord! He is your hope, your peace, your deliverer, your joy, your love. Be devoted to Him and let His Son shine on you! Let it be your lifestyle to rejoice in hope, persevere in trials and be devoted in prayer.

———————◇———————

Write all of your trials down, then all of your hopes. Put the piece of paper on the floor and dance around it, praising the Lord, rejoicing in hope!

# OCTOBER 3

One thing the Lord hates is a haughty look. A haughty spirit comes before stumbling. We are to fear the Lord and hate evil; pride and arrogance and the perverted mouth. To hate evil is wisdom. We are not to think more highly of ourselves than we ought, but to think highly of each other, becoming servants of love, givers. A bond servant is free to go if he wants to, but he has chosen to stay and be loyal out of love. Jesus was a bond servant, a love slave. He chose to give His life for us. He chose to wash His disciples' dirty feet. He could have exalted Himself, rightly, with full justice, and ruled over us, but He chose the lowly way of taking on our sins and bleeding for us. He chose the lowly way of being silent before His accusers. Let us go His way. Let us not draw attention to ourselves but to Him. Let us decrease and Jesus increase. Let us not be wise in our own sight but acknowledge Him in all our ways. He will direct our path.

---

Ask the Lord to show you any subtle area of pride or haughtiness in your life. Let Him correct it and go to Him in that secret place. Go **His** way.

# OCTOBER 4

*"If possible, so far as it depends on you, be at peace with all men." Romans 12:18*

Yes, dear brothers and sisters—take this God-given responsibility from the Lord! He is a God of peace (shalom)! His sweet and lovely presence brings peace! He is the Prince of Peace—the Great peacemaker between heaven and earth! Whatever is not of peace is not of Him. He brings peace to confirm His leading and direction when our relationship with Him is pure and right.

And how gracious and understanding the Lord is of our frail human nature. He knows how easily we fail in relationships—therefore He says, "If possible, so far as it depends on you . . . ." In other words, you are not responsible for the other person's response. If a person does you wrong, or will not forgive you, you have done your part in forgiving and trying to bring peace and unity which is God's will. He does not say to compromise the truth, but "if possible, so far as it depends on you"—be at peace. Keep a close watch on all your relationships. Humble yourself and go to the ones which are not right. Make peace and let the Lord have His way in it!

———————————◇———————————

Forgive and be forgiven. Understand and be understood. Be a peace maker in all of your relationships and be free to the glory of God!

# OCTOBER 5

*"Do not be overcome by evil, but overcome evil with good." Romans 12:21*

Precious brothers and sisters, beloved of God, let this verse minister to your hearts. Do not be overwhelmed by the darkness around you, by the evil days coming upon this earth. Look up, for your redemption draws near. The Son of God is right at the door. The coming of the Lord is at hand.

Do not be overcome by disappointments in yourself or in your brothers and sisters. Do not let the hurt take root, causing branches of bitterness in other parts of your life, hurting those around you—the last state worse than the first. Sometimes in a war there is unintentional "friendly fire" where one of us and not the enemy gets wounded. Take the wine and oil of the Comforter and get up to continue the race. Forgive, love, and understand and go on. Do not be overcome with evil. Overcome evil with good. Even with your enemies, the enemies of God, pray for a blessing—reach out in Jesus' love and overcome evil with good!

---

Pray and find a way to bless someone today who is against you or the gospel.

# OCTOBER 6

*"Secure undistracted devotion to the Lord."*
*1 Corinthians 7:35*

Dear precious one who loves God—make this a great priority in your life always. Keep simple devotion to Jesus. Do not let your life get complicated. Do not become overly busy for it is a great and subtle thief of love to Jesus. It is in doing good serving the Lord with too many activities and schedules that the evil one will snare you. You will not notice at first and then the presence of God will become dull or less in your life. Beware of this. The great men and women of God who did great things for Him, lived simple lives, undistracted, devoted to Him. They said "no" when others said "yes." They closed themselves off with Him when others spent time in fellowship or ministry. He was their Chief Delight and their Best Friend. He was the desire of their hearts. Their thoughts and hearts were in constant communion with Him—therefore their lives were devoted to Him. They heard Him and did His will. Their lives counted for God. Secure it— undistracted devotion to the Lord. Make time for it. Cut out what needs to be cut out. Add in all that He wants. Be *His* unreservedly. Fan the flames of fervent love for Jesus!

———————◇———————

Pray and revise your priorities and schedules to be undistractedly devoted to the Lord! He is the most important!

# OCTOBER 7

*"Knowledge makes arrogant but love edifies."*
*1 Corinthians 8:1*

Lord, have mercy on us—that awful sin of pride—the original sin which polluted the human race with all other sins—that raising up of self and wanting to be honored by others. How subtle it is, how often it sneaks into our motives. Or the reverse—self pity and false humility. Lord, cleanse it out of us once and for all. Keep us from desiring more and more knowledge of You in our minds without loving from our hearts. Pride goes before a fall. The Lord hates an arrogant look. The pride of life leads to destruction.

But true humility, a true servant heart, full of love—builds up. It not only builds up the one receiving it, it builds the giver in the love of the Messiah. There is nothing more satisfying than pouring out true love—the very life of the Messiah from your being—all your heart in truth and sincerity. Let us walk in His light and be full of His truth, not doing what is right because we should, but doing it because we are aglow with His love and we love others with His very heart!

---

Ask the Holy Spirit to show you any area which may be prideful or superficial. Receive His cleansing and open your heart to receive new love today!

# OCTOBER 8

*"... He (the Master) will gird himself to serve and have them recline at table, and will come up and wait on them." Luke 12:37*

Dear brother, dear sister, if you want to be great in God's kingdom, learn to be a servant of all. Be looking for ways to love the Messiah first and then others, even the unlovely. Think more highly of others, not expecting in return. Forget about yourself and glorify the Lord. Let *Him* be magnified in you. Exalt Him, acknowledge Him in every area of your life. Live for Jesus, serve Him and serve those He gives you. This is preparation for any leadership place that He may give you. Look to Him, your Lord and Master. He is your example in all of life. Jesus, the King of Kings and Creator of the Universe, stooped to come to earth, to wash men's feet, to save their souls, to heal their bodies, to deliver them from demons, to die for them, humiliated as a criminal. It was *God* who died for you. And what? And in His kingdom, *He*, *the Master*, will gird Himself to serve and will come and wait on you. *Jesus* will wait on those He finds faithfully serving.

---

Find a way to serve the Lord today, a new way, secretly between you and Him. Let it be as washing His feet. Then go and do it to your neighbor.

# OCTOBER 9

*". . . but emptied Himself (laid aside His privileges), taking the form of a bond servant, and being made in the likeness of men."*
*Philippians 2:7*

Oh how our human flesh loves to exalt itself. How it loves recognition and approval of men, even praises of men. How opposite of the Son of God who **emptied** Himself. Have you emptied yourself, or are there still areas of compromise in your life? Do you fear men at times? Are you ashamed of the Messiah at times? Oh, Lord, have mercy on us all. Keep us from striving, competition, jealousy, insecurity and lack of trust in You. Let us be like You, Jesus, and empty ourselves to be Yours at all costs— all we are and all we are not yet. Let us not exalt ourselves even in small undetected ways—let us humble ourselves. Let us die to our selfish ways. Let us forget ourselves and live for You. You, the Son of God, pure and holy, took the form of a bond servant and came into the image of man. You are forever a man, the Son of Man, although You are now exalted above all in glory. Still, You, Jesus bear the ugly scars of our sins, marred for all eternity. We will see You, whom we have pierced. Let us become **Your bondservants** so that we may bear **Your** image, endure **Your** scorn, bow to **Your** name and confess with **all that we are**, that **You are Lord**!

---◆---

Ask the Lord to let His light and truth shine through you in a way that impurities may be dealt with and His character imparted, so that who you are shows that He is Lord!

# OCTOBER 10

*"Now faith is the assurance of things hoped for, the conviction of things not seen." Hebrews 11:1*

The assurance—that "knowing deep down" from the Holy Spirit, the very confidence of God. It is not just hopeful praying, but the word from the Lord—He has spoken it into existence in your heart. It has already taken place in heaven but not yet on earth. It is the conviction so real in the spirit and by the Holy Spirit although it has not come about yet in the natural element. The prompting of the Holy Spirit comes . . . "pray for that baby to be healed," and when you do, you know it will happen even if you don't know how or exactly when. Or the Lord says, "preach the gospel to that person" and as you do, you feel it taking hold and being planted in their heart. Faith is the assurance from God of the things hoped for that are prayed for (according to His will) and not yet seen. There is also another kind of faith that pleases God which is stepping out in total trust of Him without any evidence whatsoever to prompt it, sometimes with opposite circumstances. What is the key? Obey God and act in faith.

———————————◇———————————

Make a "faith list" today of things you will trust God for. Pray through it. Choose one thing to act in faith on! Praise His name!

# OCTOBER 11

*"By your perseverance you will win your souls."*
*Luke 21:19*

He who overcomes, he who perseveres, he who finishes the race will enter into his full reward. It doesn't matter how well we start or how deep we go or how high—if we don't finish. He who is faithful unto death will win the crown. The enemy of our souls wants to cut down our faith and bring just one area of hopelessness, so he can flood our souls and steal us or even kill us. So Jesus says to persevere. It is persevering faith that wins, not just enduring passively but pursuing faith. Tribulation brings about perseverance. We must entrust ourselves to the One who is all faithful and run the race with perseverance.

Jesus said, "Ask, and it shall be given to you; seek and you shall find; knock and it shall be opened to you." Do not be weary in well doing for in season you shall reap a harvest. There is the gift of faith, given to you when you absolutely know the Lord will do something. There is also the persistent faith that keeps asking until there is a breakthrough.

Rise up, precious saint of God, soldier of the Lord, Take hold of your eternal life. Seek the Lord. Believe and receive. Pursue Him. Ask Him. Knock and the door will open. Run the race with perseverance. Glorify the King!

---

Take your faith list and find one request that you will pursue and keep asking. Be diligent and believe it will be answered.

# OCTOBER 12

*"And everlasting joy will be on their heads."*
*Isaiah 51:11*

Oh, the sweetness of His everlasting joy! Isn't it what we search for as human beings? Not fleeting happiness, not even joy itself—for it too is in seasons much more strong than at other times but the true joy of the Lord! ***Everlasting joy!*** The permanent, everlasting joy will be when we see our Lord Jesus face to face and dwell with Him forever in heaven! But there is a day to day joy that never fades. It is deep in the heart because of abiding in Jesus! It is the song that He gives to our whole being, which comes forth from deep inside. In fact, it can come forth even in sorrow if our hearts and minds are fixed on Him!

And Jesus, although He was the Man of Sorrows who took our sins—wasn't He also anointed with everlasting joy? I'm sure that He has a smile which radiates heaven itself. In Psalm 45 it says that God anointed Him with the oil of joy above His fellows. He was the fragrance of everlasting joy and purity, full of strength and enduring love! He is holy joy!

---

Consecrate yourself before the Lord to walk in His joy! Receive anointing for it by faith. Begin to sing and dance before the Lord!

# OCTOBER 13

*"I AM who I AM!" Exodus 3:14*
*"By the grace of God, I am what I am."*
*1 Corinthians 15:10*

When Moses asked, "Who are You, Lord?" God answered and said, "**I AM** who I AM." He **_is_**! He is Almighty God, the Lord, living and loving and awesome in power and might, full of splendor and majesty, to whom all of heaven bows down 24 hours a day, saying—"Holy, holy, holy, to Him who sits on the throne, who is and was and is to come! He is the Great "I AM."

This is where we begin with our own identification. Moses who had killed a man stood before the Great I AM. How great He is in forgiveness, mercy, and lovingkindness!

The Apostle Paul, who had persecuted believers said, "By the grace of God, I am what I am." He took full grace and pardon. He let the Lord transform him into one of the greatest saints who ever lived—a vessel fully surrendered and reflecting the Lord Jesus! Later he could say, "Brethren, become as I am." He knew he was an imitator of the Messiah. He didn't look back in self-pity or condemnation. He didn't walk in pride. He knew who he was. He walked in God's grace. He accepted himself, not thinking too highly or too low. Forgetting himself, he glorified the Messiah. By the grace of God, you are who you are. Glorify the Lord!

---◇---

Thank the Lord today for His grace, for who you are in Him. Forget yourself and magnify Him!

# OCTOBER 14

*"Incline your heart to understanding."*
*Proverbs 2:2*

Acquire wisdom! Acquire understanding! How important is wisdom? Often a person comes to ruin without it. But with it we need understanding—they go together as twins. Do you know that it is impossible to dislike a person whom you understand? How different the world would be with wisdom and understanding. Marriages would be put back together, and relationships would be healed. Wars would be stopped.

Have you ever been misunderstood to the point where you cried out to God? To where you felt that no one except Jesus could understand you? Didn't you feel so lonely at that moment? Didn't you cling to Jesus? How desperately we need to be understood and to understand!

Do you want to know people? To love them as Jesus did? To see them come into His glorious kingdom? Take time to understand them. Listen to them. Even more, listen to the Spirit of God for often their lips are different than their heart. Meet their needs. Care for them. Let Jesus unlock their heart through you. Understand with your heart!

———————————◇———————————

Pray and ask the Lord for wisdom and understanding in your relationships. Love with His love and understanding.

# OCTOBER 15

*"With Thee is the fountain of life." Psalm 36:9*

And what does a fountain do? It springs up gloriously in beauty, life and joy! It is continually renewed, continually receiving, continually giving! It is resurrection! Dancing! Rejoicing! Living waters that bless everyone! It is a continual flow—not only being filled and not only giving out—but both!

**You** are a fountain of Jesus' life. Do not let anything obstruct your flow from Him. Don't let anything come in between you and the Lord—no person, no thing, no emotion, no circumstances, not even yourself. **Keep your eyes on Jesus**, the source of life. Do not take your eyes off of Him. Resist distractions. Even fellowship can be a distraction. Yes, even ministry can be a distraction, or family—all good things, given by Him and ordained. But Jesus must be first continuously, for the river to flow. Let it flow lavishly! Let it become wider and longer and deeper so that your very love for Jesus reaches to people and places you never thought of. Don't look at yourself or how He uses you. **Look at Him!** Keep the river flowing. Don't look at the river. Look at Jesus! Be true to Him!

---◇---

Find a fountain today or a river. If not, draw one. Ask the Lord to help you keep your eyes on Him and let the river or fountain continuously flow!

# OCTOBER 16

*". . . for I know whom I have believed and I am convinced that He is able to guard what I have entrusted to Him until that day."*
*2 Timothy 1:23*

I know Him! I know His ways. I know Him. I have tasted of His kindness, I have waited on His will, I have experienced His faithfulness and His purity. I know Him!

Do you know Him? Have you walked with Him in a way that you know Him deeply, and you trust Him without your own understanding? Has He taken you up on the mountain tops? Has He led you through the valleys? Have you seen His shining face in the dark night of your tears? Have you been on the heights of joy with Him? Have you rested in His arms of peace and goodness? Do you know Him? Really know Him?

Then be still and know that He is God. He will be exalted among the nations. The nations are but a drop in the bucket for Him. Nothing is impossible with God. Trust Him now for that which you don't see, that which seems impossible, that which circumstances and friends say the opposite. He is able, fully able to guard and keep that which you have entrusted to Him. Our God is trustworthy. He will keep you in perfect peace.

---

Put into His hands that which is most difficult. Leave it there. Trust Him. He is trustworthy.

# OCTOBER 17

*"There is therefore now no condemnation for those who are in the Messiah, Jesus." Romans 8:1*

There is **no** condemnation! When? Now! The blood of Jesus, the Spirit of life has set me free from the law.

How often in our longings and zeal to love, we trip and fall over our weaknesses, over our doubts and unsteadiness. The flesh and human nature does not want to bow to the Lord Jesus even though our spirit has been sanctified and is bowed down in humility and love. We cannot be perfect in ourselves but we can be perfect in Jesus. He is the perfect sacrifice, the innocent Lamb of God who took our sins. We must hide in Him, dwell in Him. He is the One who is able to keep us from falling, to make us stand in the presence of His glory, **blameless with great joy**! He who began a good work in you will be **faithful to perfect it**. God is faithful. His Spirit is leading you. He will never fail you. Satan will accuse you and try to mar you. Do not look at him. Do not look at your sins and imperfections. Look at Jesus. He is perfect. You are in Him. Stay there. Look at Jesus, your perfect sacrifice!

---

Ask the Lord to help you keep your eyes on Him, to live in Him and to walk in His grace. Thank Jesus for His blood shed for you.

# OCTOBER 18

*". . . and the things which I heard from Him, these things I speak to the world." John 8:26*

Every word that came out of Jesus' mouth was from God the Father. Every word was holy. Every word was anointed. Every word intended to bless, redeem, restore, save, heal, deliver. Every word was of the kingdom of heaven, shining in His glorious light, giving life, taking us from strength to strength and glory to glory. The Holy Spirit filled every word of Jesus to the overflow. His words were not from earth, not from the human heart, but from eternity and the heart of the Father. Glory to God!

How would it be if our tongues were so disciplined and full of the fear of the Lord that we only spoke His words? (Only the Holy Spirit can tame the tongue.) Wars would stop, relationships would be healed, marriages and families would be put back together.

How blessed would be our ears if we would really hear Him, really know His will in every situation! How pleased His heart would be if we would hear and speak His words to the world!

Ask the Lord today for the fear of Him (awe and reverence) to fall upon your tongue. Ask Him to give you ears to hear Him well!

# OCTOBER 19

*"And He who sent Me is with Me; He has not left Me alone, for I always do the things that are pleasing to Him." John 8:29*

And He who sent Jesus is with you, dear precious brother, dear sweet sister! He is with **you**! He has not left you, He will never forsake you. His love for you is steadfast and beautiful! The Father did not leave Jesus alone and Jesus will not leave you alone. He will always, always come to you by His Holy Spirit if your heart is for Him. He loves you with an everlasting love and lives deep within your heart. He has redeemed you by His own holy blood.

Jesus **always** did that which pleased the Father! How often? **Always!** How blessed we would be in life if we could know that we **always** pleased the Father! Do not despair, for this is the very will of God. He is committed to teaching us patiently, day by day, how to please the Father. Do you want to please Him? Then know His word, hear His voice, do His will. **Love with His heart**. Depend completely on Him. Let **your will be His will**. Surrender totally, daily to Him. Do His will with a joyful heart whether it's easy or difficult. You will please your Father.

---◇---

Pray that your chief desire will be to do that which pleases the Father—to continually pray and obey.

# OCTOBER 20

*"The heavens are telling of the glory of God."*
*Psalm 19:1*

From the rising of the sun to the going down of the sun, the Lord's name is to be praised! How majestic is His creation! How gloriously faithful is He who creates beautiful sunrises and sunsets which we may or may not see—a demonstration of His splendor! The ocean waves, the snow-covered mountains, the forests and brooks—do they not stop us to be still before Him often? The heavens declare His glory daily! Who can look at the starry night or the fish in the sea or beautiful and unique animals or a baby's face without knowing deep inside that He is there!

The whole earth is full of His glory! It covers the earth! No government can lock it out. It is a living testimony of our living God! He pours His glory out on earth daily! The heavens speak. They have a message to all mankind. Our God is awesome and beautiful and He is love itself, forever and ever. And He, the Holy One, stepped onto earth for 33 years in His Son Jesus—to make us holy forever, to give us eternal life.

---◇---

Make a praise book full of pictures, photos, postcards and verses, declaring His beauty and glory!

# OCTOBER 21

*"Are you able to drink the cup that I am about to drink?" Matthew 20:22*

Oh, how we long to have that position with Jesus—to sit on His right and left. But only the Father knows this position. He is absolutely just and full of lovingkindness. Also there is a requirement on our part—it is the cup.

Are you able to drink the cup that Jesus drank? Do you know what it is? It is the cup of suffering. Jesus spoke much of it, yet He was full of overflowing joy! He is the joy giver, yet His life was also full of suffering and sorrow. His very purpose for coming to earth was to drink the cup of sorrow. He drank it to the dregs—until He could say, "It is finished." The weight of the world's sins were upon Him—therefore He, the author of joy and peace, became the Man of sorrows. He carried them in agony as He sweat great drops of blood in the Garden of Gethsemane. He emptied Himself to be put to torture and death. He drank the cup.

What is your cup? Every believer has a cup of sorrow to endure—even in the midst of great joy in the Lord. Will you drink the cup and have a place with Jesus? Will you go *His* way or your way? Will you deny yourself and be crucified with the Messiah? Will you let Him rise in you in resurrection?

———————————◇———————————

Find a cup and put something bitter in it to remind you of the bitter cup of sins that Jesus took for us when He died for our sins. Thank Him for it.

# OCTOBER 22

*"My Father, if it is possible, let this cup pass from Me; yet not as I will, but as Thou wilt."*
*Matthew 26:39*

Why didn't Jesus want to drink the cup? There are several reasons. There was the physical suffering and mocking and humiliation which no person would want, but Jesus was strong. He endured the 39 lashes that usually kills people. He endured heartbreak often. He was strong in spirit and soul. But the cup meant that He had to endure our sins, even become sin for us. The holy, pure, innocent Son of God. God cannot have sin in His presence yet Jesus had to become sin. It was a horror to Him. He hated sin with the utmost passion. But only His blood could cleanse us from our sins. Holy God became sin for us. It's a divine mystery. He carried our iniquities but they did not come into His Spirit.

Jesus also did not want the cup because it meant that He had to break perfect and sacred fellowship with the Father and the Holy Spirit. He has such a glorious relationship with the Father—something we know nothing about. So, He cried, "My God," not "My Father," but "My God, why hast Thou forsaken Me?" The Father had to endure the great pain of rejecting His Son in that moment. How great is His love for us! He drank the cup!

---◇---

Ask the Lord to help you drink whatever your cup of suffering is. Do it out of love for Him!

# OCTOBER 23

*". . . and His sweat became like drops of blood falling down upon the ground." Luke 22:44*

How it must have grieved our sweet Lord Jesus, the innocent Lamb of God to have our sins fall upon Him. He who knew no sin, perfect and holy had to allow things like murder, adultery, fear, anger, hatred, etc., to come upon Him. How He must have wanted the cup to pass. But how much more He desired to do His Father's will. How much more His love remained for us. This is the moment He was born for—to carry our sins. How the pain of sorrow must have hurt Him, and the agony of sickness. It must have begun in the Garden as He fell on His face before the Father. How desperate His prayers were. "Nevertheless, not *My* will but *Thine* be done." He took the cup and drank it to the ugly dregs. He must have heard the demons wickedly laughing. He drank it all. Great drops of blood began to fall from His body. His sweet heart was breaking for us. It began there when He said, "Not My will but Thy will be done." Jesus, the precious, holy Lamb, bleeding for us, bleeding for the Father, perfectly obedient. Bless Him.

---◇---

Get on your face and thank Jesus for sweating drops of blood for you. Thank Him that you are victorious over sin because of His blood and death for you.

# OCTOBER 24

*"If you abide in my word then you are truly disciples of Mine." John 8:31*

Let us take time to dwell in His word. Let us wait there until He has spoken to us. When that revelation comes let us take it into our minds and memorize it or sing it. Let it go from our minds into our spirits. Let it have its way in our will, bringing understanding, conforming us to His image. Let it teach us to act like Jesus. May we never just know about Him but really **know Him!** May we never take His precious words too lightly. May we truly be His disciples, His followers, walking in His ways, doing His will. May we know His truth, His light deep in our hearts and may we be like Him. May His truth make us free! Free of self and free of the world and free of the devil's snares.

Brothers! Sisters! Keep yourself in the love of the Messiah. Build up yourself in the Spirit. Pray in the Spirit. Dwell in His word. Let us build up our soul (mind, will, intellect) by memorizing His word. Dwell in it. Let it guard your heart and mind.

---

Choose a verse or passage that God has lit up into your spirit and memorize it or put it to music! Bless the Lord today!

# OCTOBER 25

*"At night my soul longs for Thee, indeed my
spirit within me seeks Thee diligently."*
*Isaiah 26:9*

Dear servant of God, be sure that you long for the living God, that your spirit seeks Him. Keep your heart and mind steadfast on Him, open to Him. Hear His voice and obey. Do not let distractions, even good ones, keep you from seeking the Lord. Be a diligent seeker and He will reward you with Himself—with the loveliness of His presence. Is there anything on earth better than His presence? No! His lovingkindness is better than life! His sweet presence lifts your soul to heaven where you have the peace that surpasses all comprehension. There's **nothing** as precious as Jesus! There's **no one** as precious as Him!

Do you long for Him? Is His sweet communion like a banquet of delight for you? Do you have a continual song in your heart for the Lord? Beware if your hunger and thirst for Him diminishes. Ask and receive. Come to the living waters. Grow in hunger and thirst. The more you know Him and love Him, the more you will want of Him. For He is everything! He is life! Indeed He is your very heart! Rejoice over Him!

———————————⟡———————————

Ask the Lord to give you new hunger for Himself, a fresh anointing! Drink in His love today!

# OCTOBER 26

*"Look and see if there is any pain like my pain."*
*Lamentations 1:12*

It's at that crucial point, when your pain becomes intolerable, when hopefulness surrounds you, that you can see a white speck on the horizon. It is growing bigger. It is dazzling. It breaks into the darkness around you. It is Jesus! He is walking on the water to rescue you! He walks on top of the stormy waves crashing over you. He reaches out His nail-scarred hand. He pulls you up to safety. But you can't forget how ugly the scar was and you look into His eyes. His peace floods over you as He stills the storm. In His eyes you see the depths of the pain of those scars. Marred beyond recognition. Is there any pain like His? You look again and see the heights of joy! Resurrection joy! And this is where He is taking you now—to a new morning, with fresh mercy. He who knows the depths of pain takes you to the heights of joy—in Him! Keep your eyes on Him!

---

Lay every pain and every sorrow onto His nail-scarred hands. Rise up to the new resurrection joy He has for you! Draw Jesus on the water coming to you.

# OCTOBER 27

*"Praise the Lord! For it is good to sing praises to our God; for it is pleasant and praise is becoming." Psalm 147:1*

Come sweet saint of God and praise Him! He is your promise and delight! He has **good** plans for you and not for calamity. He gives you a future and a hope! It is good to sing praises to our God! A joyful heart doeth good like medicine. Sing in the Spirit and sing in your mother tongue. Keep a song in your heart all day long. Let His peace dwell in you.

Have you noticed that when you tell someone you love them, it strengthens your love for them (and theirs for you)? It is the same with the Lord! All day long say, "I love You, Lord!" and you will begin to overflow with His love. His presence will immediately be upon you! He indwells your praises. He takes it seriously. He is totally **for** you. He loves you! Look for new ways to show Him your love. Thank Him continually for who He is and what He means to you. Keep your mind on Him and off your problems. Praise will keep the enemy away. Praise is healing and pleasant. It is becoming to you. Be dressed in it for it will give you His beauty! Let everything that has breath, praise the Lord!

---

Put on garments of praise and go on a praise fast for a week. Spend all of your free time and your quiet time praising the Lord. Seal your lips to all but His praise and see how your life changes.

# OCTOBER 28

*"See to it that no one comes short of the grace of God, that no root of bitterness springing up causes trouble, and by it many be defiled."*
*Hebrew 12:15*

Dear brothers and sisters, be sure to cling to the Lord and walk in His sweet grace. Do not fall into condemnation for God is greater and His mercy endureth forever. Be kind to the Holy Spirit. Treat Him with reverence and love! Take hold of the grace of God and don't let go. Don't fall short. Lean on Him who died for your soul. Do not fall into bitterness. Do not let it fester as an infected sore, for it will spread and grow into every area of your life. It will cause ruin and havoc to yourself and to those around you, defiling all. It will give a place to the enemy. Do not take into account a wrong suffered. Cast it to Jesus and be free. Be kind and forgiving just as the Messiah has forgiven you. If your heart is tender, use it to pour out the Messiah's love, not to be offended. Don't fall short of the grace of God.

———————————◇———————————

Pray and ask the Holy Spirit to check that there is not bitterness in your heart. If there is, forgive. Go to the person and be restored. Walk in grace.

# OCTOBER 29

*"And gathering them together, He commanded them not to leave Jerusalem, but to wait for what the Father had promised." Acts 1:4*

Dear sweet lover of God, let us be still and know that He is God. Let us keep the fiery zeal and the holiness for Him but let us also learn to wait on Him. There is a quiet trust, a knowing, a waiting, a leaning on Him which is precious to the Lord. So often, especially in the harvest, we run full of zeal to do everything. This has its place—a pouring out of our lives for Him, for them— but don't forget that He is very concerned about who we are. He wants us to be like Jesus. We need sanctification. We need to wait on Him. For we can accomplish much more by obedience than by doing. Let us use self-control from the Holy Spirit to be like Jesus and speak and do only what the Father tells us.

How quick we are to lay hands on people to receive the Holy Spirit. They must receive Him, it's true, but how much more fullness if we wait in one accord, devoted to prayer. How powerful our message if we wait and obey and if we walk in the overflow of His Spirit. Dear one, wait for what the Father has promised. Be devoted to prayer.

---◇---

Ask the Lord to give you stillness and depth in Him. Wait and be filled up to the overflow. Obey Him.

# OCTOBER 30

*". . . and after the fire a sound of a gentle blowing." 1 Kings 19:12*

After the Lord has done great and mighty things, after the attack of the evil one, comes a gentle blowing, a small still voice. It is the voice of the Lord! Yes, He is in the loud rejoicing and triumphant praise! He has made the mighty thunder and the vastness of the universe is His handiwork! He is in the roaring waves of the ocean, in the sounding of ten million trumpets and praises of angels! But He is also in the small, still voice that comes to you so intimately and tenderly. Wait for His voice in silence and you will find that He will speak to you a thousand times more than in the loud tambourine!

Maybe you feel that your voice to Him at times is still and quiet and very small. Well, the smoldering wick He will not put out, the battered reed He will not break off. He can make the smoldering wick into a blazing bon fire. He listens for your small voice amidst billions. Your voice brings Him great joy!

---◇---

Find a candle and let it burn down to a smoldering wick. Be still and know that He is God. He is pleased with your sweet voice to Him.

# OCTOBER 31

*"And they will be as mighty men, treading down the enemy in the mire of the streets in battle; and they will fight for the Lord will be with them."*
*Zechariah 10:4*

Oh soldier of God, you are on the winning side! Onward soldier of the Lord! Put on the belt of truth, the breastplate of righteousness, the shoes of the gospel of peace. Take up the shield of faith. Put on the helmet of salvation and take up the sword of the Spirit. Stand firm! Take the authority that is yours in the name of Jesus. Pray and cast out every demon of hell from high places. The blood of Jesus is against satan. He is a defeated foe. He has no authority. ***Jesus has all authority***. He is exalted above all, in the highest place! He is the truth. He is righteousness. He is the gospel of peace. He is faith. He is salvation. He is the spirit. Lift Him up above all! Claim every soul for the kingdom of heaven. You will be mighty unto the Lord in boldness, in holiness, just as little David was against the giant. You and your friends who love Jesus, will tread down the enemy. The Lord will be with you. Pray on your faces. Take hold of all He gives you. Don't let go. You will win for the Lord is with you!

———————————————◇———————————————

Pray and do spiritual warfare against the enemy. Put on the armor of God. Set the captives free. Snatch them out of the fire in the mighty name of Jesus.

# NOVEMBER 1

*"Thou hast crowned him with glory and honor."*
*Hebrews 2:7*

We are not to give glory to one another. We are not to take God's glory for He will not share it. Glory alone belongs to God. Moses wanted to see His glory but he could only see it after it passed by. His is the kingdom and the power and the glory. It belongs to God alone. Even Jesus did not take it until it was given to Him, but humbled Himself to death. He never spoke of Himself directly but said, "The Son of Man," identifying with us. Glory to God in the highest! The whole earth is full of His glory. The glory of the Lord shone around the shepherds. Here is the divine mystery—even though we cannot take it because we would tarnish it, He wants to give it to us! Jesus' last prayer was—"And the glory which Thou hast given Me, I have given to them, that they may be one as we are." He ***crowns*** us with glory and honor which we don't deserve. He wants to give **_all_** He has to us! How deep is His love! Beyond description. Gently receive His glory to be one with one another. Give Him honor. Love with His heart.

---◇---

Empty yourself of self and let the Lord fill you up to the overflow. Live for **Him**! Give Him glory and honor.

# NOVEMBER 2

*"It is good to give thanks to the Lord, and to sing praises to Thy name, O Most High; to declare Thy lovingkindness in the morning, and Thy faithfulness by night." Psalm 92:1-2*

Oh sweet believer in Jesus, it is so good, so very good to give thanks to the Lord! We must enter into His gates with thanksgiving and His courts with praise. The first step into the outer gates of His presence is a thankful heart to Him who gives us all. It is impossible to walk in the Spirit without a thankful heart. Be filled with the Spirit, speaking to one another in psalms and hymns and spiritual songs, singing and making melody with your heart to the Lord, always giving thanks for all things.

Do you lack confidence or feel unworthy? Give thanks! Do you struggle with pride? Give thanks to the Lord! Giving thanks will bring you to humility before Him and strengthen your confidence in Him. It will strengthen your love for Him and others around you. It will give you are merry heart, as medicine. For He indeed is our Most High God, our loving Father, worthy of all of our love and praises and honor forever. Declare His lovingkindness each morning and His faithfulness every night. Bless the Lord by giving Him thanks all the time.

———————————◇———————————

Pray and commit yourself to developing a life of thanksgiving to the Lord. You will live above your circumstances honoring Him!

# NOVEMBER 3

*"And the government will rest on His shoulders."*
*Isaiah 9:6*

What shall we say as nations rise against nations? When there is toil and tribulation? When we are hated by all because of the gospel? When we are brought before kings?

Oh brother, oh sister—whatever nation you are in, whatever nation you are praying for, do not be dismayed. Do not be weary in well doing for in due season you shall reap a harvest. It will not tarry. It will come. The blood of the martyrs strengthens and multiples those who follow Jesus. Pray for revival! Pray for your country or city to be brought under the Lordship of Jesus. Pray! The government does not belong to the politicians. It does not belong even to the people. It belongs to the Lord. He will carry all nations on His shoulders. In fact, He has already paid for them. He already carried them on His shoulders when He carried the cross. His precious blood was already poured out for every nation, every government. He carried their griefs and sorrows. He bore their iniquities. Jesus, the Prince of Peace has broken down every wall so that all may enter into the holy of holies!

---

Pray for your own government today and one other. Intercede against the sins of these nations. Read Isaiah 53 over each nation.

# NOVEMBER 4

*"And day by day, continuing with one mind in the temple, and breaking bread from house to house, they were taking their meals together with gladness and sincerity of heart, praising God, and having favor with all people. And the Lord was adding to their number day by day those who were being saved." Acts 2:46-47*

Do you want to please the Lord? Do you want to love Him more? Do you want to see revival? Then you must consecrate yourself upon His altar. Let Him burn out everything wrong and purify your heart, mind and soul. Then go to your brother. Get oneness of heart with your brothers and sisters. Be open and honest together before God. Hear Him and not man. Confess your sins together and be healed. Love the Lord with all that is in you and love your brothers and sisters with His supernatural love. Be in unity and see Him command a blessing over you. Keep a continual worship in your heart. Reach out together. Go from house to house. Do good to your neighbor. Show the love of the Messiah. Lead them to the Savior. See the Lord add to your numbers when you have pure and simple devotion to Him and each other with no backbiting or competition. Glorify the Lord of your heart!

---

Get with a friend or group and ask the Lord for the gifts of repentance, unity and love. Reach out together.

# NOVEMBER 5

*"Through Him, then, let us continually offer up a sacrifice of praise to God, that is the fruit of lips that give thanks to His name."*
*Hebrews 13:15*

Through Jesus we can offer up a continual praise. Let your first thoughts in the morning be a worship to Him. Give Him the first fruits of the day. Let His Spirit fill you fresh and new. Don't eat yesterday's manna. Be filled today with the new wine of His love. Do not be in a religious routine, but greet the Lord with a heart of love—as a person. It is a relationship. Meet Him in a new way. Show Him your love in a creative way. Praise and adore Him for He is more than worthy of your praise. Let there be a continual flow of His Spirit in your heart. Concentrate on Jesus. Give Him thanks all day long in every situation. If you are in a wilderness or a dark night, offer praises to Him for He is still worthy. That is real worship — when it is a sacrifice. Abraham offered up Isaac on the altar. It was a worship. When your heart is breaking, still worship Jesus. The Lord will form you into His own image. If someone praises you, offer it as an evening sacrifice of praise for all good gifts come from Him, the Father of Lights. Praise His holy name.

---

Make some kind of altar in which to offer up sacrifices of praises. Consecrate it to the Lord.

# NOVEMBER 6

*"Faithful are the wounds of a friend, but deceitful are the kisses of an enemy."*
*Proverbs 27:6*

Dear saint of God, this verse is crucifixion to bear. A parent who loves his child will discipline the child. The Lord, our loving Father and Good Shepherd, kindly disciplines us to keep us from further pain and even destruction. We can accept His discipline because we taste of His eternal love—but what about our relationships? In our oneness with each other in Jesus can we trust enough to be vulnerable?

Do you have a friend that you not only pray with but repent with, openly? Are you willing to let that friend faithfully wound you out of his or her love for you? And will you also go to that friend to wound in love and not deceive as an enemy? Will you both walk in light and truth? If you will do this, without taking into account a wrong suffered, forgiving and loving one another, the glory of the Messiah will dwell in your midst and you will be an answer to Jesus' prayer in John 17 for oneness. Bless one another in the truth and love of God.

———————————◇———————————

Ask the Lord to give you a true prayer partner with whom you can share your heart.

# NOVEMBER 7

*"But the Lord is in His holy temple; let all the earth keep silent before Him." Habakkuk 2:20*

In His holy and glorious presence, all flesh must keep silent. Let the holy hush of His Spirit fall upon you. Tremble in the fear of the Lord, for even angels cover their faces in His presence. He is awesome and powerful, full of splendor and glory! Dear saint of God, fall on your face before Him. Wait in the silence of His presence. Enjoy Him! Rest in Him! Dwell with Him in the holy of holies! For the veil has been taken away and you may enter in boldly by the blood of Jesus. Listen to Him. Let Him speak to you. Rest in His love! Wait on the Lord. Do not be in a hurry. Do not speak. Adore Him in all His splendor and holiness! Worship Him! Receive Him. Listen to His voice. Let the King desire your beauty and make you all glorious within. You were made to worship Him. He will show His deep, endless love to you. Be still and know Him. Love Him! Let His blessing flow all through you.

---◇---

Ask the Lord to help you learn to practice His presence and be still before Him as often as possible all day long.

# NOVEMBER 8

*"Enter into the joy of your master."*
*Matthew 25:21*

Dear precious one, beloved of God. Do not grow weary in well doing, for in due season you shall reap a harvest! Have you been faithful with what God has given you? Then He will trust you for bigger things. Come, you who are blessed of the Father, inherit the kingdom prepared for you. Have you been feeding the hungry with the word of God, the Bread of heaven? And with physical food too? Have you given water to the thirsty? Have you clothed the naked, visited those in prison, visited the sick? When you did it to them, you did it to Jesus! It was not just *for* Him, but *to* Him—because His love is ever upon the suffering. Whatever you have given, it's been unto Him. How pleased He is with you! Yes, it's an honor to do it unto Him—still He's so pleased. Enter in! Enter! Take hold of the joy of your master! You did it to Him! You brought Him joy!

---

Thank the Lord that the smallest act of kindness blesses Him so much! Now go to the widows, to the orphans, to the poor and to the sick! Do it unto Jesus!

*"Beloved, let us love one another, for love is from God." 1 John 4:7*

Oh that the believers in the Messiah would glorify the Lord by becoming one, perfected in unity. How often we let the flesh take over and in our selfishness end up with disputes and divisions. Not only does it give the wrong message to the world, it tears His holy body apart. We are His body. When we refuse to love and forgive, we nail Jesus to the cross over and over again. How much we grieve the sweet Holy Spirit. How we bring pain to Him, to others and to ourselves. Needless pain.

Oh, Lord help us. Have mercy on us! Change our hearts. Work on our relationships. Let us be known for our love for one another. Let our love cover our sins. Let us lay down our lives for one another. Husbands, love your wives. Parents, love your children. Friends, love one another, for love is from God and God *is* love! He *is* love! Do you want to be like Jesus? Then love one another.

———————————◇———————————

Ask the Lord to show you any relationship that's not right. Make it right. Be at peace with all, as much as you can.

# NOVEMBER 10

*"So we who are many are one body in Messiah."*
*Romans 12:5*

How beautiful is the body of the Messiah! For He has designed each one to be unique unto Himself! No one can ever take your place in the heart of God. He purposely made it that way. There's no need for competition or jealousy. You are forever special to the Lord. There is not a high and a low place, but a special place. Only you can fill that one spot. Only you can minister to the Lord and bless Him in that precious way!

Open your eyes and see the beauty of the body of the Messiah. Each one is a facet in the sparkling diamond. He made one to bless Him in giving, another in sacrifices, another in rejoicing, another for depth and stillness, another for boldness, another for gentleness.

And together we (multitudes of us) make up His counterpart—His bride. Let us see Jesus in each other. Let us truly love one another and bring glory and honor to Him. You are His and you are so beautiful!

Make a list today of the beauty He has given you and thank Him. Make another list of His beauty in others who love Him. Thank Him! Thank them!

# NOVEMBER 11

*"Lazarus, come forth." John 11:43*

When the midnight hour has come to test your faith, when all is dark and dead, when you have cried out to God over and over with seemingly no answer—wait. After crucifixion comes life, after sorrow comes joy! Only *He* can bring life. Only He can turn mourning into dancing. Rejoice for your resurrection is near! You are ever on His heart! Have you come to some devastating circumstances? Have you suffered unjustly? Then trust in your Lord, your Creator. Trust in Him, lean on Him, without understanding. Have you carried your Isaac to the altar? Is it too painful for words?

Wait, trust, rejoice! Your faithful Lord, who bore your sins in agony before you ever even looked His way, will come to you. The greater your pain, the greater will be your joy! Be brave. Suffer as He did. His light will suddenly burst in. His nail-scarred hand will lift you to the heights. You will again walk in grace and glory with your precious Lord! Come forth! He will carry you! Come forth!

---◇---

Spend some time today rejoicing in the Lord of glory—in His great resurrection power!

# NOVEMBER 12

*". . . because of the tender mercy of our God, with which the Sunrise from on high shall visit us."*
*Luke 1:78*

Yes, the Sunrise from on high, the High and Holy Son of God came to us. He indeed visited us, because of the tender mercy of our God. He Himself is the Sonrise, the Resurrection, the truth, the Life. He is our very breath. He is our praise and our delight. He is our all in all. Jesus is the Light of the world! Oh, look into the light. Look at the Son. The brightness of His countenance will purify you in an instant. Behold Him in all His beauty and glory. Let Him change you.

As you look, you will see the rays of light cast down to earth. Keep looking at the light. Follow the ray of light to your brother or sister. See them in His light. See Jesus in them. They too are beautiful because of Him. And you, yourself are beautiful when seen in His light. Don't look away and lose your first love. Don't look at your brother and judge. Look at the Son and see your brother in the sonshine. Live in the light.

———————————◇———————————

Make a picture of the Sun with great rays to remind you to behold Jesus and to see Jesus in your believing friends.

# NOVEMBER 13

*"Let not many of you become teachers, my brethren, knowing that as such we shall incur a stricter judgment." James 3:1*

Has He called you to teach, to disciple, to preach? Then you must do it. Step out in boldness and do it. Do not shrink back from your calling. But first you must count the cost. You must walk in the fear of the Lord and wait on the Holy Spirit each time you teach. Learn to give out from the overflow of His Spirit. Always give fresh, new manna. If you love Him, feed the flock. Go into the world and make disciples. Teach what you have experienced. Let His anointing rest upon you. Love those you care for with the very love of Jesus. Pour out your life. Always do right and walk in His integrity and always do it unto the Lord. Keep short accounts with people. Be open and honest. Be an example of purity before them. Do not let the sun go down on your anger. Keep a humble heart. Wash their feet. Love the Lord together with them and always lead them to love Him more.

———————————◇———————————

Ask the Lord Himself to teach you how to lead and disciple people to love Him, to share the gospel, to grow and multiply.

# NOVEMBER 14

*"But who do you say that I AM?"*
*Matthew 16:15*

Who do men say that the Messiah is? Some say He was a good Teacher. Some say He was a Prophet. Some say He was the Son of God. But who do **you** say that He is? Who is He to you? Do you know Him? Have you come to Him and been radically changed by Him? Who do **you** say that He is? Has He become your life? Do you know that He is alive?

Jesus said, "Who do you say that I AM?" He is indeed the Great I AM—God Almighty. But only the Father can reveal that to your heart—deep in your heart. It doesn't come to you by human means. You and every person on earth must have a heart and soul revelation from the Father that Jesus is God. Upon this revelation He builds His congregation, His people. Each person must come face to face with the living Son of God—that is God in the flesh. He came and dwelt among us. He died for our sins and rose again. It was God who gave His life for you. Are you His? Is He yours? Who do you say that He is!

———————————————◇———————————————

Pray and ask the Lord to show you someone you can share this truth with. Pray to be a worker in building His Kingdom.

# NOVEMBER 15

*"For He has made an everlasting covenant with me, ordered in all things and secured; for all my salvation and all my desire. Will He not indeed make it grow?" 2 Samuel 23:5*

God is faithful and full of lovingkindness. He is good. His mercy endures forever and is new each morning. He is our new song, our glory, our love. He has made a blood covenant through Jesus, the Messiah, His Son. This covenant is closer than any relative. He is your most intimate and deep relative. His covenant is forever. He has ordained all things for you through this covenant. He has secured all for you and He even lives in you by His Holy Spirit. He has ordered and secured all of your salvation for He is the way. He walks it with you. He is the Author and Perfecter of your faith. He has also ordered all of your desire. You have a new heart full of His desire. Your desire is for Him and His will, His kingdom. Jesus is committed to you. He carries out His will for you. He believes the best in you. It is a love relationship and He will indeed make it grow. Respond to His love today. Keep Him close in your heart and mind. Love Him.

---

Make a list of the ways you've grown lately and thank the Lord!

# NOVEMBER 16

*"... when Jesus saw His mother and the disciple whom He loved ...." John 19:26*

Dear sweet brothers and sisters, did you know that you can be "the one whom He loves"—I mean, whom He really loves? John was Jesus' best friend. He is the "beloved disciple." He drew the closest to Jesus, of all the disciples. Mary Magdeline drew near, not caring about man's reproach. His own mother, Mary, drew near until it was as if a sword pierced her own heart. These three had one thing in common—they loved Jesus in intimacy. It was not that Jesus had favorites which would cause jealousies and competitions. It was that they dared to draw as near as possible to Him. They stood by Him on the cross when others fled. They did not consider their own life too dear, but stood by to comfort Him in His suffering. In the middle of His agony, He blessed them from the cross. No greater love has any man than He lay down His life for His friends. What freedom He gives us as He says, "Come! Let the one who is thirsty come and take the water of life without cost." Oh let us draw close to His heart. Let us be completely His. Your intimacy with Him is in your desire. He longs for it with each one. Draw near.

———————————◇———————————

Look into the blessed eyes of Jesus. Worship Him. Draw near. Stay in His everlasting arms. Love Him!

# NOVEMBER 17

*"... always carrying about in the body the dying of Jesus, that the life of Jesus also may be manifested in our body." 2 Corinthians 4:10*

Therefore, we do not lose heart, but though our outer man is decaying, yet our inner man is being renewed day by day. I am crucified with the Messiah, nevertheless I live, yet not I, but the Messiah liveth in me. It is indeed a divine mystery. We die, yet we live. The flesh and its deeds are dying, being crucified and our spirit is living the very resurrected life of Jesus. Our own selfish desires are dying. We are being stripped of our wrong motives and wrong securities, so that we may present to Him a pure heart. At the same time, we are being filled up to the fullness of God. The Holy Spirit is flowing out of us as a river of life to those around us.

Bless the Lord for His sweet faithfulness to conform us to His image. Let us become less and Him become more. They asked John the Baptist (Immerser), "Are you the Messiah?" He was mistaken for Jesus. Let us be so like Him that people will see Him and glorify Him in our presence. Submit to His dealings. Be filled with Jesus.

---

Make a fresh surrender to the Lord today. Let Him have His way in your life, in every circumstance. Trust Him. The Lord is good!

# NOVEMBER 18

*"Surely our griefs He Himself bore, and our sorrows He carried." Isaiah 53:4*

Dear precious one of God, have you been wounded, forsaken, trodden down? Have you felt the heartbreak of losses? Let Jesus be the lifter of your head today. He is your Healer and your faithful burden bearer. Underneath are His everlasting arms. He suffered the loss of all things for you in His death. The nails were in His blessed hands and feet for six hours—for you. The crown of thorns was jammed onto His head—for you. He knows your suffering. He knows you to the core. He is your comforter. Cast your sorrows upon Him. Give Him each tear drop. He bore it for you. He carried it. He still carries it. He intercedes for you. His holy blood cleanses you. After sorrow comes joy! Joy unspeakable. This trial is not worthy to be compared with the glory we will have with Him there. Throw your sorrows onto Jesus. Take His hand. Let Him lift you up and give you His peace.

---

Make a cross. Nail onto it your sins, your sicknesses, your sorrows, and rejections.

# NOVEMBER 19

*"I am crucified with the Messiah, nevertheless I live, yet not I but the Messiah liveth in me."*
**Galatians 2:20**

What does it mean to be crucified with the Messiah? Is it dying to the world and being devoted to Him? Yes, that is the first step. That is the outer crucifixion. What does it mean in depth? It means taking up your cross daily and following Jesus. His call is to enter into the fellowship of sufferings and being conformed to His death. Have you been hurt because of your faith? So was He. Have you been challenged and mocked? So was He. Have you been betrayed by a friend? So was He. But you have not suffered to the point of bloodshed. You will not suffer separation from the Father. In the measure that you share His sufferings, you will indeed know the power of His rising. You must drink the cup of His suffering in order to reign with Him. Some do not want this intimacy with our precious Lord, but you do. You will be more sensitive because He is sensitive. You will hate sin and love holiness as He does. You will feel God's heartbreak over the world's rebellion to Him. You will feel the depth of His love (as He laid down His life). His persecutions will come to you. His Spirit will flow through you and His heart will be your heart.

---

Write on a piece of paper all the ways that you identify with the Messiah and His sufferings. Add verses of encouragement and put it on the wall.

# NOVEMBER 20

*"Glory in His holy name."* **1 Chronicles 16:10**

Holy, Holy, Holy, is the Lord! Holy is His name forever. Let us glory in His holy name. Let us lift up His name in honor and He will draw all men unto Himself. Just mention of His holiness, just a simple song worshipping His holiness brings His holy presence! He comes so gently and in quietness but also in majesty and power. How beautiful is His holy presence. How He waits for you to invoke it. He longs to pour Himself upon you—His bride!

Dear beloved child of God, let it be your chief desire to walk in His holiness and bring His holy presence everywhere you go and in all you do and say.

And when you gather in His holy, holy, name—wait on Him—desire Him! He will come to you with His precious holy presence. Glory in His holy name, now and always.

Take time to be with Him. Fall on your face and wait. Let Him fill you full. Glory in His holy name.

# NOVEMBER 21

*"Greet one another with a holy kiss."*
*Romans 16:16*

What a glorious blessing when we see Jesus, the Son of God, in each other! As we walk in the fear of the Lord we truly do greet one another with a holy kiss. Sometimes it is His love shining in each other's eyes, sometimes it is in worshipping or praying together. Sometimes it is in reaching out to each other or in loving someone who is an outcast or unlovely. Sometimes it is in humbling ourselves before each other. But the holy kiss is always there if we are filled with His Holy Spirit. The holy kiss is there.

Psalm 2 says, "Kiss the Son." Song of Solomon 1:2 says, "May he kiss me with the kisses of his mouth." His loving-kindness is better than life. "Kiss" means "worship" (an upward kiss to God). He is our Beloved, our Blessed Bridegroom in heaven! He longs for our kisses, our worship! Is your heart full of Jesus? Is it overflowing in adoration? It can be. In an instant, with just one look into His sweet, holy eyes of love. Stay in the holy of holies with Him. Kiss the Son of God with a holy, holy kiss.

---

Worship the Lord and pray in the Spirit. Be filled with the wine of His love. Give Him a holy kiss.

# NOVEMBER 22

*"... the bridegroom came and those who were ready went in with him to the wedding feast; and the door was shut." Matthew 25:10*

Dear precious ones who love God, be ready for the Masters' call. For He will come at midnight or when you least expect it. Behold the Judge is right at the door. In these dark days when morality is increasingly perverted and the door to evil opens more and more, be ready, be on the alert. Pray and stay alert. Be faithful and sensible for He is near, right at the door. Don't be without understanding. Stay close to the heart of God. Let His heartbeat be your heartbeat. Do not be distant in your relationship with Him. Do not stay at one plateau for you will surely sink down. Do not be satisfied but seek the Lord always. Hunger and thirst for Him. Let Him anoint you with fresh oil. Don't live on yesterday's manna. Hear His voice today. Be filled with the precious oil of His Spirit. Don't quench His Spirit but walk in the overflow, in the intimacy. Let your lamp be full of His word and His Spirit at all times, for He is coming soon and the door will be shut.

———————————◇———————————

Carry a little flashlight around with you all day to remind yourself to stay filled with the Spirit of God. Be ready for His return.

# NOVEMBER 23

*"My soul clings to Thee." Psalm 63:8*

Dear lover of God, are you clinging to Him today? Are we not like the Israelites who clung to the Lord when life was difficult and did not cling so much when they were blessed? Maybe we don't let go of Him or forget Him, but we coast—and we hurt Him. In our hearts we love Him but are we diligently seeking Him? Are we entering into the closeness that He longs for? Are we held in His arms? Clinging to Him? Are we loving Him and pursuing Him with all of our heart, mind and strength?

Keep going dear saint of God. Do not grow weary or lax. Keep your heart full of thankfulness and praise so you can enter into the holy place. For He has anointed you above your companions. He longs for you to have sweet communion with Him—that you may know the length and width and depth of His love, being filled up to His fullness. He loves to show you His kind love and mercy and grace. Enter into oneness with Him. Dwell there in His love. He is your love, your life. Adore Him.

———————————————◇———————————————

Meditate today on what it means to cling to your sweet Lord and to dwell in that holy place with Him. Let His light and love warm your heart today.

# NOVEMBER 24

*"Pray for the peace of Jerusalem. May they prosper who love you." Psalm 122:6*

Could it be that the Lord has set a precedence with His holy people (Jew and Gentile in love with Jesus, "Yeshua," the Messiah)? The Lord told Abraham, "those who bless you will be blessed and those who curse you will be cursed." The Lord, through the Apostle Paul said, "I am not ashamed of the gospel. It is the power of salvation to all those who believe, to the Jew first and then to the Gentile." Jesus said He was sent to the "Lost Sheep of Israel" first. Why? Does God have favorites? No. The Jews are chosen to be His instruments in reaching the nations— to bless the world—to reach out. And what about Jerusalem? We are to pray for her peace—peace within her walls and prosperity in her palaces, for the sake of the house of the Lord. There in the Holy City, the King of Glory died and rose again! Maybe in the peace of Jerusalem, the nations will also have peace (Shalom)—the blessing will multiply!

---◇---

Pray today for Jerusalem and Israel, the Prime Minister, the Rabbis. Pray for her with all your heart.

# NOVEMBER 25

*"But thanks be to God for His indescribable gift." 2 Corinthians 9:15*

Oh dear loved one of God, put on a thankful heart today. Let your whole being overflow with gratitude. In this you will find joy. Keep yourself in the love of God. Keep your eyes on Jesus. Jesus! Precious, unspeakable gift of God! How can we ever fathom the very depth of His love for us? ***Thanks be to God!*** Give Him thanks today! Pour out your heart in thanksgiving to Him this day for His indescribable gift of Jesus! Sing unto Him! Dance unto Him! Rejoice in Him with gladness! Let your every breath praise the Lord! Do you know that the surpassing grace of God is in you? He reveals His gift of Jesus and His glory through you! Will you too be a gift of glory for the Lord? Will you let His light and life and love shine through you? Let this surpassing grace come forth and bear fruit. The unspeakable gift, the glorious treasure of God is *in* you! Shine, sweet servant of God! Glorify Him! His love and grace rest upon you! Thanks be to God for His indescribable gift—Jesus!

———————————⋄———————————

Find a new way to express your thanksgiving to the Lord for Jesus! Bless Him with all your heart today!

# NOVEMBER 26

*". . . while we look not at the things which are seen, but at the things which are not seen; for the things which are seen are temporal, but the things which are not seen are eternal."*
**2 Corinthians 4:18**

Yes, the Lord has made it so we have no excuse for not believing. All of creation reveals the glory of God. The physical, all of it on earth, is but a representation of the spiritual and the eternal. All of it. The sun and the moon and stars reveal God's faithfulness to the righteous and the unrighteous. The seed buried in the ground and later blossoming full of life reveals the crucifixion and resurrection of Jesus. The coming together in marriage reveals the oneness of the Father, Son, and Holy Spirit and the coming union of Jesus with His people. The growth of a baby into childhood, youth and adulthood reveals our spiritual growth from the time of our conversion. The physical is but a prelude to the eternal. We are just pilgrims of the Most High God passing through this land. Our home is in heaven. Let us not look at the temporal but at Him, the eternal, full of glory and light, the eternal King—Jesus!

---

Weigh all of your concerns today in the light of eternity! Keep God's prospective in your heart and heaven in your eyes!

# NOVEMBER 27

*"Lord, You know all things; You know that I love You." John 21:17*

Jesus had asked Peter three times, "Do you love Me?" It was restoration for the three times Peter had denied Him. The first two times Jesus used the word "agape" meaning unconditional, unending, godly love. Peter had answered that he loved Jesus but he answered with the word "phileo" meaning man's limited human love. The third time Jesus asked with "phileo." Peter said, "Lord, You know all things; (You know my heart) You know that I love (phileo) You." At that point Jesus said (not in words)—"I'll take it!" He received Peter's phileo love and entrusted him to feed the sheep. How gracious of our sweet Lord to take what we little humans can offer—so insufficient at times. But He only needs a mustard seed to build a big tree. The widow in 2 Kings 4 only had a jar of oil left but she obeyed the word of the Lord by faith. She offered what she had to the Lord and He multiplied it just as He multiplied the fishes and loaves. The Lord is full of compassionate understanding. He knows our frame. Give Him all, even if it's little and let Him fill up the rest to overflowing.

———————◇———————

Offer up to the Lord today an area where your faith is small. Give Him all of it and wait and pray and see Him graciously fill up what is lacking and much more. Put a drop of oil in a jar to remind you.

*"I dwell on a high and holy place, and also with the contrite and lowly of spirit." Isaiah 57:15*

Rise up, O saint of the Lord! Rise up! Go up to the high places where the air is pure and full of His glory. It is the Most High God, the Creator of the Universe who calls you. He is your dearest Friend, your Good Shepherd, your Heavenly Father. He is the most gentle and intimate One. He alone knows you in depth and understands you. He alone loves you with everlasting love.

And how can you go up higher to Him? He dwells in a holy place, with the contrite and lowly of spirit. Yes, you must bow down to go up higher. You must break and let go of self. You must be lowly and humble like Jesus, who washed His disciples' feet, who was crucified for you. A contrite (crushed) heart is pleasing to Him. It is soft and tender towards Him. He can lead and love you better. To rise up to the high and holy place with the Lord, you must bow down and love Him.

———————————◇———————————

Ask the Lord to show you areas where you need to bow to Him. Bow and adore Him. He will lift you up!

# NOVEMBER 29

*"For the redemption of his soul is costly."*
*Psalm 49:8*

Yes, beloved, the redemption of your soul is so very costly. For it cost our dear Lord untold agony, grief and death. Whoever shall save his life shall lose it, but whoever loses his life for Jesus' sake shall find it. What does it profit a man, if he gains the whole world and loses his soul? What will a man give in exchange for his soul? Some count their life as valuable as a bottle of liquor. Some sell their soul for material wealth. Some for power or fame.

To follow Jesus will cost you everything. Are **you** willing to lose **all**, that you might really **know** Him? Are you ready to be persecuted by the religious? To be imprisoned for your faith? To be betrayed by your family or slandered? Jesus said that some of us will be miraculously delivered and some will be put to death, for His name's sake. He said we would be hated by all. By your **perseverance** you will win your souls. Be on guard that your heart may not be weighed down and you fall into a trap. Keep on the alert, praying at all times so that you may stand before the Son of God. Pay the cost. Abandon yourself to Jesus.

---◇---

Make a fresh surrender to the Lord. Give Him all. Be willing to do anything for Him. Breathe in the fresh aroma of His Spirit upon you today!

# NOVEMBER 30

*"Keep yourselves in the love of God, waiting anxiously for the mercy of our Lord Jesus, the Messiah to eternal life." Jude 21*

Yes, we must keep ourselves in the love of God for His lovingkindness is everlasting—it endures forever. The love of God is shed abroad in our hearts. All love is from God. Without Him there is no love and no life. His love is of eternal nature. It is not human, like ours. It is not surface, but full and rich and deep, changing all that it touches forever. A person who professes to belong to the Messiah but has not had their life changed, is not a real believer yet. The Messiah's love is the strongest power in the universe. It changes evil to good, deception to truth, death to life, punishment to grace, blemish to purity and holiness. It is the love of the Messiah that is shed abroad in our hearts. His blood shed for us demonstrates His love. No greater love has any man than he lay down his life for his friends. Daily, Jesus pours out His ocean of love. It is there always, forever. Daily, we must take it. He was crushed for our sins, a Man of sorrows. He took our pains and rejections. We are free to keep ourselves in the love of God. Jump into His sea of love!

---

Let your heart meditate on His vast and eternal love today! Take it fresh and new into your heart. Put away all else. Draw an ocean full of His love!

# DECEMBER 1

*"And while He was praying the appearance of His face became different, and His clothing became white and gleaming." Luke 9:29*

While He was praying—His holy face became different, glowing with the glory of heaven. Even His clothes were shining. The light and love of heaven and eternity went clear through His pure body and heart. His majesty and splendor were seen.

Dear sweet soldier of the Lord, as you go forth in His name, full of His Holy Spirit, let all that you say and do be hallowed by His presence in prayer. He will transfigure you as you go! You will not notice, but He will do it! You will never be the same! The people around you will never be the same! The things you do will never be the same! Even the most practical thing will be sealed by His Holy Spirit. Your face will be different. ***You will be like Jesus!*** He will continually transfigure you. Do not be overly concerned with the outer appearance, but let His radiant glow be in you! Jesus took on a human body and even though our bodies are passing away—they are changed—different—for they are the temple of the Holy Spirit.

---

Pray for His holy presence on all that you do and say. Stay in His presence on your face and worship until the glory falls. Exalt Him! Love Him!

# DECEMBER 2

*"But many who are first, will be last; and the last first." Mark 10:31*

Do you see with God's eyes? Do you see the glory of Jesus in the believers around you or are you critical, judging and prejudiced? If you are any of these negative things then you have lost your first love for Jesus. Turn your eyes back on Him. Let Him fill you again with His own love, His own ears and eyes—to see as He does. Think on that which is true, honorable, pure and worthy of praise. Begin again to thank the Lord. See His face in your brothers' and sisters' eyes. Love with His heart.

Those who are outcasts, those who are unnoticed, unrecognized and left out, those who are rejected and thrown away (including unborn babies)—they will be first in God's kingdom. Those old people who have been forgotten, those holocaust victims—they will be first. Those widows and orphans, those who suffered—they will be honored first when the records are set straight. But those who take His glory now, who love the limelight and all the attention—those who lift themselves up—they will be last. God is perfectly fair and just for all of eternity.

———————————◇———————————

Pray today and go seek an outcast person or an older, lonely person and pour out the love of the Messiah upon them! Bless God!

# DECEMBER 3

*"I will lift up my eyes to the mountains; from whence shall my help come? My help comes from the Lord, who made heaven and earth. He will not allow your foot to slip." Psalm 121:1-3*

Life is not always fair, but God is **always** fair. He is just and full of lovingkindness. The earth is full of valleys, hills, plains and mountains—and so is life. It is a series of ups and downs, crucifixtions and resurrections.

Do we always expect sunshine? If we had it we would dry up for it is more difficult to be intimate with the Lord in times of abundance than in times of great distress and trials. If we had all rain we would soon be washed out with discouragement and sorrow. But the Lord knows what we need, what we can take and how to deliver us and heal us. He knows how to order our seasons. He knows how to purify our hearts. He knows how to accomplish His purposes and make us into the likeness of Jesus! This is His will if we follow Him with all of our hearts. Are we willing to go to the mountain tops and even down into the valleys to follow the Son of God wherever He leads us? Will you trust Him today with every valley and every mountain? He will not let your foot slip!

———————————◇———————————

Draw a picture of valleys and mountains. Add on Psalm 121:1-3.

# DECEMBER 4

*"Now let me die, since I have seen your face,
that you are still alive." Genesis 46:30*

When Jacob (Israel) saw that his son Joseph was still alive he was content to die and go to heaven. His life's purpose, and even more was completed. He had obeyed God and come to the last chapter. Now Jacob could close his eyes as he surrendered his last breath.

When Simon, righteous and devout (looking for the consolation of Israel, with the Holy Spirit upon him) saw the baby Jesus (Yeshua), he took Him into his arms and blessed God saying, "Now Lord, Thou dost let Thy bondservant depart in peace, according to Thy word; for mine eyes have seen Thy salvation, which Thou hast prepared in the presence of all peoples, a light of revelation to the Gentiles and the glory of Thy people Israel."

Have your eyes seen Him? Have you seen Jesus? Have you walked with Him, obeyed Him, loved Him? Are you growing in Him still? Is He your very breath? Your life? Is He all that matters to you? Is Jesus the purpose and fulfillment of your life? Will you be content at the end of your life to say, "My eyes have seen Thy salvation, let me, Your servant depart in peace?"

---

If you are unsure of God's leading or next step for your life, seek Him in fasting and prayer so that you may fulfill all His purposes for you!

# DECEMBER 5

*"And since we have gifts that differ according to the grace given to us, let each exercise them accordingly." Romans 12:6*

God is so gracious, so just, so giving! He alone knows what is best for us and what to give us at just the right moment. He knows what to ask of us. He is always *for* us. He is always with us. God is always good.

Jesus' high priestly prayer in John 17 is the one thing that will cause us to really bring His kingdom and will on earth. He prayed that we would be one, as He and the Father and the Holy Spirit are one. Are we one? Do we love each other as He and the Father and the Spirit love each other? Are we one in our congregations?

We need to celebrate! Yes, we need to celebrate the differences and love one another without moral or spiritual compromise! Let us take the opposite spirit of the world and the flesh and the powers of darkness. Celebrate the gifts your friend has, or your brother has. Thank God that he's different from you and that you are both created uniquely to glorify God in a special way that no one else can. Do not envy. *Celebrate* the differences! It is a spiritual warfare! Celebrate!

---

Ask the Lord to help you make a list of all the qualities of a person very different from you. Now thank the Lord for each quality! Amen!

# DECEMBER 6

*"The judgments of the Lord are true; they are righteous altogether. They are more desirable than gold; yes than much fine gold; sweeter also than the honey and the drippings of the honeycomb. Moreover, by them Thy servant is warned; in keeping them there is great reward."*
*Psalm 19:9-11*

Even in His judgment, the Lord is kind and full of goodness. He judges and corrects us with the purpose of leading us into holy, loving fellowship with Himself. His desire is to spend all of eternity pouring out His lovingkindness to us—but we must be in the place where He can do it. His judgments are true and righteous. Let us desire His fatherly correction and help. Let even the trials He allows become as gold, making us pure in heart, conforming us to His image. Let His words and the prompting of His Holy Spirit be sweet like honey. Let us taste and see that the Lord is good! Let us trust Him to warn us and keep us from straying. Even good things and good people can distract us from the Lord and His purposes. Let us keep hearing, keep seeing, keep running the race with Jesus, for He is our great reward. In Him is an abundance of eternal treasure. Let His pure judgments help and guide you.

---

Ask the Lord to correct you even in small things by His Holy Spirit, that you may walk more intimately in Him—to please Him!

# DECEMBER 7

*"It is not those who are healthy who need a physician, but those who are sick; I did not come to call the righteous, but sinners." Mark 2:17*

Yes, Jesus came for the poor in spirit—those humble enough to know that they can do absolutely nothing without Him.

You cannot come to God in salvation without realizing that you have nothing to offer in that direction. Nothing. Your most holy efforts will not get you into heaven, for you are marked with sin that was inherited into the human race. Your own righteousness is stained. God is perfectly pure and holy with a blaze so bright that you would disintegrate before Him. Only the blood of Jesus will save you. Nothing else.

Isn't it the same as we walk with Him? Do we dare to look at a brother or sister with judging eyes? Do we dare to exalt ourselves above anyone else? No! Only the blood of Jesus, even now, can save you today. You are continually being saved by His blood daily. And when you are barely hanging on—that's when His amazing, abundant grace floods you entirely. It is His loving grace, His kindness of repentance that carries you. You were lost and He found you and He carries you still!

---◇---

*Get on your knees and ask the Lord to show you His amazing grace this day! It's free! Swim in it!*

# DECEMBER 8

*". . . for now I know that you fear God since you have not withheld your son, your only son from Me." Genesis 22:12*

"Now I know," says the Lord. He knows. He seeks to give us pure, holy hearts, overflowing with His own precious love. His great desire is His love in us! That we would fear Him, honor Him, bow down in our hearts to Him all day long. For He alone is worthy. He alone is worthy of all of our praise—of our lives. He who is holy and sits upon the throne loves us deeply, beyond our comprehension, with eternal love.

How do we show our love for Him? Is it not in the same as He does for us? He gave His dearest. He gave His only Son. He gave the best. He gave His heart. Who is our dearest? Who is our best? Will we give that precious one to the Lord and not withhold? Abraham gave his only son, the promised one from God, the joy of his life. He feared God. He honored the Holy One. He trusted in His love. Does God know us? Do we fear Him?

---

Today, in stillness and soberness offer to the Lord the one you love the most. Put that one into His hands as a love offering. Fear God!

# DECEMBER 9

*"... for with the Lord there is lovingkindness, and with Him is abundant redemption."* Psalm 130:7

All the purposes of God are filled with His love and redemption. He continually restores. The minute something is wrong or there is hurt or pain, His redemption processes begin. He even does more than what is needed. He turns evil to good for those who love Him. We do not consciously feel this in times of sorrow. He will do the impossible. Trust Him. He always restores to better things. We must hold onto Him. Be faithful to Him. Do not let bitterness get into your heart. Forgive and cling to Jesus, the Great Forgiver. Spend time with Him. Keep His word in your heart and act on it. Wait and you will hear Him. You will see Jesus coming to you, walking on the waves of the storms of your life. Endure until He comes. He always restores and redeems. He has purposes for you. Your life will become as pure gold through the difficult times. He is the Master goldsmith and He is making you shine from within. He is perfecting you. Jesus, your precious Redeemer is holding you. Submit to Him.

———————————◇———————————

Find something in your household (photos, etc.) that you can redeem. Keep it in a place to cherish and let it remind you that Jesus redeems you!

# DECEMBER 10

*"Trust in the Lord with all your heart and do not lean on your own understanding. In all your ways acknowledge Him and He will make your paths straight." Proverbs 3:5-6*

Oh how easy it is to trust the Lord when things are going our own way—but what about when His purposes or circumstances go in another direction? Or when heartfelt prayer goes unanswered? That is the test! What about when things seem to go the opposite of what you prayed for? Do you still trust Him? What about a sudden break in a relationship that is painful? What about a seemingly unfair situation where you are the brunt of it? What about a sudden death or suffering illness? What does your heart say to God during those times? Do you inwardly accuse Him? Do you honestly question Him? Do you ignore Him? How will you stand the test? Dear precious, beloved one! This is the best time to cast all your cares upon Him and trust Him. Trust God! Do not—do *not* lean on your own understanding. He holds you. He loves you. He sees the outcome. Trust Him— especially at those times. Acknowledge Him. Let Him direct your path. Your love for Him will grow deeper and you will be more like Jesus!

———————————◇———————————

Write your heart questions down in a time of pain. Cast them up to Him and receive greater ability to trust Him!

# DECEMBER 11

*"A joyful (merry) heart makes a cheerful face.*
*But when the heart is sad, the spirit is broken."*
*Proverbs 15:13*

Oh that precious medicine of joy! It heals the soul. Laughter is good and healthy for your soul.

Ask the Lord today for a merry and joyful heart! Let it burst out of you! Rise up in your soul and be filled with His joy—with His presence! Ask and you will receive. He loves to give you His joy! Jesus was the most joyful human being to walk this earth! He even sang with His disciples after the bread and wine, on His way to Gethsemane. He sang even though He was going to be killed soon. He endured the cross for the joy set before Him! His joy was to see the salvation of mankind! He had the anointing of joy above His companions because He walked in righteousness and hated evil. Jesus was filled with great joy! Enter into the joy of your Master! He wants His joy to be full in you! The fruit of the Holy Spirit is joy! Make His joy complete by being one with Him and other believers. The joy of the Lord is your strength.

———————————————◇———————————————

Ask for His joy! Receive it as a gift and act on it by singing or clapping or dancing or praising! Walk in it!

# DECEMBER 12

*"The Lord's lovingkindnesses indeed never cease, for His compassions never fail. They are new every morning. Great is Thy faithfulness."*
Lamentations 3:22-23

His love *never* fails. *Never*. It never ceases. It cannot, for it is filled with Him. It *is* Him—God is love. He is alive forever and His love never fails. He will never ever let you down or leave you. His resurrection spirit is in you and it is growing in bright intensity, not diminishing. Be filled today with His love and you will succeed and not fail. You will overcome in all situations. You will stand strong when persecuted. You will be like Jesus.

And His mercy is new every morning. His sweet compassions never fail. How good the Lord is to give us *new* mercies each morning. He is so tender. He is the God of new beginnings.

Take His new mercy this morning and run the race full of Him! Run as if to win! Be filled up with His love and compassion in all that you do, with everyone you meet. You are His. Pour yourself out. Give His love. Give it. Make a difference in this world today. His love never ever fails!

————————————◇————————————

Find tangible ways today to pour His love and mercy out. Pursue finding the sick, the old, the widows, orphans, prisoners.

# DECEMBER 13

*"I solemnly charge you in the presence of God . . .*
*preach the word; be ready in season and*
*out of season." 2 Timothy 4:1-2*

There will come a time very soon when people will not endure sound doctrine—they will not even want to hear, and the freedom to tell them of salvation will be taken away. Your own faith will be tested for the enemy will try to deceive even the elect. The anti-Messiah himself will come preaching something so similar, acting so holy that it might deceive many who follow God. There will be persecution all over the earth. What will you do at this time? Will you hide in fear and believe secretly? It will never work. The fear will overtake you. You must trust God to give you the anointing to overcome and persevere. How are you now? Are you bold with the message of the Messiah? If not, ask for that gift. It is His heart cry that you preach the word, the gospel—in season and out of season. That means when it is comfortable for you and hearts are open—also when it is difficult and you are mocked. When it is painful. Do it, for you are His soldier. Prove your love for Him. Preach the word in season and out of season.

---

Get into the presence of God and ask Him to open doors for you to share the gospel and preach the word. It's His will. He will do it.

# DECEMBER 14

*"But you, be sober in all things, endure hardship, do the work of an evangelist, fulfill your ministry." 2 Timothy 4:5*

But you . . . you! The Lord is saying to **you**—be sober in all things. Get wisdom and understanding daily from the Lord. Stay walking in the fear of God. Keep your heart pure and your tongue from evil. Be alert, stay in prayer. Know what the Lord is doing. Keep your eyes on Him—on Jesus. Do not waiver. Do not go to the right or left. Dwell in Jesus. He is the vine, you are the branch.

Are you surrendered to Him? Is He your Lord? Then follow Jesus! Where is He leading? To crucifixion! Follow Him. Is there pain in your life? Endure this hardship. Is it too much? Be like Jesus. By His Holy Spirit, endure it.

Do the work of an evangelist! To this you were called—to make God known. Jesus hung on the cross for this purpose—to give salvation. You are living for this—to pour out your life as He did—to make Him known. Fulfill your ministry—make Him known. It was His last command. Go! Tell them! Bring His good news of eternal life!

———————————◇———————————

Consecrate yourself to the Lord to be a witness for Him at all times. Do not shrink back. Do the work of an evangelist.

# DECEMBER 15

*"That with one accord you may with one voice*
*glorify the God and Father of our Lord."*
*Romans 15:6*

Will you accept, forgive and love one another as Jesus has done this for you? Will you lay aside your pride and understand one another for the unity of His body which He prayed for? Will you do it without compromising the truth but with love in your heart? Will you be a servant to Jesus and to each other as He was?

"That they may be as one, as We are one, that the world may know that Thou didst send Me." Will you love one another as a shining light to this world which desperately needs Jesus and is in danger of perishing? He has given you His Holy Spirit that you may glorify Him in this way! Do it! Be in one accord. Live for Jesus and for others, not for self. Lay your life down as He did. Be poured out wine on His altar and broken bread for His body.

And when you worship, join in with heaven, because your little voice among the billions of people and angels matters to Him! He listens for you. If it were only you He would be pleased. Only you can bring to His heart your love.

---

Commit yourself today to bring unity to the body of the Messiah in some way and to worship the Lord more steadfastly in all you do and say and in special times.

# DECEMBER 16

*"But God demonstrates His own love toward us, in that while we were yet sinners, the Messiah died for us." Romans 5:8*

Dear saint of God, have you ever felt that you have let God down? Did it crush you and break your heart? With all your being you only want to please Him. Take courage, cheer your heart, rise up from the ashes to His beauty. You have not disappointed Him as you think, for He is **for** you, not against you. Before you knew Him, when you openly (maybe unknowingly) rebelled against Him, He loved you so much that He died for you. He demonstrated His deep, unconditional love when you didn't even care about Him. Much more then, having now been justified by His blood. You are saved by His life given when you were His enemy. How dear and precious and priceless you are to Him now that you love Him. Take His mercy fresh and new each day. He is faithful to complete His work in making you into His image. He is so in love with you. His love never fails and yours doesn't either, only your mind needs renewing. Your spirit is in union with Him. Bless His holy name. He who is faithful calls you. Embrace Him today.

———————————◇———————————

Take time to embrace the Lord fully today. Take in His tender love. Forgive yourself as He forgives you.

# DECEMBER 17

*"I will never desert you, nor will I ever
forsake you."* Hebrews 13:5

*". . . and lo I am with you always, even to the
end of the age."* Matthew 28:20

Faithful, faithful God! Who is like Him? Who is faithful like Jesus? No one. Underlying all of His character traits, (such as holiness, love, mercy, graciousness) is His strong faithfulness. Bless You, Lord! We would all perish if it wasn't for His faithfulness. There are some who push His grace and continue sinning willfully after salvation. They walk in danger of trampling the Son of God. But for those who really love Him and serve Him with all their hearts, He is there—always, always faithful. He will never let you down, never. He is faithful to the end. He will never leave you alone. Do you feel lonely? Well, He's there with you anyway. And He will never forsake you or turn against you. Faithful, faithful God. We are not like that. If we are crossed in a sensitive area or betrayed, our flesh rises up to get revenge. Who could ever endure what Jesus went through without bitterness? In His Spirit alone, could it be done. Faithful, faithful God. Rest in the sea of His faithful love. Drink it in and you too will be faithful to Him, unto death.

---

Ask the Lord to help you to be continually faithful in small things so that your life will glorify Jesus in being faithful in the fiery trials.

# DECEMBER 18

*"Follow Me, and I will make you fishers of men." Matthew 4:19*

Do you want to have God's heart? Then follow Jesus! Do you want to see God worshiped and adored in heaven and on earth? Follow Jesus! Do you want to be a fisher of men, like Him? Follow Jesus! Follow Jesus and *He* will make you a fisher of men. He doesn't say, "Only evangelists follow Me." He doesn't say "Get trained and follow Me." He doesn't say, "Some of you follow Me if you want to." He says, "FOLLOW ME!" All of you. *He* will teach you. *He* will take away your fears. *He* will use you. *He* will do it. He longs for someone to have *His* heart to reach the lost. What were His thoughts as He was crucifiied? To save the lost. Billions do not know the Messiah today. One can reach 100's or 1,000's if they have *His heart*. Follow Jesus! Let Him teach you and use you. Do not be apathetic. Reach out! Your life will influence for heaven. Follow Jesus, the great Fisher of souls! Follow Jesus!

---◇---

Consecrate yourself to reach out in some way (verbally, written, or in action) every day, for Jesus. Make Him known and loved!

# DECEMBER 19

*"For of His fulness we have all received, and grace upon grace." John 1:16*

Oh, the sweet lovingkindness of Jesus! We behold His glory, full of grace and truth! Jesus is full of truth. He knows you. He knows your weaknesses, your sadnesses, your failures, your sins. He knows the absolute truth about you. Long before you looked His way, He loved you with the heart of His Father, with an everlasting, unfailing love—God's love! He knew the truth then and He knows it now. His love is sacrificial and holy.

Jesus is full of grace. By grace you are saved and grace alone, so that no man may boast. It is the pure work of God alone. His grace is sufficient. He gives grace and glory. He does not give us what we deserve. He gives us grace. He pours out His love, His kindness, His favor—unconditionally. You are free of the sin which entangles you! You are free to be filled with His glory! Be free in His grace! Receive His fullness today! It is free! It is for you now! Receive grace upon grace!

———————————◇———————————

Find a way to share the grace of God with someone today. Give them your unconditional love, the love of the Messiah today!

# DECEMBER 20

*"Behold, the nations are like a drop from a bucket." Isaiah 40:15*

Even the nations themselves are but a drop in the bucket for the Lord! Nothing is impossible with God! Absolutely nothing! Are you facing a difficult, impossible situation? Cast it upon the Lord for He is a God of the impossible. Step out in faith and trust Him for a miracle—His way, in His timing. Do not give up—the nations are a drop in the bucket. Lift up your heads, O ye gates, that the King of glory may come in! Oh kings of the earth, be warned! Oh leaders, be discerning! Worship the Lord with awe and reverence. Rejoice with trembling. Do homage to the Son! Kiss (worship) the Son of God, lest He become angry and you perish in the way. How blessed are those who take refuge in the Lord! The nations are only a drop! He is the Almighty God, Creator of the universe! He is full of tender mercy and love for you! Nothing is impossible! Trust Him! Lean on Him! He is worthy! He is powerful! He is Lord!

---◇---

Put the most impossible prayer request into His hands. Do not take it back. Begin to thank Him for the answer! Now pray for a particular nation.

# DECEMBER 21

*"Let every valley be lifted up, and every mountain and hill be made low." Isaiah 40:4*

Your King, Jesus (Yeshua), comes to you, humble and endowed with salvation. Shout in triumph! Rejoice greatly! A voice is calling, "Clear the way for the Lord in the wilderness; make smooth in the desert a highway for our God. Behold, the Lamb of God who takes away the sin of the world." He scatters those who are proud in heart. He brings down rulers from their thrones. He exalts the humble. Let every valley be lifted up. Let the humble and broken and poor in spirit come and seek His face. He will lift them up. Let the prideful and the arrogant be made low. He cuts down and He lifts up. He judges with perfect mercy. He has regard for those who fear and reverence Him. He fills the hungry soul and sends the rich away empty. He remembers you in His rich mercy. The Mighty One will do great things for you. Humble yourself in the sight of the Lord and He will lift you up high, unto Himself. Bow to Him and you will walk on the heights with Him. Make your path straight to the Lord.

---

Thank the Lord for any humbling circumstances in your life, for He will lift you up to Himself.

# DECEMBER 22

*"Glory to God in the highest, and on earth, peace among men with whom He is pleased." Luke 2:14*

Glory, glory, glory to God! Glory to God in the highest! Give Him glory today! Honor Him. Worship and adore Him! Go into the holy of holies and look at His beautiful face. He is the highest! Bow down and adore Him. Let your mouth and your heart be full of love for Him! When He is glorified in the highest, peace will come among men and good will on earth.

Imagine if you were on the hill with the poor and simple shepherds. *They* heard the angels, not the ones who studied the law in the temple. They had pure and simple, childlike hearts, able to humbly receive.

Do you desire pure and simple devotion to Jesus? Open your heart daily and walk with Him in the light. Rid yourself of busyness and distractions. Make a place for Him. Then you will hear Him speak to you. Your heart will thrill and rejoice as the angels did. Glory to God in the highest for sending His holy Son Jesus to us!

---

Be still before the Lord! Hear Him! Now rejoice before Him! Glory! Glory! Glory! Glory to God in the highest!

# DECEMBER 23

*"Behold, the bondslave of the Lord; be it done to me according to your word." Luke 1:38*

Dear beloved one, can you say these words as Mary did? She was about to deliver God's Son, the Savior who would also deliver her from her own sins. She was highly favored of God, the most blessed woman to live. But she had a price to pay. The moment she said, "Let it be done according to your word," trusting the angel of God, she had to face misunderstanding and false accusation. She was a humble, plain girl, a peasant. She had to face her parents and the townspeople who might uphold the law and stone her. She had to face the possibility of losing Joseph and having a false stain upon her family's name. She was young and yet would carry the responsibility of raising God's Son. One day a sword of sorrow would pierce her heart as she saw her Son, her Savior hanging on the cross. But Mary believed God. She loved God. She went forth in His will, not her own, risking all. She stood for Him and He stood for her. She became the one in whom all generations call "blessed." Amen!

---

Take a step in prayer today and determine to stand for the Lord and His purposes. Count the cost and be "blessed."

# DECEMBER 24

*"My soul exalts the Lord, and my spirit has rejoiced in God my Savior."* Luke 1:46-47

Rise up my soul, rise up! Rise up to the call of the Lord, your Most High God! Give Him honor and glory and praise this day for He has done great things for you! Exalt the Lord! Exalt His holy and beautiful name! You were made to praise Him. Only you can praise Him in your own way, no one else can. He waits for you. He listens for your sweet voice. You are His song of joy! You bring Him joy! Exalt Him! Lift Him up and He will draw all people unto Himself. Rejoice in Him today! Find a way to thank Him in everything! Cast every care and sorrow upon Him. He cares for you. Receive His love fully today! Let it lift you up to His throne of grace and glory! He has regard for you, His humble servant. His eyes are continually upon you—always—forever. Rise up to Him today. Love Him back. Worship and adore Him with all your heart for He is pleased with you!

———————————————◇———————————————

Find a new place, outside or inside and dance unto the Lord! Fill His heart with your love this Christmas Eve!

# DECEMBER 25

*"For today in the city of David there has been born for you a Savior who is the Messiah, the Lord." Luke 2:11*

Today is the day of your salvation. If you hear His voice do not harden your heart. Today is the day of salvation. This is the day that the Lord has made, let us rejoice and be glad in it. Today, a Savior has been born for you. For *you!* Who is this Savior? He is the Messiah, the Lord. He is God Himself in a human body. It was *God* who laid in that manger for you. *He* is your incomprehensible, unfathomable, unspeakable gift this Christmas. He gave Himself. He humbled Himself. He sweat great drops of blood for you. He let His hands and feet be pierced for you. He suffered and died for you. *God!* In a woman's womb as a seed, in a manger, on this earth walking, talking, loving, healing, and on the cross. *God!* And then—*up*, up from the grave. *Risen* for you. *God!* God, your Savior! Born for you. Rise up today, dear beloved one. Take His sweet hand. Take the gift! Give yourself in total abandonment to the One who gave Himself for you. Love Him. Serve Him. Be His.

---

Find a place in a park or yard and make a manger. Worship the Lord there this Christmas morning! Glory to God!

# DECEMBER 26

*"For mine eyes have seen Thy salvation which Thou has prepared in the presence of all peoples." Luke 2:30*

Have your eyes seen His salvation? Have you really seen Jesus, God's holy sacrifice for you? God has given Him to you— the gift of salvation. God has given His Son to you! Have you received Him? Has He forgiven your sins? Have you received a new life from Him? Do you really know Him and walk with Him daily? Is He your very life? Then your eyes have seen His salvation! Yet it is still a precious and glorious divine mystery— that God would become a Man and give Himself, for His nature is pure and holy love. God *is* love. And what does love always do? It gives and gives and gives. It gives completely without holding back. Have you given yourself completely to Him? Are you His love offering? The Lord is a Giver of good gifts. He gave His best. He gave His all. He gave Jesus—a light of revelation to the Gentiles and a glory to Israel. My eyes have seen the salvation of God!

———————————————◇———————————————

In your heart, look upon the manger, look upon His death for you and the empty tomb. See the salvation of God!

# DECEMBER 27

*"For I am already being poured out as a drink offering."* 2 Timothy 4:6

Do you know that you were created for the Lord? He made you for Himself so that He could have a love relationship with you forever. You were made to praise and worship Him—and isn't that a chief desire and a joy to you? Times in worship are peaceful and full of the glory of your love for Him. How quickly He comes to you! His love is deep. You were made to pray and to ask for His will and His kingdom on earth—to pray for family and congregations and cities and nations! He has given you an awesome responsibility.

You were made to dwell in His word and digest it so that your life is full of Jesus—then to give it all away to others. You were made to preach the gospel and to be a blessing to everyone. You *are* a blessing if you're walking with Jesus. He has others in mind when He blesses you, for you are to give it out—to grow and multiply. Be fruitful and multiply. Let your life be poured out as a drink offering for others to know Him and love Him. Pour yourself out and you will have peace.

———————————◇———————————

Ask the Lord to give you the honor of being poured out for others in new ways.

# DECEMBER 28

*"Hallowed be Thy name." Matthew 6:9*

Do you hallow His name? Is the beautiful and powerful name of Jesus (Yeshua) so very holy to you? Does it hurt you when His name is misused or misunderstood? Is His name precious to you? Does the sound of it stir up your love for Him? Do you love to say His name and to praise Him by the names of His character?

Do you hallow His name in worship? Do you linger there, longing for more? Is it like sweet wine to your lips? Do you hallow His name in prayer? Do you love to go into your prayer closet and be with Him, the One you dearly love? Do you hallow Him so much that you spend a lot of time with Him praying His will? Do you love to bow down to Him in reverence, to fall on your face and wait on Him? Do you cut other activities out so you can be with Jesus?

Do you long for your loved ones and even for cities and nations to hallow His name?

———————————◇———————————

Meditate on His name, His person—hallow His name! Write His holy name and keep it with you all day.

# DECEMBER 29

*". . . looking for the blessed hope and the appearing of the glory of our great God and Savior, the Messiah, Jesus." Titus 2:13*

Lift up your eyes, holy saint of God! Look into His beautiful face. Be still in His presence. Look with holy eyes. Look for the blessed hope! Look for Jesus! Look! Oh please look! Forget all the things that weigh you down. Cast them away as a hindrance. Don't let them come near you. Keep your eyes on Jesus. Let your heart groan for the blessed hope of His appearance. He is great and mighty and omnipotent. He is the Lord of Lords! Almighty and holy God! He is full of never ending glory! Awesome and glorious! Who is like Him! Look, dear one! Look! Look for His glorious appearance—our great God and Savior the Messiah! Look for Him!

As you look, your heart will be purified. Let His peace fall upon you as you wait. He is your glorious Bridegroom in heaven. He longs to be united with you. Look! For in a little while He will come. He is right at the door. All eternity will open. You will be like Him! Look for the blessed hope! Look!

———————————◆———————————

Draw two big eyes and put them in the place you worship to remind you to look for the blessed hope!

# DECEMBER 30

## *"Amen. Come Lord Jesus." Revelation 22:20*

Oh, come Lord Jesus! Come! We, Your bride long for You! You alone are pure love! You alone are holy! You alone are worthy! You are beautiful and awesome above all else in the universe! You are full of splendor and majesty! We adore You!

Come, dear one who loves Jesus! Come and bow down and worship Him. Your King is coming to you. His kingdom is coming upon this weary earth. If anyone is thirsty, let him come to Jesus! He is coming quickly and His reward is with Him. You will see the Son of Man coming in a cloud with power and great glory! He is the Resurrection and the Life! Come to Jesus, all who are weary and heavy. Let the children come to Jesus, do not hinder them, for such is the kingdom of heaven. The hour is approaching. The Son of man is coming.

Oh come, Lord Jesus! We long to see You face to face. We long for Your tender embrace. We were made for You! Come, Lord Jesus! Come!

———————————◇———————————

Commit to share the gospel as a lifestyle so that people will come to Jesus—for He is coming soon!

# DECEMBER 31

## *"Worship God." Revelation 22:9*

Come dear saint of God, beloved of the Almighty, come and bow down. Come and fall on your face before His glorious presence. Wait before Him in silence, in awe of His holiness. Worship Him in reverence. Be still and know that He is God. Worship Him in holy array. Worship Him with all your heart, mind, soul and body—a living sacrifice, holy and acceptable to Him. Worship Him in Spirit and in truth, with a pure heart. Adore Him who lives forever. Send a holy kiss up to Him who is and who was and who is to come. Celebrate the Lord who is beautiful and beyond words of praise, who is eternal love. Bless God in heaven who is your wisdom. Dwell in the depth of His love. He is supreme. He is your Sovereign King. He is your joy and praise and peace beyond comprehension. Take hold of His heart and adore Him. Thank Him over and over. Fall in love with Him over and over. Live in the holy of holies with Him. Serve Him. Obey Him. Honor Him. Make Him known. Make His praise glorious. Let your life worship Him. Please Him. Love Him. For He is glorious and full of majesty and splendor. He alone is worthy, and awesome. He, the living God, is in love with you. You are His bride and one day you will be united with Him forever, not only beholding Him, but embracing Him, crying, "Holy, Holy, Holy," Give Him glory! Do His will! Do all that is in your heart for God is with you! Worship God!

---

Consecrate yourself anew as a holy sacrifice of worship unto the Lord to do His will no matter what the cost and to love Him with all of your heart. Worship God!

# ORDER FORM

BRIGHT MORNING STAR can be a blessing to your family and friends every day of the year! The Lord can use it to speak to them in personal ways that will change their lives. It would be a perfect gift for birthdays, holidays, or the New Year. Also, a perfect gift for your Bible Study group or Congregation.

*Save up to 20% on an order of two or more books.*

|  | Quantity | Price | Amount |
|---|---|---|---|
| BRIGHT MORNING STAR ..................... | x $ | = | $ |

(I book: $14.95, 2–4 books: $13.50 each, 5 or more books: $11.99 each)

California residents add sales tax ........................................................... $_____

Shipping & Handling ............................................................................. $_____
(Add $2.50 for the first book, plus $0.75 for each additional book.)
Note:  If you cannot afford a book, please write a letter and send what
       you can. We will help you.

TOTAL ORDER AMOUNT .................................................................... $_____
(enclose check or money order, no cash or C.O.D.'s)

---

Make check or money order payable to: Virginia van der Steur
Mail order to:   Virginia van der Steur
                 P.O. Box 4121
                 Seal Beach, California 90740-8121

Please print your name and address clearly:

Name _____

Mailing address _____

City _____

State or Province_____ ZIP or Postal Code _____

Telephone Number (_____) _____

Foreign orders must be submitted in U.S. dollars and are shipped by uninsured surface mail.

God bless you as you minister to those you love through Jesus, the BRIGHT MORNING STAR!

*For those of you who prayed to ask Jesus to forgive your sins and come into your heart as you began this book or as you read it, please write to me at the above address. I am interested in your life and would love to hear from you! The Lord bless you and keep you and make His face shine upon you; and be gracious to you. The Lord lift up His countenance on you and give you SHALOM!*